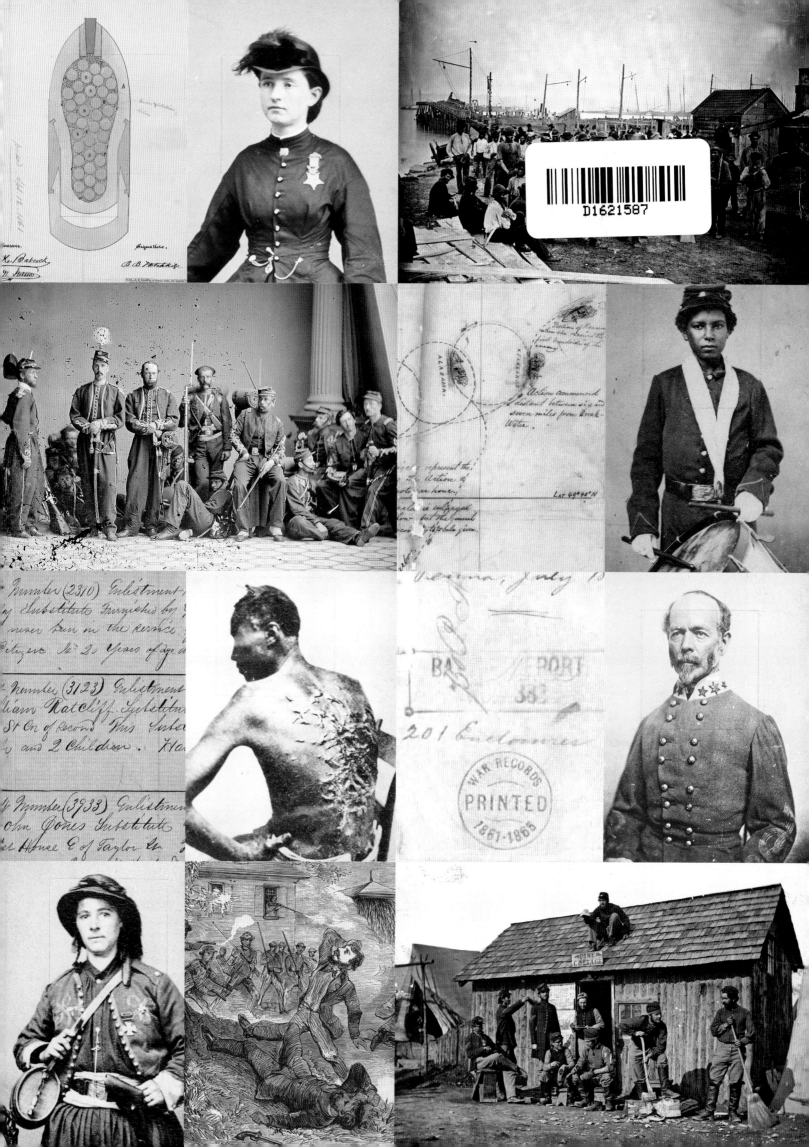

D1621587

This book is based on the exhibition "Discovering the Civil War," presented at the National Archives' Lawrence F. O'Brien Gallery in Washington, DC, in two parts: "Beginnings," from April 30, 2010, to September 6, 2010, and "Consequences," from November 10, 2010, to April 17, 2011. It was written by the National Archives Experience's special exhibition team, led by Senior Curator Bruce Bustard, as well as historians and other contributors with connections to the National Archives and Records Administration.

Copyright 2010
The Foundation for the National Archives

First published in 2010 by GILES
an imprint of D Giles Limited
4 Crescent Stables, 139 Upper Richmond Road
London, SW15 2TN, UK
www.gilesltd.com

LIBRARY OF CONGRESS CATALOGING-IN-PUBLICATION DATA
Discovering the Civil War / by the National Archives Experience's "Discovering the Civil War" Exhibition Team with a message from David S. Ferriero, Archivist of the United States; foreword by Ken Burns.
    p. cm.
"This book is based on the exhibition "Discovering the Civil War," presented at the National Archives' Lawrence F. O'Brien Gallery in Washington, DC, in two parts: "Beginnings," from April 30, 2010, to September 6, 2010, and "Consequences," from November 10, 2010, to April 17, 2011."
    Includes bibliographical references and index.
    ISBN 978-1-904832-91-1 (hardcover) -- ISBN 978-0-9841033-2-4 (softcover)
1. United States--History--Civil War, 1861-1865--Exhibitions. 2. National Archives (U.S.)--Exhibitions. I. Center for the National Archives Experience. II. Foundation for the National Archives.
    E468.D56 2010
    973.7--dc22
    2010027924

ISBN: 978-1-904832-91-1 (hardcover edition)
ISBN: 978-0-9841033-2-4 (softcover edition)

All rights reserved

No part of the contents of this book may be reproduced, stored in a retrieval system, or transmitted in any form or by any means, electronic, mechanical, photocopying, recording, or otherwise, without the written permission of the Foundation and the Publisher.

All measurements are in inches (and centimeters); Height precedes width precedes depth.

FOR THE FOUNDATION FOR THE NATIONAL ARCHIVES
Thora Colot, *Executive Director*
Christina Gehring, *Publications and Research Manager*
Patty Reinert Mason, *Senior Editor*

FOR THE NATIONAL ARCHIVES AND RECORDS ADMINISTRATION
Marvin Pinkert, *Executive Director, Center for the National Archives Experience*
Christina Rudy Smith, *Director of Exhibits*
Bruce I. Bustard, *Senior Curator*
Benjamin Guterman, *Copy Editor*

EDITOR
Sharon Barry

DESIGNER
Ellen Burns Design

FOR GILES
Proofreader: David Rose
Produced by the Publisher, an imprint of D Giles Limited
Printed and bound in Hong Kong

PHOTOGRAPHIC CREDITS: The majority of items reproduced in this book are from the holdings of the National Archives and Records Administration, which, unless otherwise noted, supplied the photographs.

FRONT COVER (NATIONAL ARCHIVES EDITION)
Top row, left to right: Patent drawing for Hotchkiss projectile, 1862 [Record Group (RG) 241]; Dr. Mary Walker, ca. 1866 [111-B-2112]; "Negro laborers at Alexandria, near coal wharf" [111-B-400]

Second row, l. to r.: Soldiers of a New York Zouave regiment [111-B-5886]; Map of the courses sailed by the USS *Kearsarge* and the CSS *Alabama* during their battle, 1864 [RG 45]; "Taylor–Drum Boy, 78th Regt. USCT, US Colored Infantry" [165-JT-302]

Third row, l. to r.: Page from the Record of Statements of Substitutes Sent from these Head Quarters 3rd Cong. District N.Y. Capt. S.B. Gregory Provost Marshal [RG 110]; The scars from a whipping on a slave's back [165-JT-230]; Union Gen. George Meade's report on Battle of Gettysburg [RG 94]; Confederate Gen. Joseph E. Johnston, ca. 1865 [111-B-1782]

Fourth row, l. to r.: "Mary Tepe . . . traveled with the 114th Pennsylvania" [79-TP-2148]; The shooting of Edward Gorsuch; "Pine Cottage," soldiers' winter quarters [111-B-256]

FRONT COVER (TRADE EDITION FOR GILES)
Men on the deck of the USS *Monitor*, 1862 National Archives, Records of the Office of the Chief Signal Officer [111-B-246].

DISCOVERING
THE CIVIL WAR

BY THE NATIONAL ARCHIVES EXPERIENCE'S
"DISCOVERING THE CIVIL WAR" EXHIBITION TEAM

WITH A MESSAGE FROM DAVID S. FERRIERO

ARCHIVIST OF THE UNITED STATES

FOREWORD BY KEN BURNS

DOCUMENTARY FILMMAKER

THE FOUNDATION FOR THE NATIONAL ARCHIVES, WASHINGTON, DC

IN ASSOCIATION WITH D GILES LIMITED, LONDON

CONTENTS

Drummer boy, 78th U.S. Colored Troops

National Archives, Records of the War Department General and Special Staffs [165-JT-302]

Nº 35.153,

B.B. Hotchkiss' Improvements in

Explosive Projectiles.

Patented May. 6. 1862,

$1.50

CLASSIFICATION
35.153
DIVISION

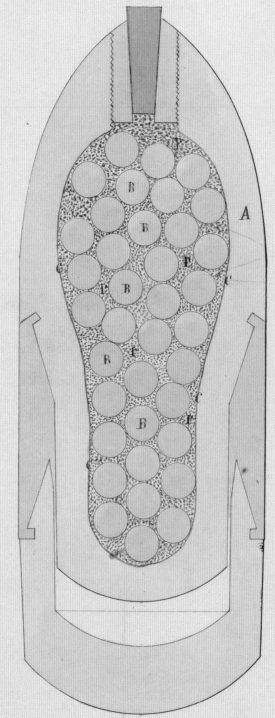

Witnesses,

G. H. Babcock

D. W. Stetson

Signature,

B. B. Hotchkiss.

35,153.—B. B. Hotchkiss, of Sharon, Conn., for Improvement in Explosive Projectiles:
I claim, first, An explosive projectile, in which the contents are
solidified, substantially in the manner and so as to secure the advantages set forth.
Second, I also claim the employment in such projectile of an adhe-
sive lining, C, substantially as described, so as to increase the adhe-
sion of the solidified contents to the interior of the shell.

MESSAGE FROM THE ARCHIVIST

DAVID S. FERRIERO, ARCHIVIST OF THE UNITED STATES

In my first year as Archivist of the United States, I could not have asked for a better debut than to open the National Archives' latest exhibition, "Discovering the Civil War." Commemorating the 150th anniversary of the transformative event of the 19th century, this exhibition, shown in our nation's capital and around the country, is remarkable in several ways.

First, it draws from one of the richest reservoirs of records in our holdings, millions of official documents, photographs, maps, and letters about the Civil War. We hold not only the records of the Union forces but also the so-called "Rebel Archives," captured Confederate records. And we have the records of the Freedmen's Bureau, the agency charged with assisting African Americans in the transition from slavery to citizenship.

Second, the exhibition uses these records in creative ways that inspire people young and old to explore further. The very concept that there are still new discoveries to be made about the Civil War, and that the research is an adventure, advances our goal of increasing interest in and access to the nation's records. The clever use of modern lenses, like social media, to take a fresh look at the 19th century makes this exhibition truly distinctive.

Finally, the exhibition has a scope and scale worthy of its subject matter. The 6,000-square-foot national traveling version—shown in two parts in the historic National Archives Building in Washington, DC—is the largest traveling exhibition we have put together in decades.

I hope the exhibition, and the stories and images in this accompanying catalog, will inspire you to visit the National Archives—not only as a tourist, but as a researcher—to conduct your own exploration of the Civil War, or to investigate another topic of interest. The billions of Federal Government records in the National Archives are held in trust for the American people. I invite you to use them to make your own discoveries.

B. B. Hotchkiss's patent drawing for "Explosive Projectiles (for rifles)," May 6, 1862

National Archives, Records of the Patent and Trademark Office

FOREWORD

KEN BURNS, DOCUMENTARY FILMMAKER

Too often, we Americans make the mistake of telling our history from the top down, thinking that focusing solely on a succession of Presidential administrations, punctuated by wars, gets it. It does not. This top-down approach misses so many seemingly small but fascinating and compelling stories, and so many so-called "ordinary" people whose lives are immeasurably significant. It is clear that in actuality a bottom-up approach leads us towards a truer and deeper understanding of our nation—past and present.

At the National Archives, we engage in a bottom-up exploration of our history—one that goes beyond the dry dates and facts and events of our history books to excavate a living, breathing history we are ourselves a part of, we ourselves are still forging.

This bottom-up approach to history is of incalculable value because it engages our citizens in the practical work of democracy. It is possible to come to the National Archives and see how this massive and remarkable resource works, and that is what I have endeavored to do as a private citizen, as a filmmaker, and now as a member of the Foundation for the National Archives.

The power of ordinary lives to transform our history is at the heart of the mission of the National Archives, which preserves and makes accessible to all people their own history. As a filmmaker engaged in telling the story of American history for more than 30 years, I have relied on this incredible institution in every instance, for every film. Inevitably, my original view of the subject matter at hand changed and evolved and grew as I discovered new aspects of my subject—things I would not have been able to unearth anywhere else.

Such was the case more than 20 years ago, as I was finishing the editing on my film *The Civil War.* One day I received a package from the National Archives. Inside were facsimiles of documents about the actions of a certain Union General Averill in the newly created State of West Virginia in the summer of 1863. It was too late to include any of this in the film, but, still, I began reading.

Clockwise from left: Dr. Mary Walker, ca. 1866 [111-B-2112]; Unidentified Native Americans, ca. 1860–65 [111-B-3738]; "Mary Tepe . . . traveled with the 114th Pennsylvania," ca. 1863 [79-TP-2148]; "Three 'Johnnie Reb' prisoners captured at Gettysburg," 1863 [200-CC-2288].

It seems that Averill was able to capture a group of Confederate cavalrymen in a small skirmish. The Southerners were mostly from Captain McClanahan's Co. of Virginia Horse Artillery. They were, in the fascinating details of these records, completely outgunned. Three men were killed, 5 wounded, and 13 were made prisoners and sent to Camp Chase in Ohio to be eventually paroled in March 1865. The records at Camp Chase are sketchier, but they do record receiving, processing, and releasing (paroling) the prisoners. They were a fairly nondescript bunch. Most seem to have come from Bathe County, Virginia. None were slaveholders, or looked to have much interest in the constitutional issues. One fellow was described as being 5 feet, 4 inches tall, with a dark complexion, gray eyes, and dark hair. He said he was a blacksmith in life and stated to the copyist, a Mr. R.W. Pearson, that he had been forced to join the Confederate Army. Another copyist, a Mr. Jameison, places the group of "rebels" at Cox's Wharves on the James River near City Point on March 11 or 12, 1865, where all records of the men disappear.

I was struck by the impersonal nature of the papers and yet a sense that real Americans had lived through this war. Had been touched by it. Fought. Were captured. Held prisoner. Released. Shod horses. Maybe in the top-down version of things they didn't matter much, but in someone's history they do, and that makes for a different kind of history.

And speaking of a different kind of history, that Confederate blacksmith captured at Moorefield, West Virginia, and imprisoned at Camp Chase in Ohio . . . his name was Abraham Burns—my great, great grandfather.

In the moment of this discovery—this connection to my personal American history—I felt a profound sense of intimacy with our national narrative and the huge magnificence of the National Archives, where literally billions of records are stored.

I hope you will join me in your own bottom-up exploration of the Civil War, through the treasure house of documents in the National Archives, and through the Archives' latest traveling exhibition: "Discovering the Civil War."

The exhibition, detailed in the pages that follow, invites you to look beyond the battlefield to the everyday struggles of ordinary people. I cannot guarantee you will find someone from your own family, as I did when I researched the Civil War. But I know you will make your own bottom-up connections to our shared national story. I hope you will be transformed the way I was, in the realization that history, as William Faulkner said, is not "was," but "is."

That is what this exhibition stands for, and what the National Archives is all about.

ACKNOWLEDGMENTS

Both the exhibition and the publication, *Discovering the Civil War*, were enormous undertakings that required large teams of contributors and countless examples of collaboration over the course of five years. At the National Archives, the "Discovering the Civil War" exhibition team was led by Marvin Pinkert, Director of the Center for the National Archives Experience, Christina Rudy Smith, Director of Exhibits, Bruce Bustard, senior curator, and Thora Colot, Executive Director of the Foundation for the National Archives. Team members included Will Sandoval, Jennifer Johnson, Ray Ruskin, Michael Hussey, Karen Hibbitt, James Zeender, Darlene McClurkin, and Amanda Perez. The exhibit text was copyedited by Maureen MacDonald, and the publication text by Benjamin Guterman.

The Foundation for the National Archives, under the direction of Thora Colot, made the exhibit and this book possible. Christina Gehring and Patty Reinert Mason managed and coordinated the book project. Franck Cordes, Stefanie Mathew, and Meg Daniel Nelson played key roles in bringing "Discovering the Civil War" to completion, and intern Caroline Corley provided valuable administrative support.

Ken Burns, documentary filmmaker and Vice President of the Foundation's Board of Directors, made valuable suggestions at several points during the exhibition development process and wrote the Foreword to this publication.

Ellen Burns designed this publication. Sharon Barry served as writer-editor.

The Jackson Brady Design Group designed the exhibition. The computer interactives and audio experiences in the exhibition were created by Cortina Productions, Inc. The exhibition fabricators were ExPlus and Sparks Exhibits & Environments Corporation. Avitecture, Inc. was responsible for audiovisual and information technology integration.

The process of selecting items for "Discovering the Civil War" was guided by a number of archivists throughout the National Archives, who also served as subject matter specialists for the project: Trevor Plante, Kenneth Kato, Reginald Washington, Jane Fitzgerald, V. Chapman Smith, Walter Hill, Deanne Blanton, Connie Potter, Keith Kerr, Holly Reed, Brenda Kepley, Edward McCarter, Eugene Morris, Timothy Mulligan, and John Deeben.

Other National Archives staff members who made contributions include: Adrienne Thomas, Michael J. Kurtz, Catherine Farmer, Katherine Chin, Patrick Kepley, Daniel Falk, Michael Jackson, Kahlil Chism, Leslie Simon, Dorothy Simmons, Jessie Kratz, Peter Brauer, Pat Anderson, Rutha Beamon, Thomas Nastick, Mitchell Yockelson, Mark Meader, Christina Kovac, Christina Hardman, Elizabeth Campbell, Netisha Currie, Susan Cooper, Miriam Kleiman, Laura Diachenko, James Garvin, Timothy Edwards, Dave Adams, Vernon Early, Miranda Perry, Annette Williams, Jason Schultz, and Alison Gavin.

Conservator Terry Boone led the conservation work for the exhibition, along with Yoonjoo Strumfels, Susan Page, Annie Wilker, Allen Johnson, Lisa Isbell, Amy Lubick, Lauren Varga, Sara Shpargel, Anne Witty, Steven Loew, Kathy Ludwig, Jana Dambrogio, Gail Harriman, Morgan Zinsmeister, Cathy Valentour, Daniel Dancis, Holly Dewitt-McIntyre, Richard Whittington, Doug McRae, Joyce Lin, Melina Avery, Anna Friedman, Jen Herrman, Mark Ormsby, and Margaret Kelly. The scans of documents and photographs in the exhibition and in the book were done by Michelle Farnsworth and Jennifer Seitz, assisted by Michael Horsley, Amy Young, Erin Rhodes, Sheri Hill, and Jeff Reed.

We especially thank President Edward L. Ayers of the University of Richmond who read and commented on the catalog text, and Professor Joseph Reidy of Howard University who carefully read the exhibition scripts and improved them. Other historians who contributed to the project were Chandra Manning, Anne Sarah Rubin, and Tyler Anbinder.

The late Budge Weidman, volunteer manager of the Civil War Conservation Corps, along with her husband, Russell Weidman, supported "Discovering the Civil War" from its inception. Budge was a devoted Civil War buff, a passionate volunteer, an advocate for the National Archives, and a dear friend of the Foundation for the National Archives.

We dedicate this book in her memory.

In the exhibition's Prologue area, a modern-day archivist explains that "Discovering the Civil War" is about examining evidence and exploring unexpected twists and turns, not about battles, chronology, or facts.

National Archives photograph by Earl McDonald

Mary Tepe, traveled with the 114th Pennsylvania Infantry and served as laundress, nurse, cook, and sutler. This photograph was taken around 1863.

National Archives, Records of the National Park Service

INTRODUCTION

It ended almost 150 years ago. But Americans still discuss, debate, and disagree about the Civil War. No one alive today lived during this momentous conflict. Time and myth have filtered our views of the war.

So how do we know what happened?

Very often, the answer lies in records left by the participants themselves. Much of that evidence—letters, orders, diaries, maps, telegrams, photographs, and broadsides—is preserved in the National Archives of the United States. This catalog, based on the exhibition "Discovering the Civil War," takes a fresh look at that conflict through little-known stories, seldom-seen documents, and unusual perspectives. It invites you to examine the evidence found in records, consider and ask questions about that evidence, listen to a wide variety of voices from the Civil War era, and make up your own mind about the struggle that almost tore apart these United States.

A New Kind of Civil War Exhibit

On April 1, 1961, the National Archives opened a major exhibition in Washington, DC, to commemorate the centennial of the Civil War. It was organized chronologically from Fort Sumter to Appomattox and covered the military, political, technological, and diplomatic history of the war. It never mentioned slavery, emancipation, African American troops, or the Freedman's Bureau.

Almost 50 years later, on April 30, 2010, "Discovering the Civil War" opened—just in time for the war's sesquicentennial. Rather than the traditional chronological approach, this exhibition—like this catalog—was organized thematically.

Rather than repeat what others have already done, the exhibit focused on the centrality of records as historical evidence. Its title reflects the fact that much has been discovered about the Civil War over the last 50 years, that new Civil War stories are continually being uncovered and re-examined, and that understanding the Civil War means engaging personally with its people and their era. The title also speaks to our goal of providing you with the opportunity to discover the Civil War for yourself by exploring—and asking questions about—a wide variety of documents.

Expanded Cast of Characters

"Discovering the Civil War" introduces a far wider cast of characters than are found in traditional exhibitions about the Civil War. You will meet not only generals, diplomats, and military heroes but also laborers, slaves, nurses, deserters, and guerrilla fighters. This catalog, like the exhibition, does not dwell on charges, flanking movements, or battlefield turning points. Instead, it brings the often extraordinary experiences of "ordinary" people to the forefront. It challenges you to think about how these men and women experienced the war and how the choices they made contributed to the larger story of the Civil War.

Here you will confront and investigate topics such as slavery, emancipation, and the African American experience during the war. You will meet a wide spectrum of Americans ranging from a "foreign-born" citizen from New York applying for Confederate citizenship, to an escaped slave writing home to his wife, to petitioners from Maine asking for repeal of the Fugitive Slave Act.

This 1862 photo shows an unidentified African American with members of the 2nd Georgia Battalion. Slave labor assisted the Confederacy in many ways, but it was illegal for black men to join the Confederate Army until just before the end of the war.

National Archives, Donated Materials in the National Archives

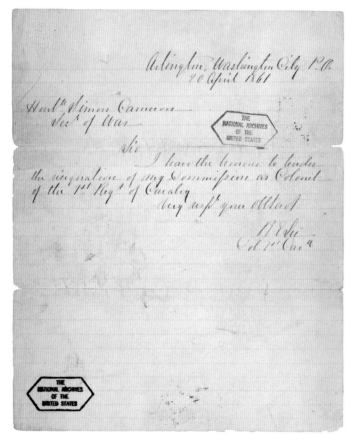

Robert E. Lee was among the hundreds of officers who resigned their commissions in the U.S. Army, Navy, and Marine Corps when their home or adopted states seceded. Lee became General of the Confederate Army.

National Archives, Records of the Adjutant General's Office, 1780's–1917

New Documents and Experiences

The documents reproduced in this catalog represent some of the highlights from the exhibition, which was the most extensive display ever assembled from the National Archives' wide-ranging and incomparable Civil War holdings. Here you can explore records usually seen only by historians. You will find famous milestone documents such as Robert E. Lee's resignation from the U.S. Army and telegrams between President Lincoln and his generals. But you will also encounter many revealing but less well-known documents such as the unratified 13th amendment of 1861, a message from a Southern governor rejecting Lincoln's call for troops to put down the rebellion, and a draft of the Confederate Constitution.

Patent drawings for tents, weapons, artificial limbs, and other military and medical devices illustrate the inventions developed to fight the war and care for the wounded. Pension records reveal that Frank Thompson, who served in the Union Army, was a woman. A Chinese-language message to Prince Kung, thanking him for not allowing Confederate ships to enter Chinese ports, demonstrates that the Civil War was, in a very real sense, a global war.

You can also see examples of the interactive experiences that helped the exhibit bring the Civil War into the 21st century. One page illustrates an interactive graphic novel about the Confederate raider *Alabama* and its sinking by the USS *Kearsarge*. An image of a giant on-screen web demonstrates the strong pre-war relationships that existed among Northern and Southern military leaders.

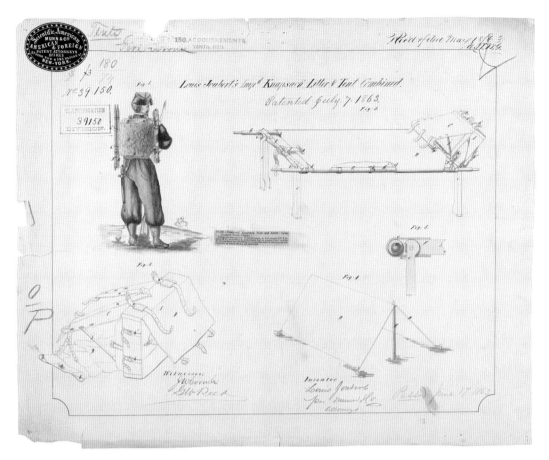

Louis Joubert patented this multi-purpose device in 1862 that could serve as a tent, knapsack, or litter.

National Archives, Records of the Patent and Trademark Office

Finally, through the essays included with each chapter, you will get an insider's look at the process of discovery that historians and other researchers experience themselves as they explore documents in the National Archives.

Your Chance to Discover

We invite you to take this unprecedented opportunity to peer inside history and uncover for yourself the fascinating and complex stories revealed in the records of the National Archives.

Join researchers to unlock secrets, solve mysteries, and uncover new stories and fresh perspectives in the records of the Civil War. Read about some of the exciting discoveries researchers made as they created "Discovering the Civil War." And find out for yourself how records bring history to life.

We hope that you will ask questions, be surprised and excited by what you find, connect personally with the past, and in this way discover the Civil War.

Both the North and South used a variety of measures to raise and retain fighting forces. This broadside solicited recruits for the 9th Regiment of New Hampshire Volunteers.

National Archives, Records of the Provost Marshal General's Bureau (Civil War)

FORT SUMTER TAKEN DETAIL

The rebel flag flies over Fort Sumter in Charleston, South Carolina. On April 12, 1861, after decades of growing strife between North and South, Confederate artillery opened fire on this Federal fort. Union forces surrendered 34 hours later. On May 6, the Confederate Congress passed a resolution that amounted to a declaration of war against the United States. The Civil War was on.

National Archives, Records of the Public Buildings Service [121-BA-914A]

CHAPTER 1

BREAKING APART

In 1859 the prospect that the United States would break apart and plunge into civil war seemed remote. Few Americans could have imagined a war that would last four years, destroy much of the South, kill 620,000 soldiers and sailors, and free 4 million slaves. Yet just two years later, it happened.

- What led to the secession of the South?
- Were there efforts to avoid war?
- How did the South try to forge a national identity?

Explore the documents that follow for answers to these and other questions about the origins and onset of the Civil War.

PETITION

For the Establishment and Protection of Freedom in the Territories of the United States.

To the Congress of the United States:

The undersigned, citizens and electors of the State of *New York* residing in *Covington & Perry*, in the county of *Wyoming*, respectfully pray that Slavery and the Slave-trade may be expressly prohibited by act of Congress in all the Territories of the United States.

NAMES.		NAMES.	

ABOLITIONISTS PETITION CONGRESS

Starting in the 1830s a small but growing movement advocated the abolition of slavery in the United States. After 1850 abolition's appeal spread to those who feared slavery's expansion into the territories. Abolitionists collected hundreds of thousands of signatures on petitions to Congress, like this one from citizens of New York. As abolitionist agitation increased, Southern whites became increasingly outspoken in their defense of slavery.

National Archives, Records of the U.S. House of Representatives

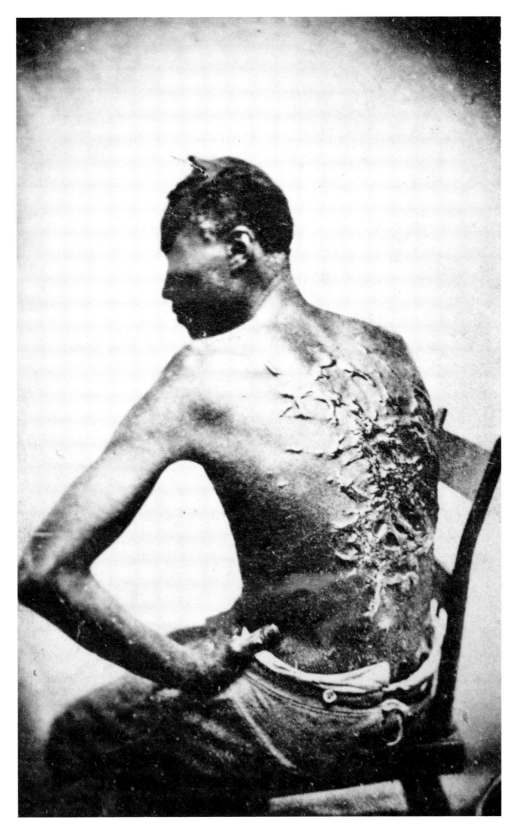

SCARS OF SLAVERY

This 1863 photograph of the former slave "Peter," displaying scars from his overseer's whippings, was widely reproduced as evidence of slavery's cruelty. The image was sometimes paired with a photo or drawing of "Peter" after his enlistment in the U.S. Army. "Peter" was sometimes identified as "Gordon."

National Archives, Records of the War Department General and Special Staffs [165-JT-230]

CHRISTIANA RESISTANCE (1851) DETAIL

The shooting of slave owner Edward Gorsuch by a fugitive slave led to the largest mass indictment for treason in American history. The trial took place on November 24, 1851, at Independence Hall in Philadelphia, Pennsylvania—the same building where both the Declaration of Independence and the Constitution had been adopted.

Reproduced from William Still, The Underground Railroad *(1872)*

The Christiana Resistance: Traitors or Heroes?

On November 6, 1849, four black men—Noah Bailey, Nelson Ford, George Hammond, and Charles Ford—escaped from slave owner Edward Gorsuch and fled north from Baltimore County, Maryland, to the small town of Christiana, Pennsylvania. The following year, Congress enacted the Fugitive Slave Act, strengthening the Federal Government's role in returning runaway slaves, requiring states to return slaves to their masters, and reducing the legal protection offered to runaways. On September 11, 1851, Gorsuch and a posse arrived in Christiana with Federal warrants for his escaped slaves. He was accompanied by a U.S. marshal.

The fugitives had taken refuge at the home of William Parker, a former slave and the leader of a local self-defense organization. Gorsuch's posse surrounded the Parker house. Alerted by the blow of a horn, armed members of the African American community rushed to the house. A tense standoff ensued.

Two local white men, Castner Hanway and Elijah Lewis, arrived and advised the posse to leave. Then the confrontation turned violent. One fugitive knocked Gorsuch to the ground and shot him. The slave owner was clubbed repeatedly and died. Several other members of the posse and crowd were wounded.

Hanway, Lewis, and 36 others—including William Parker, Noah Bailey, and Nelson Ford—were indicted on the charge of treason. Hanway was tried first. His trial began on November 24, 1851. In response to the Government's charge of treason, Hanway's defense attorney asked:

Sir—Did you hear it? That three harmless, non-resisting Quakers, and eight-and-thirty wretched, miserable, penniless negroes, armed with corn-cutters, clubs, and a few muskets and headed by a miller, in a felt hat, without a coat, without arms, and mounted on a sorrel nag, levied war against the United States. Blessed be God that our Union has survived the shock.

On December 11, after deliberating only 15 minutes, the jury in the case of *The United States of America vs. Castner Hanway* found Hanway not guilty. Federal prosecutors refused to prosecute any of the other indictments. But the bitter controversy over the Fugitive Slave Law still divided the country. Over the next 10 years, black men and women would continue to seek freedom, and tensions over slavery and its extension would threaten to break the bonds between North and South.

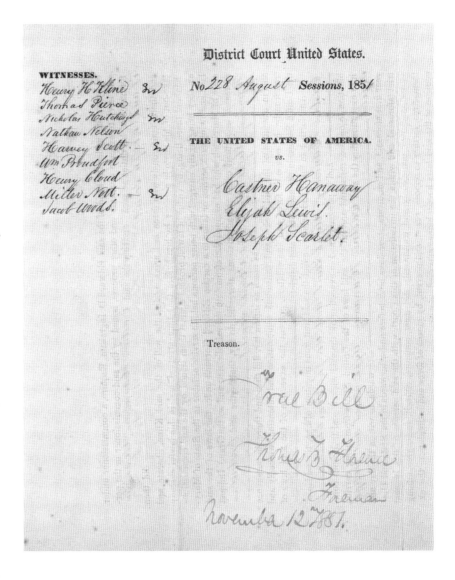

INDICTED FOR TREASON DETAIL, SELECTED PAGE
The Government charged that those indicted "did traitorously assemble and combine against . . . the United States." This is the indictment for Castner Hanway, a local white man and the only person to be tried.

National Archives at Philadelphia, Records of the District Courts of the United States

BLOODY KANSAS

The Kansas-Nebraska Act, enacted by Congress in 1854, empowered the people living in a territory to decide the question of slavery there. People for and against slavery rushed to the territory of Kansas, and civil war erupted over whether the territory would become a slave or free state. This newspaper clipping describes one of many bloody battles between abolitionists and slavery supporters. Both sides created governments and applied for statehood. In 1861 Kansas was admitted to the Union as a free state.

National Archives, Records of U.S. Army Commands,
1821–1920

THE JOURNAL,
EXTRA.
LEAVENWORTH CITY, AUGUST 16th.
MORE OUTRAGES!!
COL. TITUS MURDERED!
Nine Hundred Abolitionists with Five pieces of Artilery at Lecompton!!
The City Surrounded!!

Mr. Rodrigue, Express, has just arrived, bringing intelligence of the attack on Col. Titus's house, and the probable murder of the entire party. There were 30 men in the house, and as it was surrounded by at least 400, there is no possibility of the escape of a single man.

Another portion of the Abolition forces attacked the House of G. W. Clark, Indian Agent. About two hours after the destruction of Col. Titus' House, and while the Express was leaving, the roar of the cannon was distinctly heard. *Lane is in the field.* Andrew Preston, Esq., wounded. Mr. Sisterre killed. Mr. Clowes killed, Editor Southern Advocate. killed. Lecompton is hourly expected to be attacked.

Up citizens of Kansas and come to the rescue. All the women and children of Lecompton are driven from the city and are now coming to this city. *Action! Action!! Action!!!*

JOHN BROWN IN KANSAS

This mural by John Steuart Curry, entitled *The Tragic Prelude* (1941), shows abolitionist John Brown in Kansas. It hangs in the Kansas State Capitol in Topeka, Kansas. In 1859 Brown led a slave revolt in Harpers Ferry, Virginia. He was captured, tried, and executed.

National Archives, Records of the National Park Service [79-CWC-3F (10)]

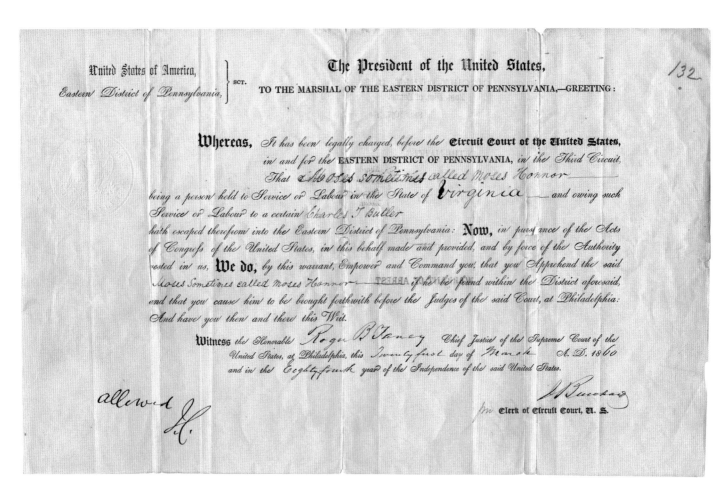

ESCAPED SLAVE RECLAIMED

This is an arrest warrant for Moses Honnor, a slave from Virginia who escaped to Pennsylvania in August 1859. It is part of the court record documenting his owner's successful efforts to capture Honnor. Congress had strengthened the Fugitive Slave Act as part of the Compromise of 1850. The law made it easier for masters to reclaim their "property," strengthened the Federal Government's role in returning slaves, and reduced a slave's legal protection.

National Archives at Philadelphia, Records of District Courts of the United States

LINCOLN ELECTED PRESIDENT

This photograph was taken by Alexander Hesler on June 3, 1860. Just over five months later, on November 6, Lincoln would win the Presidential election. Within two months of his election, South Carolina would become the first Southern state to leave the Union.

Donated Materials in the National Archives [200-FB-3C-1]

List of the Votes for President and Vice President of the
United States for the constitutional term, to commence
on the 4th day of March, 1861.

Number of Electoral votes	States	For President				For Vice President			
		Abraham Lincoln of Illinois	John C. Breckenridge of Kentucky	John Bell of Tennessee	Stephen A. Douglas of Illinois	Hannibal Hamlin of Maine	Joseph Lane of Oregon	Edward Everett of Massachusetts	Herschel V. Johnson of Georgia
8	Maine	8				8			
5	New Hampshire	5				5			
13	Massachusetts	13				13			
4	Rhode Island and Providence Plantations	4				4			
6	Connecticut	6				6			
5	Vermont	5				5			
35	New York	35				35			
7	New Jersey	4			3	4			3
27	Pennsylvania	27				27			
3	Delaware		3				3		
8	Maryland		8				8		
15	Virginia			15				15	
10	North Carolina		10				10		
8	South Carolina		8				8		
10	Georgia		10				10		
12	Kentucky			12				12	
12	Tennessee			12				12	
23	Ohio	23				23			
6	Louisiana		6				6		
7	Mississippi		7				7		
13	Indiana	13				13			
11	Illinois	11				11			
9	Alabama		9				9		
9	Missouri				9				9
4	Arkansas		4				4		
6	Michigan	6				6			
3	Florida		3				3		
4	Texas		4				4		
4	Iowa	4				4			
5	Wisconsin	5				5			
4	California	4				4			
4	Minnesota	4				4			
3	Oregon	3				3			
303		180	72	39	12	180	72	39	12

The whole number of the Electors appointed to vote for President and Vice President of the United States is 303
Of which a majority is 152

I now announce to the two Houses of Congress, the state of the vote for President of
the United States, to be,

For Abraham Lincoln, of Illinois 180
For John C. Breckenridge, of Kentucky 72
For John Bell, of Tennessee 39
For Stephen A. Douglas, of Illinois 12

And the state of the vote for Vice President of the United States, to be,
For Hannibal Hamlin, of Maine 180
For Joseph Lane, of Oregon 72
For Edward Everett, of Massachusetts 39
For Herschel V. Johnson, of Georgia 12

I therefore declare, that Abraham Lincoln, of Illinois, having received a
majority of the whole number of Electoral votes, is duly elected President of the United States,
for four years, commencing on the fourth day of March, 1861.—

And that Hannibal Hamlin of Maine, having received a majority of
the whole number of Electoral votes, is duly elected Vice President of the United States
for four years, commencing on the fourth day of March, 1861.—

The business for which the two Houses were assembled having been finished
the Senate will now return to its chamber.

NOT EXACTLY A LANDSLIDE

The Presidential election of 1860 was a four-way race among Republican Abraham Lincoln, Democrats Stephen A. Douglas and John Breckenridge, and Constitutional Union party nominee John Bell. Lincoln won only 40 percent of the popular vote. But as this list shows, he won 180 out of 303 electoral votes, including most of the North. Douglas came in second but won only 12 electoral votes.

National Archives, Records of the U.S. Senate

THE CONSTITUTION

OF THE

CONFEDERATE STATES OF AMERICA.

1 We, the people of the Confederate States, each State acting for itself

2 and in its sovereign and independent character, in order to form a permanent

3 Federal Government, establish justice, ensure domestic tranquility, and se-

4 cure the blessings of liberty to ourselves and our posterity—to which ends we

5 invoking the favor and guidance of Almighty God—do ordain and establish

6 this Constitution for the Confederate States of America.

ARTICLE I.

SECTION 1.

1 All legislative powers herein delegated shall be vested in a Congress of

2 the Confederate States, which shall consist of a Senate and House of Rep-

3 resentatives.

SECTION 2.

1 1. The House of Representatives shall be composed of members chosen

SELECTED PAGE

"WE, THE PEOPLE OF THE CONFEDERATE STATES . . ."

Adopted on March 11, 1861, the Constitution of the Confederate States resembled the Constitution of the United States. It differed in its emphasis on each state's "sovereign and independent character," its reference to "Almighty God," and its six-year term for President. The document explicitly granted citizens the right to hold property in slaves, and to take slaves from state to state. The Confederacy banned the importation of slaves from other nations.

National Archives, War Department Collection of Confederate Records

THE SOUTH GAINS A KEY STATE

Wealthy and strategically located, Virginia initially refused to join the seven Southern states that seceded after Lincoln's election. But when Lincoln called for 75,000 troops to suppress the rebellion, the Virginia Convention reversed course. It passed this Ordinance of Secession on April 17, 1861, by a vote of 88 to 55. A statewide vote held a month later supported its decision.

National Archives, General Records of the Department of State

An Ordinance to Repeal the Ratification of the Constitution of the United States of America by the State of Virginia, and to resume all the rights and powers granted under said Constitution.

THE PEOPLE OF VIRGINIA in their ratification of the Constitution of the United States of America adopted by them in Convention on the twenty fifth day of June in the year of our Lord one thousand, seven hundred and eighty eight having declared that the powers granted under the said Constitution were derived from the people of the United States, and might be resumed whensoever the same should be perverted to their injury and oppression; and the Federal Government having perverted said powers not only to the injury of the people of Virginia, but to the oppression of the Southern slaveholding States:

Now, therefore, we, the People of Virginia do declare and ordain that the Ordinance adopted by the people of this State, in Convention, on the twenty fifth day of June, in the year of our Lord one thousand seven hundred and eighty eight whereby the Constitution of the United States of America was ratified, and all acts of the General Assembly of this State ratifying or adopting amendments to said Constitution are hereby repealed and abrogated; that the Union between the State of Virginia and the other States under the Constitution aforesaid is hereby dissolved; and that the State of Virginia is in the full possession and exercise of all the rights of sovereignty which belong and appertain to a free and independent State. And they do further declare that said Constitution of the United States of America is no longer binding on any of the citizens of this State.

This ordinance shall take effect, and be an Act of this day when ratified by a majority of the votes of the people of this State cast at a poll to be taken thereon on the fourth Thursday in May next, in pursuance of a schedule hereafter to be enacted.

DONE IN CONVENTION in the City of Richmond on the seventeenth day of April, in the year of our Lord one thousand eight hundred and sixty one, and in the eighty fifth year of the Commonwealth of Virginia.

Angus R. Blakey
John Rand Chambliss   John Janney — President
Geo. Wythe Randolph   Geo. W. Taylor   U.S. Cecil   James M. Ruffey
James P. Holcombe   Geo. Blow Jr   Addison Hall
Williams Carter Wickham   Samuel G. Staples
George W. Richardson
John Tyler
John Goode Jr.
Edmd. Morris
Wm. W. Boyd   Lewis D. Isbell
James H. Cox   Benj. F. Wysor
John L. Marye   George Wm. Brent   James C. Bruce
Saml. C. Williams   James M. Strange   James Gustavus Holladay
Marmaduke Johnson
Hugh M. Nelson
Wm. Campbell Scott
K. B. French   John Critcher
Robt. Turner   Robert C. Kent
A. J. Gray   Saml. Woods
Jno. M. Speed

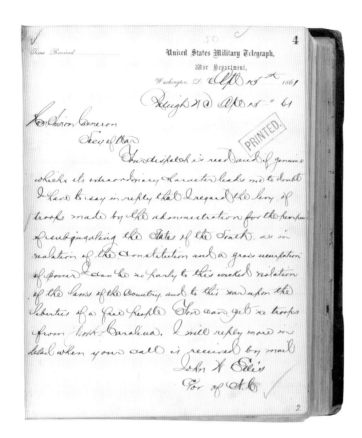

"YOU CAN GET NO TROOPS FROM NORTH CAROLINA"

Secretary of War Simon Cameron asked North Carolina to provide two regiments in response to President Lincoln's request for volunteers to squash the rebellion. The Governor of North Carolina replied with this message condemning the Federal Government's attempts at "subjugating the States of the South." About a month after Lincoln's proclamation, on May 20, North Carolina seceded from the Union.

National Archives, Records of the Office of the Secretary of War

JEFFERSON DAVIS LEADS THE SOUTH

Jefferson Davis served as President of the Confederate States of America from 1861 to 1865, its entire history. This photograph was taken around 1860.

National Archives, Records of the Office of the Chief Signal Officer
[111-B-4146]

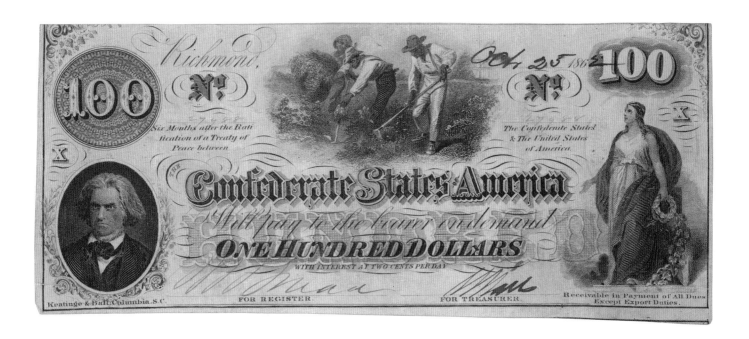

MONEY TALKS

Confederate currency reflected the new nation's self-image. The drawings on its bills emphasize the commerce and wealth of Southern society. Some highlight the importance of cotton to the Confederate economy. Others honor heroes such as Virginia-born George Washington and officials such as President Jefferson Davis and Vice President Alexander Stephens. Slaves appear healthy, happy, and well treated.

National Archives, Records of the Office of the Bureau of Accounts (Treasury)

REBEL ARCHIVES STAMP

A unique feature of many Confederate records held by the National Archives is this oval stamp marking them as "Rebel Archives." Shortly after the fall of Richmond in April 1865, the U.S. military issued orders to capture as many Confederate documents as possible. These "Rebel Archives" would serve as evidence in any trials of Confederate leaders. After the assassination of President Lincoln, efforts to locate official Confederate documents were redoubled to determine if there had been a conspiracy. Once the records were received in Washington, DC, clerks from the War Department marked individual documents with this stamp.

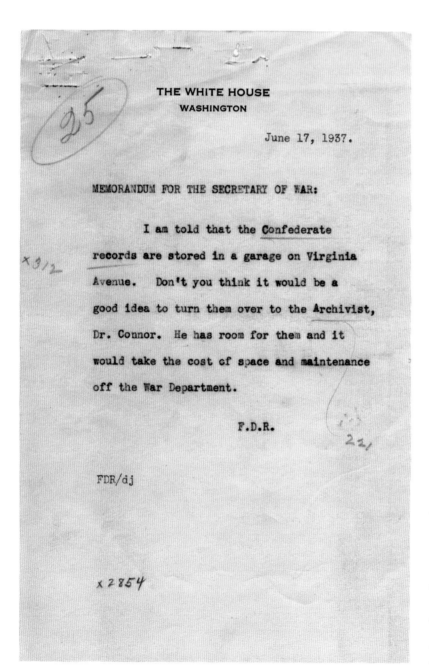

THE WHITE HOUSE
WASHINGTON

June 17, 1937.

MEMORANDUM FOR THE SECRETARY OF WAR:

I am told that the Confederate records are stored in a garage on Virginia Avenue. Don't you think it would be a good idea to turn them over to the Archivist, Dr. Connor. He has room for them and it would take the cost of space and maintenance off the War Department.

F.D.R.

FDR/dj

Records of a Defeated Nation

On April 2, 1865, with defeat at hand, Confederate officials fled the capital of Richmond, Virginia, with the most important government records. They burned some records in Richmond and along the escape route. Union forces captured many others, and the U.S. War Department preserved them. Over the next 73 years more Confederate records were donated to the War Department.

In 1938 the War Department transferred these records to the National Archives. They became the War Department Collection of Confederate Records—by far the Archives' largest group of Confederate records.

A NEW HOME FOR CAPTURED RECORDS

In June 1937 President Franklin Roosevelt sent this note asking if Confederate records under Secretary of War Harry H. Woodring's control should go into the National Archives. Eventually, the agencies reached an agreement, and over the next few years most of the War Department's records were transferred to the National Archives.

National Archives, Franklin D. Roosevelt Presidential Library and Museum

A "SENSATION IN THE CHAMBER"

Kenneth Kato

There were attempts to preserve the Union, including a compromise proposed by Kentucky Senator John J. Crittenden in 1860. One volunteer fire company from Pennsylvania came up with a novel way of expressing support for "Crittenden's Compromise."

As civil war threatened the United States, debates and concerns were not limited to statesmen and military commanders. Young men in communities throughout the country would be risking their lives in the event of such a calamity. Beyond elections and rallies, petitions were the most effective means voters had of letting Congress know how people felt about an issue.

In central Pennsylvania, members of a volunteer fire company took time out from the company's centennial celebrations to communicate their views on the escalating crisis. Their flag petition, described by their Senator as "some sensation in the Chamber," expressed their hopes for peace, proud patriotism, and awareness of the nation's heritage.

Struggles for Compromise

The 1860 Presidential election weighed heavily on the members of Congress as they returned to Washington for a new session. The Republican nominee and victor, Abraham Lincoln, had run on a platform prohibiting slavery's spread into new territories and states. Loose talk in the slaveholding South about secession was turning to action. In his last annual message to Congress, President James Buchanan sounded a note of impending doom. He condemned secession as unconstitutional. He concluded, however, that the Constitution prohibited any forceful effort at preventing secession.

The period from December 1860 to March 1861 would be one of the most critical periods in the country's history. Throughout those desperate weeks, Senators and Representatives searched for a magical combination of proposals that would unite rather than divide the country. Many proposals were advanced. One suggestion was to separate slave states and territories from free ones by extending the Missouri Compromise line (36° 30') to the Pacific Ocean. Another advocated letting citizens of new states decide the status of slavery there.

Crittenden's Proposal

Each house of Congress established a special committee to craft legislation to resolve the crisis. Kentucky Senator John J. Crittenden was among the members of the Senate committee. Many looked to him as the successor of the Great Compromiser, the late Henry Clay. Crittenden was under great pressure to break the deadlock that prevented any compromise proposals from advancing in Congress.

Kentucky Senator John J. Crittenden proposed a compromise to help break the deadlock in Congress and preserve the Union. DETAIL

National Archives, Records of the Office of the Chief Signal Officer [111-B-4219]

When South Carolina seceded on January 3, 1861, Congress had made no progress. Senator Crittenden's proposals for compromise had gone nowhere. But he proposed a radical solution to the crisis suggesting that a national referendum be held on his package of proposed Constitutional amendments. He hoped that an unambiguous judgment from the country would erode congressional obstacles. Senator Stephen Douglas of Illinois, the champion of popular sovereignty, immediately endorsed Crittenden's proposal, and Pennsylvania Senator William Bigler introduced a bill to authorize the national referendum.

Crittenden was respected by both sides of the sectional dispute over slavery in the territories, and his compromise bills had the best chance of interrupting the momentum for secession.

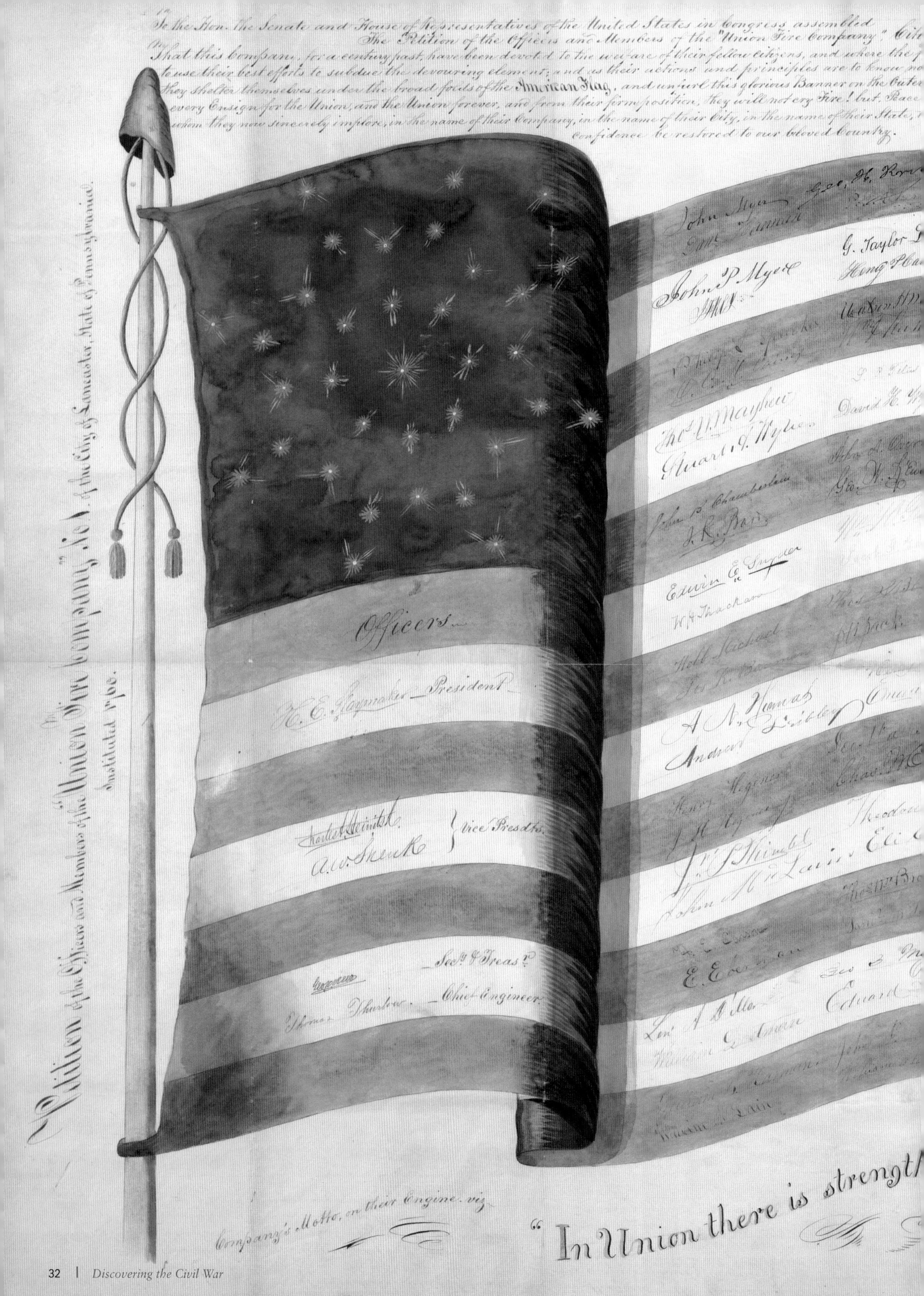

To the Hon. The Senate and House of Representatives of the United States in Congress assembled

The Petition of the Officers and Members of the "Union Fire Company" Cit...

That this company, for a century past, have been devoted to the welfare of their fellow citizens, and where they...

to use their best efforts to subdue the devouring element, and as their actions and principles are to know no...

they shelter themselves under the broad folds of the American Flag, and unfurl this glorious Banner on the outer...

every Ensign for the Union, and the Union forever, and from their firm position, they will not cry Fire! but... Peace...

whom they now sincerely implore, in the name of their Company, in the name of their City, in the name of their State...

confidence be restored to our beloved Country.

Officers

H. E. Slaymaker — President

Charles Heinitsh
A. W. Shenk } Vice Presdts.

Sec'y & Treas'r

Thomas Thurlow — Chief Engineer

Company's Motto, on their Engine, viz.

"In Union there is strength"

the City of Lancaster, Penna. _____ Most Respectfully Represents,

...mes threatened the greatest destruction, they never stopped to inquire the cause, but rushed...

...West, no North, no South, but only the love of their fellow men, and perpetuity of the beloved Union...

...d on the highest pinnacles, until every mountain has its host, and every host its Ensign, and...

...Peace !" until their voice be heard, and their fervent prayers be granted, by their Hon. Representatives...

Crittenden or Bigler Compromise Resolutions, or any other of similar import, so that Peace and)

And they will ever Respectfully pray &c.

We lend our aid in time of need."

"The Petition of the Officers and Members of the 'Union Fire Company'" of Lancaster, Pennsylvania, supporting the Crittenden Compromise. February 6, 1861

National Archives,
Records of the U.S. Senate

To the Senate of the United States:

The petition of the undersigned CITIZENS OF PHILADELPHIA, without distinction of party, respectfully showeth :

That they earnestly pray your honorable body, to pass the resolutions introduced by the HON. MR. CRITTENDEN, of Kentucky; a copy of which is hereunto annexed, or resolutions embodying the same principles and measures, believing that this course will be acceptable to your constituents in all sections of our country, and will have the effect of allaying the present unhappy excitement.

RESOLUTIONS
Introduced into the Senate of the United States, by the Hon. Mr. Crittenden, of Kentucky, on the 18th of December, 1860.

Whereas, Alarming dissensions have arisen between the Northern and Southern States as to the rights to the common Territory of the United States, it is eminently desirable and proper that such dissensions should be settled by the constitutional provisions which give equal justice to all sections, whereby to restore peace. Therefore,

Resolved, By the Senate and House of Representatives, that the following articles be proposed and submitted as an amendment to the Constitution, which shall be valid as a part of the Constitution, when ratified by conventions of three-fourths of the people of the States.

First, In all the Territories now or hereafter acquired north of latitude 36 degrees 40 minutes, slavery or involuntary servitude, except punishment for crime, shall be prohibited ; while south of that latitude it shall remain ; and in all territory south of that latitude, slavery is hereby recognized as existing, and not to be interfered with by Congress, but be protected as property by all departments of the territorial goverment during its continuance as a territory. When territory north or south of such line, within such boundaries as Congress may prescribe, shall contain the population necessary for a member of Congress, with a republican form of government, it shall be admitted into the Union on an equality with the original States, with or without slavery, as the Constitution of the State may prescribe.

Second, Congress shall have no power to abolish slavery in places under its jurisdiction, or in States permitting slavery.

Third, Congress shall have no power to abolish slavery in the District of Columbia, while it exists in Virginia or Maryland, or either. Congress shall never, at any time, prohibit the officers of the Government, or members of Congress, whose duties require them to live in the District of Columbia, and bringing slaves, from holding them as such.

Fourth, Congress shall have no power to hinder the transportation of slaves from one State to another, whether by land, navigable rivers, or sea.

Fifth, Congress shall have power by law to pay the owner who shall apply, the full value of the fugitive slave in all cases when the marshal is prevented from discharging his duty, by force or rescue, made after the arrest. In all such cases the United States shall have power to sue the county in which such violence or rescue is made, and the county shall have the right to sue the individuals who committed the wrong in the same manner as the owner could sue.

Sixth, No future amendments shall affect the preceding articles, and Congress shall never have power to interfere with slavery in the States where it is now permitted.

A PETITION FROM PHILADELPHIA

Many Americans—including the "Citizens of Philadelphia" who wrote this more standard petition—saw the Crittenden Compromise as a solution to the "alarming dissensions . . . between the northern and southern states."

National Archives, Records of the U.S. Senate

The proposed amendments protected slave interests, settled the slavery question, and preserved the Union by

- restoring the Missouri Compromise line (36° 30') and extending it to the Pacific, with the line marking the boundary between slave and free territories
- reducing congressional authority to regulate slavery in Federal jurisdictions
- guaranteeing full compensation to slave owners prevented from recovering their property
- changing the Presidential term to a single six-year term; and
- prohibiting any future constitutional amendments from modifying or replacing these amendments and all other provisions concerning slavery.

Flag Petition

On February 6, 1861, in the midst of the debate over the Crittenden proposals, Senator Bigler presented a most unusual petition to the Senate. It was a large color drawing of the American flag waving from a pole topped by a liberty cap and draped with braid. The petition asked Congress to pass the "Crittenden or Bigler compromise Resolutions, or any other of similar import" in order "to resolve the sectional crisis."

This colorful document was created for the Union Fire Company, No. 1, of Lancaster, Pennsylvania, which was celebrating its centennial in 1860. The company's membership had included a signer of the Declaration of Independence (George Ross), a President (James Buchanan), state and local leaders, and many veterans from the Colonial wars, the American Revolution, and more recent conflicts. Unlike many other urban volunteer fire departments, the Union Fire Company had remained an organization made up of sober men of standing and had not degenerated into a club of drunken thugs.

The centennial celebrations honored the company's respectability and century of service. A parade capped a two-day summer festival. At the end of the parade, the Lady Friends of the Union Fire Company, No. 1, presented the volunteer firemen with "a beautiful silk American flag, with golden stars set in a ground of deep blue." Its pole was topped with a liberty cap in red velvet decorated with silver stars.

Volunteer fireman and artist J. Franklin Reigart used the centennial flag and pole as the model for the petition. Above the waving flag was the company's plea to Congress. Beside the pole was the title "Union Fire Company, No. 1." And below the flag was the company's motto: "In Union there is strength. We lend our aid in time of need."

The petition described how the volunteer firemen headed "where the fiercest flames threatened the greatest destruction." They "never stopped to inquire the cause, but rushed, to use their best efforts to subdue the devouring element." As citizens "devoted to the welfare of their fellow citizens," they asked Congress to follow their attitude and ignore regional interests in favor of national interests. After calling for passage of either the Crittenden or Bigler compromises, the company's officers and men signed their names along the stripes of the flag.

Senator Bigler later described to the company the Senate's reception of their memorial, closing with hope for "an adjustment that may save for a time what remains of the Union, but no one can tell what a day may bring forth."

Fate of the Compromise

But time was not on the side of the peacemakers. Neither Crittenden's nor Bigler's proposals were ever taken up. Instead, the House of Representatives passed a constitutional amendment that prohibited any amendments concerning the domestic institutions of the states, including slavery. In the closing days of the Congress, the Senate narrowly passed the House resolution.

Lincoln was inaugurated President on March 4. The states of the Upper South seceded. A Confederate States of America was established. The Confederate forces began firing on Fort Sumter on April 12, 1861, and the Civil War began.

As a result of the war, the Union Fire Company's meeting in May 1861 was "the smallest meeting held" by the company. Many of the men had joined state militia in response to President Lincoln's call for a Union Army. Eventually, a company of Pennsylvania soldiers became known as the Union Guard because so many of the Union Fire Company's members made up its ranks. In July 1862 the company voted to lower its flag for 15 days for the many former firemen killed during the Peninsular Campaign.

NOTE ON SOURCES

The petition from the Union Fire Company, No. 1, can be found in Records of the U.S. Senate, Record Group 46. The Fire Company's history was written by Alfred Sanderson and privately published in 1879 on the occasion of Lancaster's first professional fire department. See *Historical Sketch of the Union Fire Company, No. 1, of the City of Lancaster, Penna., From 1760 to 1879*. The classic account of the "secession crisis" is David M. Potter's *Lincoln and His Party in the Secession Crisis* (1942, reprinted 1995) as well as Allan Nevins' *The Emergence of Lincoln: Prologue to Civil War, 1859-1861* (1978, reprinted 1992). An interesting discussion of petitions to Congress can be found in William Lee Miller's *Arguing about Slavery: John Quincy Adams and the Great Battle in the United States Congress* (1995). Amy S. Greenberg's *Cause for Alarm: The Volunteer Fire Department in the Nineteenth-Century City* (1998) focuses attention on the world of the volunteer fireman in an urban setting.

BECOMING A CONFEDERATE CITIZEN

Joel Walker

When the Civil War erupted, citizens like Benjamin Bennett—a native of New York living in the South—suddenly found themselves aliens in their own land. How did they become Confederate citizens?

September 12, 1861, was a hot, humid day in Mobile, Alabama. Germans, Irishmen, Norwegians, and Swedes pulled at their collars and wiped their brows as they waited for the 73-year-old law clerk to prepare the form that would enable them to declare their intention to become naturalized citizens. The clerk, John A. Cuthbert, patiently crossed out certain words on the form and replaced them with handwritten ones. Wherever the word "United" appeared, four times on each page, he slashed it out and wrote in "Confederate." Then he completed the declaration with the future citizen's name, the country (or state) of former citizenship, and the promise to renounce former allegiance.

Moving to Mobile

John Cuthbert came to Mobile 24 years earlier, in 1837, when he acquired the *Sans Souci* estate on Mon Louis Island. He left a successful law and political career in Georgia, where he had served as a United States Congressman and had a town named after him, to cast his lot with the growing port city on Mobile Bay. In 1860, Mobile was the 27th largest city in the United States of America, with a population of 29,258. Now, just a year later, it was the fourth largest city in the Confederate States of America. It was beginning to bustle.

Mobile was blessed with valuable natural features, agricultural advancement, and progressive technology. Mobile Bay, along with the two rivers that flowed into it, provided natural access from the sea into the Southern interior. The invention of the cotton gin and the subsequent advance of King Cotton had opened up this interior, and two railroad lines now led out of Mobile—one heading northeast and the other northwest. The combination of transportation corridors and an expanding hinterland attracted workers from other parts of the country and around the world. They were needed to build, sail, load, and unload ocean-going ships. It was these new workers who appeared before John A. Cuthbert, clerk of the Confederate States District Court of Alabama, Southern Division, to declare their intention to become citizens of the Confederacy.

Becoming Naturalized, Confederate-Style

The basic process for becoming a naturalized citizen in the new Confederacy remained very similar to that in the United States. Individuals needed to live in the country for five years and declare their intention to naturalize at least two years before becoming citizens. Two exceptions to the United States process made the Southern method unique.

In August 1861, the Confederate Congress enacted a law allowing foreigners already in the Confederate military to become citizens immediately by taking an oath administered by their commanding officer. There was no need to declare one's intention. Nor was there a need to live in the country for five years.

The second exception dealt with alien enemies—foreigners from a country at war with the Confederacy. Since the War of 1812, the United States did not allow any alien enemy to declare his or her intention to become a citizen, let alone become one. This was not the case in the Confederacy.

Benjamin Bennett Declares his Intention

And so on September 12, 1861, Benjamin C. Bennett, a 28-year-old carpenter from New York, declared his intention to become a citizen of the Confederacy. He renounced "all allegiance and fidelity to . . . the state of New York, and the government of the United States." The Confederate States had been at war with the United States (and thus New York) since shots were fired at Fort Sumter earlier that year on April 12.

Bennett was one of 16 "foreigners" who declared their intention to naturalize that September day, the first day that any Confederate declarations were recorded in the Mobile court. It was a full eight months since Alabama seceded from the Union on January 11, and John A. Cuthbert used the same bound volume of declaration forms that had been used by the United States District Court of Alabama. On page 54, Cuthbert began slashing out "United" and replacing it with "Confederate." The last completed form, signed by Cuthbert, is dated June 7, 1862. It declares Kentucky-born Clayton A. Mobley's desire to naturalize. Mobley's form is on page 208. On the intervening pages, foreigners from Ireland, England, Sweden, Norway, and Germany declared their intention alongside others from "foreign lands" such as Rhode Island, Pennsylvania, Ohio, and New Jersey.

Following the Record Trail

What became of these future citizens of the Confederacy? Many can be found in the military records of the Confederacy. Some appear in the 1870 U.S. Census and subsequent censuses. No Benjamin C. Bennett born in New York and living in Alabama shows up in Alabama after the 1860 census. There are Benjamin Bennetts and B. C. Bennetts in the records of Alabama's Civil War regiments, but it's not clear if they are

Confederate

UNITED STATES OF AMERICA, } So. Div.
SOUTHERN DISTRICT OF ALABAMA. }

Be it Remembered, That Benjamin C. Bennett
personally appeared before me Confederate   Clerk of the District
Court of the United States for the District aforesaid, on this 12th   day of
September   in the year of our Lord one thousand eight hundred and
fifty-sixty one,   who upon his solemn oath, doth depose and say, that he is a native of
of New York,

now residing in the State of Alabama—that he has been in the United States
years—that he is aged   years or thereabouts—that it is *bona fide* his
intention to become a citizen of the Confederate United States, and absolutely and entirely to renounce and
abjure all allegiance and fidelity to every foreign Prince, Potentate, State or Sovereignty and
particularly to the State of New York, & the government of the United States; & that he doth acknowledge the authority of the government of the Confederate States.

IN TESTIMONY WHEREOF, I have hereunto set my hand and
affixed the seal of said Court at Mobile, this day and date
above written.

John A. Cuthbert

Clerk.

ALIEN IN ALABAMA

In 1861, Benjamin C. Bennett, "a native of New York" living in the South, had to go to the District Court of Alabama to change his legal status. On this form he declared his intention to become a Confederate citizen and to "renounce . . . all allegiance and fidelity to . . . the government of the United States." As you can see, the process required some modification of the existing form.

National Archives at Atlanta, Records of the District Courts of the United States

the same Benjamin C. Bennett who declared his citizenship intention on September 12, 1861.

And what of John A. Cuthbert? He finished the bound volume of declarations in 1862 and completed an index of all hopeful new citizens, both U.S. and Confederate, which he recorded on the backs of the final few forms. Last mention of him in Federal records is in the 1880 census. He was again practicing law in Mobile, Alabama, and living as a boarder at the residence of John and Kate Williams. He died a year later at the age of 93.

NOTE ON SOURCES

The bound volume *Declaration of Intention 1855-1859, 1861-62* in Records of the U.S. District Courts, Southern District of Alabama, Record Group 21, documents a wide variety of native countries and, during the 1861-62 years, native states of those declaring for citizenship. But the forms say little about who these people were, what they did, or even how old they were. Finding these individuals in the 1860 U.S. Census and correlating name with place of birth not only determined biographical details but established the growing cosmopolitan nature of Mobile, Alabama. The Alabama Department of Archives and History's online *Civil War Soldiers Database* identified their role in the war. William M. Robinson's *Justice in Grey: A History of the Judiciary System of the Confederate States of America* (Harvard University Press, 1941) referred to a number of the declaration forms in the bound volume mentioned above, including that of Benjamin C. Bennett, in its explanation of the Confederate naturalization process. *The Biographical Directory of the United States Congress* documented much of the life of Confederate Clerk John A. Cuthbert.

THE CONSCRIPT BILL!
HOW TO AVOID IT!!
U. S. NAVY.
1,000 MEN WANTED, FOR 12 MONTHS

Seamen's Pay, - - - - - - - $18.00 per month
Ordinary Seamen's Pay, . : . . . 14.00 " "
Landsmen's Pay, ... 12.00 " "
$1.50 extra per month to all, Grog Money.

$50,000,000 PRIZES!

Already captured, a large share of which is awarded to Ships Crews. The laws for the distributing of Prize money carefull
protects the rights of all the captors.

PETTY OFFICERS,—PROMOTION.—Seamen have a chance for promotion to the offices of Master at Arms, Boatswain'
Mates, Quarter Gunners, Captain of Tops, Forecastle, Holds, After-Guard, &c.
Landsmen may be advanced to Armorers, Armorers' Mates, Carpenter's Mates, Sailmakers' Mates, Painters, Coopers, &c.
PAY OF PETTY OFFICERS,—From $20.00 to $45.00 per month.
CHANCES FOR WARRANTS, BOUNTIES AND MEDALS OF HONOR.—All those who distinguish themselves i
battle or by extraordinary heroism, may be promoted to forward Warrant Officers or Acting Masters' Mates,—and upon thei
promotion receive a guaranty of $100, with a medal of honor from their country.
All who wish may leave HALF PAY with their families, to commence from date of enlistment.
Minors must have a written consent, sworn to before a Justice of the Peace.

For further information apply to U. S. NAVAL RENDEZVOUS,
E. Y. BUTLER, U. S. N. Recruiting Officer,
No. 14 FRONT STREET, SALEM, MASS.

FROM WRIGHT & POTTER'S BOSTON PRINTING ESTABLISHMENT, No. 4 SPRING LANE, CORNER OF DEVONSHIRE STREET.

CHAPTER 2

RAISING ARMIES

In early 1861 the U.S. Army consisted of only about 14,000 men. The U.S. Navy was even smaller and scattered around the world's oceans. The new Confederate States of America had to create an army and navy from scratch.

Yet just four years later, millions of men had fought on both sides.

- How did the North and South build such huge armed forces so quickly?

- What motivated men to enlist?

- What if you didn't want to serve?

- What happened to those who resisted?

The documents that follow provide evidence that both North and South took far-reaching measures to raise and retain their fighting forces.

JOIN THE NAVY AND GET RICH!

In July 1863, when the U.S. Congress instituted a draft, many men sought to avoid Army service. The U.S. Navy still relied on volunteers for manpower. It used this broadside to convince potential recruits that service in the Navy would be much more financially rewarding than service in the Army. The Confederate Congress enacted the first national draft in American history more than a year earlier, in April 1862.

National Archives, Naval Records Collection of the Office of Naval Records and Library

YOUNGSTERS AT WAR

This drummer boy, who served with the 78th U.S. Colored Troops, was one of more than 10,000 troops under the age of 18 who enlisted in the Union Army. About five percent of Confederate Army troops were under the age of 18.

National Archives, Records of the War Department General and Special Staffs
[165-JT-302]

INTEGRATED BUT NOT EQUAL

This U.S. gunboat, probably the *Mendota*, had an integrated crew. Many of the black crew members were recently freed slaves. About 18,000 black men served in the U.S. Navy, but black sailors served only in the lowest ranks.

National Archives, Records of the Office of the Chief Signal Officer [111-B-129]

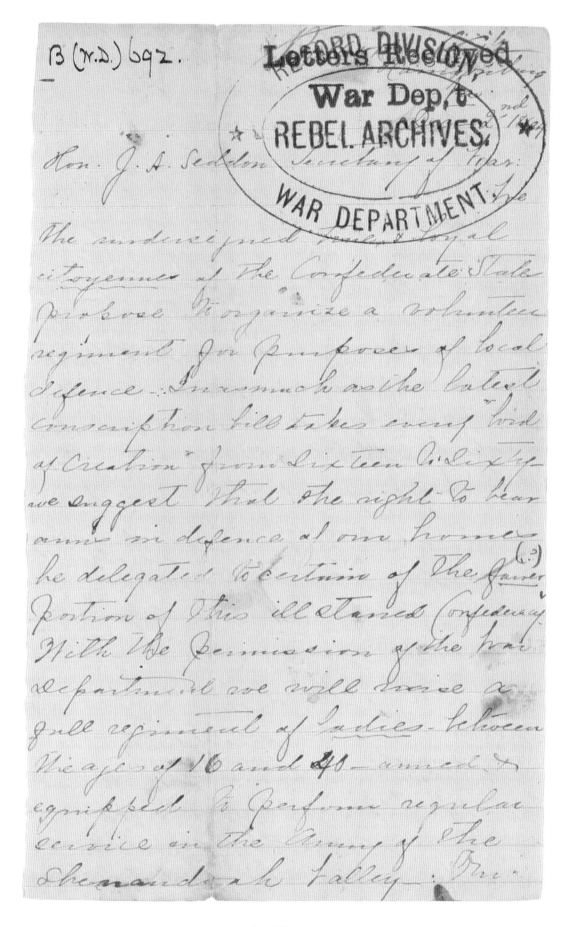

WHY NOT LET WOMEN FIGHT? SELECTED PAGE

In late 1864, a group of women from Harrisonburg, Virginia, wrote to Confederate Secretary of War James Seddon offering to "raise a full regiment of Ladies between the ages of 16 and 40 . . . " The Confederate War Department replied that it was "not quite ready to call the Ladies to our help in the Field. The Men of the Country it is hoped will suffice."

National Archives, War Department Collection of Confederate Records

APPEAL TO VIRGINIA MEN

A close look reveals that this impassioned 1861 broadside refers to western Virginia, not the American West. It was issued in Augusta County, Virginia, by Michael G. Harman, a wealthy hotel owner, planter, and slaveholder. He was also quartermaster and chief recruiter for western Virginia. Many volunteers from Augusta County formed the 52nd Virginia Infantry. Early in the war, men volunteered for patriotic reasons. As the war dragged on, the armed services resorted to financial incentives, the draft, and recruiting agents.

National Archives, War Department Collection of Confederate Records

Headquarters, Va. Forces,

Staunton, June 7th, 1861.

To Arms! To Arms!!

BRAVE MEN OF THE WEST!!

Drive back the insolent invaders who insult you by their presence on your soil. Our little band of Volunteers have been forced from Phillippa by the *ruthless Northern foe* led on by traitors and tories. It is for you now to rally to the field and **AVENGE THE INSULTED HONOR OF WESTERN VIRGINIA.**

To-day I send to your assistance a force of *Artillery, Cavalry, Infantry* and *Rifles.* To-morrow

AN ARMY WILL FOLLOW

sent to your aid by your patriotic President, JEFFERSON DAVIS, and your noble Governor, JOHN LETCHER.

Arms, Ammunition and Uniforms will be supplied you at your places of rendezvous.

M. G. HARMAN,

Major Commanding.

WANTED! 200 NEGROES.

By direction of Lieut. Gen. Pemberton, Commanding Department of Mississippi and East Louisiana, I call upon the Planters of Lowndes and adjacent counties for Negroes to complete the fortifications.

For every negro furnished, including cooks, the Quartermaster's department will pay $1 25 per day—owners to feed their negroes. Tents or other shelter will be provided by the Government.

Good and experienced overseers will be employed to stay with and take charge of the laborers.

Report on Monday morning, 3rd Nov. in front of Court House.

JNO. ADAMS,

Col. C. S. Army.

SLAVES IN THE CONFEDERATE ARMY

The Confederate Army used slaves as cooks, servants, and teamsters. They also built fortifications. This advertisement called on slave owners to provide slaves—and receive payment for their labor in return.

In March 1865, just weeks before the end of the war, the Confederate Congress passed legislation allowing its army to recruit black troops. But it did not promise the troops freedom in return for their military service.

National Archives, War Department Collection of Confederate Records

TO COLORED MEN!

FREEDOM,

Protection, Pay, and a Call to Military Duty!

On the 1st day of January, 1863, the President of the United States proclaimed FREE-
DOM to over THREE MILLIONS OF SLAVES. This decree is to be enforced by all the power of
the Nation. On the 21st of July last he issued the following order:

PROTECTION OF COLORED TROOPS.

"WAR DEPARTMENT, ADJUTANT GENERAL'S OFFICE,
WASHINGTON, July 21.

"*General Order, No. 233.*

"The following order of the President is published for the information and government of all concerned:—

EXECUTIVE MANSION, WASHINGTON, July 30.

"'It is the duty of every Government to give protection to its citizens, of whatever class, color, or condition, and especially to
those who are duly organized as soldiers in the public service. The law of nations, and the usages and customs of war, as carried on
by civilized powers, permit no distinction as to color in the treatment of prisoners of war as public enemies. To sell or enslave any
captured person on account of his color, is a relapse into barbarism, and a crime against the civilization of the age.

"'The Government of the United States will give the same protection to all its soldiers, and if the enemy shall sell or enslave any
one because of his color, the offense shall be punished by retaliation upon the enemy's prisoners in our possession. It is, therefore,
ordered, for every soldier of the United States, killed in violation of the laws of war, a rebel soldier shall be executed; and for every
one enslaved by the enemy, or sold into slavery, a rebel soldier shall be placed at hard labor on the public works, and continued at such
labor until the other shall be released and receive the treatment due to prisoners of war.

"'ABRAHAM LINCOLN.'"

"'By order of the Secretary of War.
"'E. D. TOWNSEND, Assistant Adjutant General.'"

That the President is in earnest the rebels soon began to find out, as witness the following order from his Secretary of War:

"WAR DEPARTMENT, WASHINGTON CITY, August 8, 1863.

"SIR: Your letter of the 3d inst., calling the attention of this Department to the cases of Orin H. Brown, William H. Johnston,
and Wm. Wilson, three colored men captured on the gunboat Isaac Smith, has received consideration. This Department has directed
that three rebel prisoners of South Carolina, if there be any such in our possession, and if not, three others, be confined in close custody
and held as hostages for Brown, Johnston and Wilson, and that the fact be communicated to the rebel authorities at Richmond.
"Very respectfully your obedient servant,
"EDWIN M. STANTON, Secretary of War.

"The Hon. GIDEON WELLES, Secretary of the Navy."

And retaliation will be our practice now—man for man—to the bitter end.

LETTER OF CHARLES SUMNER,

Written with reference to the Convention held at Poughkeepsie, July 15th and 16th, 1863, to promote Colored Enlistments.

BOSTON, July 13th, 1863.

"I doubt if, in times past, our country could have expected from colored men any patriotic service. Such service is the return for
protection. But now that protection has begun, the service should begin also. Nor should relative rights and duties be weighed with
nicety. It is enough that our country, aroused at last to a sense of justice, seeks to enrol colored men among its defenders.

"If my counsels should reach such persons, I would say: enlist at once. Now is the day and now is the hour. Help to overcome
your cruel enemies now battling against your country, and in this way you will surely overcome those other enemies hardly less cruel,
here at home, who will still seek to degrade you. This is not the time to hesitate or to higgle. Do your duty to our country, and you
will set an example of generous self-sacrifice which will conquer prejudice and open all hearts.
"Very faithfully yours,
"CHARLES SUMNER."

PROMISE TO BLACK TROOPS

After President Lincoln issued the Emancipation Proclamation on January 1, 1863, the U.S. Army began recruiting
black men in earnest. The Confederate government regarded captured black soldiers as fugitive slaves, not prisoners
of war. It threatened to execute or sell them into slavery. This broadside reassured potential black recruits that the
U.S. Government would treat *all* of its troops as soldiers—and retaliate in the event of Confederate mistreatment of
black U.S. soldiers.

National Archives, Records of the Adjutant General's Office, 1780's–1917

The Curious Case of James Gorman

This rare example of a Civil War recruitment notice points to a mystery. When the United States first authorized a draft on March 3, 1863, James Gorman had already served in the U.S. Army for about 18 months, with Company A of the 6th New Jersey Infantry. In May 1863, Gorman was wounded and captured briefly by Confederate forces during the Battle of Chancellorsville. The rest of his service seems to have been mundane—until May 11, 1864, when he was fatally wounded at the Battle of the Wilderness in Virginia.

Less than two months later, this draft notice was issued for Gorman. It is unclear why he was drafted after his death. It could be a simple bureaucratic mistake. Records in his military service file suggest some confusion around his name. An 1866 request for records about a Joseph Gorman who served with the 6th New Jersey, received a reply that Joseph Gorman could not be found in the records.

DEAD BUT STILL DRAFTED
This document is a rare and unusual example of a Civil War draft notice.
Donated Materials in the National Archives

RIOTS IN NEW YORK
In mid-July 1863, when Federal officials began enrolling men for the draft, riots erupted in New York City. This illustration of police charging on the rioters appeared in the August 3, 1863, issue of *Harper's Weekly*. More than 5,000 troops arrived—many directly from the Battle at Gettysburg. Nevertheless an estimated 20,000 rioters ruled the city for four days, and 119 people died. Rioters targeted New York's African American community, burning the Colored Orphan Asylum and driving many blacks out of the city.
Courtesy of the New York Public Library

CHARGE OF THE POLICE ON THE RIOTERS AT THE "TRIBUNE" OFFICE.

Representative Recruit

No. 39.

~~SUBSTITUTE~~

VOLUNTEER ENLISTMENT.

District

STATE OF   *3 sub dis of* **TOWN OF**

Columbia   *Washington DC*

I, *John S. Staples* born in the State of *Pennsylvania*, aged *Money* years, and by occupation a *Laborer* DO HEREBY ACKNOWLEDGE to have agreed with *Abraham Lincoln*, Esq., of *3 sub district of District of Columbia* to become his ~~SUBSTITUTE~~ in the Military Service, for a sufficient consideration paid and delivered to me, on the *first* day of *October*, 1864; and having thus agreed with said *Abraham Lincoln* I DO HEREBY ACKNOWLEDGE to have enlisted this *first* day of *October* 1864, to serve as a **Soldier** in the **Army of the United States of America**, for the period of *One* ~~THREE YEARS~~, unless sooner discharged by proper authority: I do also agree to accept such bounty, pay, rations, and clothing, as are, or may be, established by law for soldiers. And I do solemnly swear that I will bear true and faithful allegiance to the **United States of America;** that I will serve them honestly and faithfully against all their enemies or opposers whomsoever; and that I will observe and obey the orders of the President of the United States, and the orders of the Officers appointed over me, according to the Rules and Articles of War.

SWORN and subscribed to, at *Washington DC* this *1* day of *October* 1864.

BEFORE ___   *John S Staples*

Capt 1 Reg VRC
Provost Marshal
DC.

Representative

We certify, on honor, That we have carefully examined the above-named ~~Volunteer Substitute~~ agreeably to the Regulations, and that, in our opinion, he is free from all bodily defects and mental infirmity which would in any way disqualify him from performing the duties of a soldier; that he was entirely sober when enlisted; that he is of lawful age, (not under 18 years;) and that, in accepting him as duly qualified to perform the duties of an able-bodied soldier, and as a ~~Substitute~~ *Representative* in lieu of *Abraham Lincoln* ___ drafted in *Not liable to draft* ___, 1864 we have strictly observed the Regulations which govern in such cases. This soldier has *blue* eyes, *brown* hair, *dark* complexion; is *5* feet *3* inches high.

Capt 1 Reg VRC Provost Marshal

___ Commissioner of Board.

___ Surgeon of Board.

Board of Enrollment of *th* Dist. of *Col*

LINCOLN'S SUBSTITUTE

In both the North and South many men who were drafted hired substitutes to take their place for a going rate of $200 to $275. President Lincoln was well over the age to be eligible for the draft. But he sponsored a soldier, 19-year-old J. Summerfield Staples from Pennsylvania, through a program known as "representative recruits." Staples has come to be known as Lincoln's "substitute."

National Archives, Records of the Adjutant General's Office, 1780's–1917

FORM I.

Bond to be given by Persons claiming Exemption under the 2d clause of the 4th Article, 10th Section of the Act of Congress, Approved February 17, 1864.

THE CONFEDERATE STATES OF AMERICA:

State of *Georgia*

KNOW ALL MEN BY THESE PRESENTS, That We, *Lycurgus S Rees* of *Columbia* County, in the said State, *James B Neal Security* of *Columbia* County, and *John E Smith Security* of *Columbia* County, in the said State, are held and firmly bound unto the Confederate States of America, in the penal sum of *Ten Thousand* Dollars to be paid to the said Confederate States of America; for which payment well and truly to be made and done, we bind ourselves, and each of us, our heirs, executors and administrators, jointly and severally, firmly by these presents.

Sealed with our seals and dated this _____ day of *May* in the year of our Lord one thousand eight hundred and sixty *four*.

Whereas, the above bound *L S Rees* has applied for the exemption of *himself* as a *Farmer or Agriculturalist* under the fourth article of the tenth section of the Act of Congress, approved 17th February, 1864, entitled "An Act to organize forces to serve during the War," there being upon the farm or plantation of the said *Lycurgus S Rees* for which exemption is sought, *Fifteen* able-bodied slaves between the ages of sixteen and fifty, within the meaning of said act; and which application is to be granted upon the satisfactory execution of this Bond:

Now THE CONDITION OF THIS OBLIGATION IS SUCH, That if the above bound *Lycurgus S. Rees* shall deliver to the duly authorized Officer or Agent of the Confederate States, at *Thomson depot G RR*, or at such other place as may be directed by the Secretary of War, or his duly authorized Officer or Agent, within twelve months from the date hereof, *Fifteen hundred* pounds of Bacon, or, at the election of the Government, its equivalent in Pork, and *Fifteen hundred* pounds of nett Beef, (said Beef to be delivered on foot,) to be paid for by the Government at the prices fixed by the Commissioners of the State, under the Impressment Act, and shall sell the marketable surplus of provisions and grain now on hand, and which he may raise from year to year while this Exemption continues, to the Government, or to the families of soldiers, at prices not exceeding the prices fixed by the Commissioners of the State, under the Impressment Act; and shall in all other respects faithfully conform to the requisitions of the said Act, under which the said *L S Rees* is exempted, according to the true intent and meaning thereof, (he being entitled to the commutation therein provided upon compliance with the terms thereof,) then this obligation to be void and of no effect, or else to remain in full force and virtue.

Signed, Sealed and Delivered in presence of

R140 1884

James B. Neal (SEAL)

(SEAL)

Robert Martin J. P.   *John E Smith* (SEAL)

APPLYING FOR EXEMPTION

Many Southern whites believed the Confederate draft favored the rich. The "twenty Negro law," for example, exempted planters with 20 or more slaves. In February 1864 that requirement was reduced to 15 slaves, and Georgian Lycurgus Rees—who had "fifteen able-bodied slaves"—applied for an exemption as "a Farmer or Agriculturalist." In return he agreed to furnish the Confederate War Department with 1,500 pounds of beef, bacon, or pork.

National Archives, War Department Collection of Confederate Records

DESERTERS.

$360 REWARD !

I will give thirty dollars reward for the arrest and delivery to me, or lodgment in jail, with due notice to me, so that I can secure them, of each of the following deserters from Company D, Russell's Rangers, 4th Ala. Cavalry, C. S. A.

George B. Collins.—Has dark hair, eyes and skin, is about 5 feet, 10 inches high, weighs about 150 pounds, and is about 23 years old. Residence, near Valhermoso Springs, Morgan county, Ala.

J. W. Ennis.—Has dark hair, blue eyes, fair complexion, 5 feet 6 or 8 inches high, weighs about 160 pounds, and is about 26 years old. Residence, near Brooksville Blount county, Ala.

John O. Feemster.—Has dark hair, blue eyes, fair complexion, 5 feet 8 or 10 inches high, is about 21 years old. Weighs about 165 pounds. Residence, Red Hill P. O., Marshall county Ala.

Wm. M. Feemster.—Has dark hair, blue eyes, fair skin, is about 5 feet 8 or 10 inches high, weighs about 165 lbs. and is about 18 years old. Residence, near Red Hill P. O., Marshall county, Ala.

John M. Lee.—Has light hair, blue eyes, fair skin is about 5 feet 8 inches high, weighs about 170 lbs., and is about 21 years old. Residence, near Vienna, Madison county, Ala.

Newton Rone.—Has dark hair, eyes and skin, is about 5 feet 6 inches high, weighs about 130 lbs, and is about 19 years old. Residence, near Blue Spring P. O., Morgan county, Ala.

Wiley B. Sherrol.—Has dark hair, eyes and complexion, is about 5 feet 9 in high, weighs about 170 lbs, and is about 22 years old. Residence, near Danville, Morgan county, Ala.

J. H. B. Smallwood.—Has light hair, grey eyes, fair complexion, is about 6 feet high, weighs about 170 lbs, and is about 22 years old. Residence, on Cane creek, Marshall county, Ala.

Wiley Vinzant.—Has dark hair, grey eyes and dark complexion, is about 5 feet 7 inches high, weighs about 150 lbs. and is about 22 years old. Residence, Gandy's Cove P. O., Morgan county, Ala.

N. B. Whalen.—Has black hair and eyes and dark complexion, is about 5 feet 10 inches high, weighs about [....] is about 23 years old. Residence, Red Hill P. O., Marshall county Ala.

James W. Ennis, John O. Feemster, Wm. M. Feemster, John M. Lee, and Newton Rone, enlisted at Big Spring, Marshall county, Ala., July 9, 1863.

George B. Collins, Wily B. Sherrol, Wiley Vinzant and N. B. Whalen, enlisted at Falkville, Morgan county, Ala., and J. H. B. Smallwood enlisted at Guntersville, Ala., on and about the 15th Aug't, 1862.

Nathenial Homes.—Has dark hair, blue eyes, light complexion, is about 6 feet high weighs about 165 lbs., and is about 23 years old. Residence, Mount Alvis P. O., Blount county, Ala. Enlisted at Falkville, Morgan county, Ala., Aug 5, '62.

Isaac I. Hoyle.—Has dark hair, eyes and complexion, (right four finger shot off) is about 5 feet 8 inches high, weighs about 130 lbs, and is about 20 years old. Residence, near Apple Grove, Morgan county, Ala.—enlisted at Falkville, Morgan county, Ala., Aug. 5 1862.

Address

Capt. Wm. H. TAYLOR.

Company D, Russell's Rangers, 4th Ala. Cavalry, Shelbyville, Tenn.—april2—3m.

Deserter---$30 Reward.

CAMP, RUSSELL'S REGIMENT ALABAMA CAVALRY,
HEADQUARTERS, UNIONVILLE, April 28, 1863.

THIRTY dollars reward will be paid for the apprehension, or safe delivery in jail, or nearest Military Post, for the following named deserter from my Co. (D.) Russell's Regiment Alabama Cavalry:

Thomas H. Love—Has fair complexion, grey eyes, light hair, five feet six inches high, weighs about 125 pounds. Residence near Somerville, Alabama, and was enlisted at Big Spring, Alabama, July 9, 1862, to serve for three years or the war.

Address,

W. H. TAYLOR, Capt.,
Commanding Co D., Russell's Reg't,
may7—tf. Alabama Cavalry.

WAR DEPARTMENT,
Provost Marshal General's Office,
WASHINGTON. D. C., *October 6, 1864.*

To *Major Thomas Duncan,*
3rd U. S. Cav'y
A*c*t. Ass't Provost Marshal General,

Davenport, Iowa,

The "Daily Reports of the state of the draft," received at this office, disclose the fact that an extraordinary proportion of drafted men fail to report for examination. You will immediately adopt the best course you can devise to secure the arrest of the delinquents, and, *under no circumstance, permit them to lurk within your jurisdiction.* You will, whenever necessary, invoke the aid of such military authorities as are within your reach, and request the co-operation of the civil authorities.

JAMES B. FRY,
Provost Marshal General.

OFFICIAL:

Theo McMurtrie

Captain, and Act. Ass't Adjt. Gen.

REWARD FOR DESERTERS

This clipping offers a $30 reward for each Confederate deserter listed. Both the United States and the Confederacy were hurt by desertions. Confederate Army desertion rates for the entire war were about 12 percent, but desertion varied by geography. In Virginia, for example, desertion peaked in 1862 and then held steady. Many Confederate deserters took off for a few weeks to visit family or help with farm work, and then returned to their units. But others left permanently, and some organized guerrilla bands to resist capture.

National Archives, War Department Collection of Confederate Records

"ARREST . . . THE DELINQUENTS"

Resistance to the Union draft necessitated this memorandum from the War Department. About 20 percent of draftees never reported. Enrolling officers were sometimes beaten, run out of town, or shot at. Antidraft sentiment was especially strong in the Midwest, where antiwar Democrats (called "Copperheads" by Republicans) organized rallies and hid draft evaders.

National Archives at Kansas City, Records of the Provost Marshal General's Bureau (Civil War)

WHO WERE THE SUBSTITUTES?
Bruce I. Bustard

One option available to men who were drafted but didn't want to serve was to purchase a substitute to serve in their place. An 1863 Provost Marshal's report on substitutes from Brooklyn, New York, provides fascinating details about their backgrounds and service experiences.

For those fed up with romantic popular culture depictions of the Civil War, Martin Scorsese's 2002 *Gangs of New York* provided a chilling alternative. Scorsese's film—which starred Daniel Day Lewis, Leonardo DiCaprio, and Cameron Diaz—depicted life in New York City's Five Points slum during the mid-19th century as rife with corruption, anti-immigrant sentiment, racism, and class warfare. It gave us a "War of the Rebellion" that was more about poor New Yorkers battling government in the streets and feeling its hard hand of repression than it was about saving the Union, crushing secession, or freeing slaves.

But whatever its achievements or failures as film or historical narrative, *Gangs of New York* made its viewing public more aware of the Civil War draft. In one memorable scene, poor Irish immigrants arriving in New York harbor are conscripted right off the boat, just after they watch coffins return from the war zone. In the film's climax, gang violence is dwarfed by more widespread carnage: the 1863 New York City draft riot, with its anti-black violence and armed conflict with Union troops.

The characters who inhabit *Gangs of New York* came to mind one day as I sat in the National Archives Central Research Room reading through records relating to the Civil War draft and looking for documents to include in the "Discovering the Civil War" exhibit. A small loose-leaf notebook containing brown lined paper, much like those students use to write exams, caught my attention. Across its front was written, "Record of Statements of Substitutes sent from these Head Quarters 3rd Cong. District N.Y. Capt. S. B. Gregory Provost Marshal."

The book contained the names of men who had volunteered to join the U.S. Army as substitutes for others who had been drafted. It listed each substitute's name, the individual who paid the substitute to take his place, and the recruiting agent. It also contained details such as the substitute's address, age, occupation, and marital status. As such, this report was much like others in the Archives: a straightforward accounting needed for government records at the time, and now a valuable resource for social historians trying to decipher Civil War era patterns and trends. It was not, I thought then, a document easily understood or enjoyed by the general public.

This sketch entitled "Recruiting in the New York City Hall Park in 1864" appeared in *Frank Leslie's Illustrated* on March 19, 1864.

National Archives, Records of the Office of War Information

This page from the "Record of Substitutes" describes substitute George Speidel as "just arrived from Germany." Another substitute, John Smith, had "been in the country since last Sunday." SELECTED PAGES

National Archives at New York City, Records of the Provost Marshal General's Bureau (Civil War)

But a closer reading of this "substitute book" proved much more rewarding. Each entry in the book contained brief phrases that made its subject human and intriguing. For example:

- **Louis (Lewis) Buck** was 22 years old, born in Germany, and had "been a seaman about 10 years."
- **John Dempsey** was a "horse trainer" who had "Just arrived from Liverpool, England; has been in the country 5 days."
- **Robert Horton** "was a slave in North Carolina; came on here with the 9th New York Vols. as a servant to one of the officers."
- **Henry Quick** "had been in the Rebel service was a prisoner and took the oath of Allegiance and was released"

Here were New York's *real* enlistees, not Scorsese's cinematic ones. I wanted to know more about them. What were their stories? Why did they enlist? What became of them?

The Draft Begins

In 1862, the Confederacy enacted the first national draft in American history. The North followed on March 3, 1863, when President Lincoln signed the Enrollment Act. It mandated the enrollment for conscription of all eligible men between the ages of 20 and 45, with those younger than 36 to be drafted first. Exemptions from service were provided for hardship and for physical and mental disabilities, but not for occupation or religious beliefs. The draft created by this law was administered by the U.S. Army and thus enforced by Federal power.

A man who was drafted had several alternatives if he did not qualify for an exemption and did not want to serve. He could "fail to report" and take his chances evading the draft and jail. He could pay a $300 commutation fee that would free him from his obligation for this draft, but not subsequent ones. Or he could find an individual who was willing to serve in his place and pay that "substitute" the going rate, initially at the start of the war around $200 to $275. Purchasing a substitute allowed an individual to avoid service for the duration of the war.

The first draft took place in September 1863. For administrative purposes, drafts were organized by congressional district. I was disappointed to discover that Five Points was in New York City's 4th Congressional District, not the 3rd, where the "Record of Substitutes" originated. New York's 3rd Congressional District covered Brooklyn, then a separate city from New York. In 1860, it was a community of close to 300,000 people. The busy Brooklyn Navy Yard employed 6,000 men.

Occupations and Backgrounds

But while the origins of the substitute book ruled out direct parallels with *Gangs of New York*, its stories still fascinated me. I found these by researching the individuals listed as well as by analyzing statistical data drawn from the book. The most common occupation listed in the book, for instance, was "sailor." Twenty-one of the 70 names had some sort of work experience at sea. Several substitutes in the book had previous

This Confederate service record shows that Henry Quick served in the 8th South Carolina Infantry.

National Archives, War Department Collection of Confederate Records

After fighting for the Confederacy, Henry Quick filled out this form to enlist as a volunteer substitute in the Union Army.

National Archives, Records of the Adjutant General's Office, 1780's–1917

service with the U.S. Navy, while others had been in foreign navies.

- **William Jones** had been "a seafaring man all his life" and had been in the Royal Navy.
- **Maurice Downey**, a 23-year-old laborer from Ireland, had served on the Mississippi River aboard the *"Gen. Bout Essex."*
- **Andrew Matthews**, who sported a tattoo of a "crucifix on right arm," "had been a cook for Admiral Farragut," and had been "discharged in consequence of the loss of the ship."

"Laborer" was the second most frequently listed occupation. Others included "calico printer," "shoemaker," and "photographist."

The ethnic backgrounds of some of the men listed in the "Record of Substitutes" did parallel Scorsese's depiction of Union substitutes as "just off the boat." Fifty substitutes were either listed as "alien" or were, according to their service records, born somewhere "other than the United States." A few were very recent arrivals. Others were native born or had been in the country for years.

- **Diedrich Kloppenbury**, a former "Hanoverian Army" soldier, had been in America for "about six weeks."
- **William Haines** had only "been in New York about 5 days."
- **Thomas Lillis** was born in Ireland but was a U.S. citizen "from Conn. Has been in this country for 10 years."

- **Felix O'Neil**, described as "a waiter," was born in New York but had worked as a nurse in Bellevue Hospital "for the last 18 months" before his enlistment.

Military Experiences

A few of the substitutes left no military service record. The documentation of those who did made these men three-dimensional and enabled me to follow their military careers.

- **Private Buck**, for example, didn't seem cut out to be a soldier. After enlisting in Company B of the 176th New York Infantry in September 1863, he deserted by March 1864. Captured and put into confinement while awaiting trial, he deserted again on July 20.
- **Private Dempsey** had a career plagued with sickness. The 27-year-old "horse trainer" joined the 47th New York Infantry in October 1863, but by February 1864 he was in the hospital in Hilton Head, South Carolina. He was discharged on June 2, 1864, "unable to lift any weight with his hands."
- **Henry Quick** did indeed serve in the 8th South Carolina Infantry, as confirmed by his Confederate service record. As a Union soldier with the 176th New York Infantry, he briefly became a corporal, was reduced in rank, and worked as a cook until he was mustered out in April 1866.

- **Robert Horton,** a former slave, is a mystery. Three Robert Hortons who served with the U.S. Colored Troops (USCT) are listed in the National Park Service's Civil War Soldier and Sailor database. None seem to be the same man listed in the "Record of Substitutes." Did this Robert Horton fail to enlist? Was he one of a few African Americans who served in units that were not part of the USCT?

The service records of other substitutes hint at equally dramatic stories.

- **Private Felix O'Neil** was charged and convicted of "Robbery and Intoxication" and served three months imprisonment, possibly at the Dry Tortugas off the Florida coast.
- **Henry Hoffman,** a 38-year-old "just in from Germany," had six years experience in the "Hanoverian Army." He was wounded and taken prisoner at the Battle of Olustee, Florida, on February 20, 1864. Transferred to the infamous Confederate prisoner-of-war camp at Andersonville, Georgia, Hoffman died of dysentery on July 23, 1864.
- **Thomas Farrell,** a former Confederate, was captured at the Battle of Gettysburg. After taking the oath of allegiance, he went to New York City and was confronted by a sergeant who forced him to join the 176th New York Infantry. Sent to Bonnet Carre, Louisiana, he was court martialed and confined to prison in December 1863. After becoming ill, he was sent to a hospital in Annapolis, Maryland. He deserted in November 1864.

And Still More Questions

The "Record of Substitutes" leads to other records in the National Archives and to more questions as well. Are the men listed in any way representative of substitutes as a group? What happened to those who survived the war? Did they or their families apply for military pensions? Can they be found in the 1870 census? Who were the men who paid to escape military service? What happened to them? Who was Captain Gregory?

Answering questions such as these would require many more months of research, in and out of the Archives. Some could never be answered except, perhaps, through a talented novelist's or filmmaker's imagination. But I leave the "Record of Substitutes" amazed that so many stories can be teased out and so many questions raised by a single document.

NOTE ON SOURCES

The "Report of Statements of Substitutes" is among Records of the Provost Marshal General's Bureau (Civil War), Record Group (RG) 110, held at the National Archives, New York City (I first saw the book in Washington, DC, before it was "regionalized.") The Compiled Military Service Records of the men listed in the book are held among the Records of the Adjutant General's Office, 1780's–1917, RG 94. The Confederate service records of Henry Quick and Thomas Farrell are in War Department Collection of Confederate Records, RG 109. The best general history of the Civil War draft is *We Need Men: The Union Draft in the Civil War* (DeKalb, 1991). There are few modern studies of Civil War substitutes. Tyler Anbinder's article, "Which Poor Man's Fight? Immigrants and the Federal Conscription of 1863," *Civil War History* 52 (December 2006), demonstrates that poor immigrants usually preferred volunteering as substitutes to conscription.

Much of the research for this essay was conducted by Esther Berumen, a Florida State University graduate student interning with the National Archives exhibits office during the summer of 2008.

As this casualty form reveals, substitute Henry Hoffman died of dysentery at the Andersonville, Georgia, prisoner-of-war camp.

National Archives, Records of the Adjutant General's Office, 1780's–1917

CHAPTER 3

FINDING LEADERS

Both Abraham Lincoln and Jefferson Davis faced a Herculean task in raising and training huge armies and navies on very short notice. Although it was relatively easy to train privates and seamen, it was much more challenging to find and train capable officers who could command hundreds or thousands of men.

- How did Lincoln and Davis find good military leaders?
- Where did these officers come from?
- How did these men know each other?

Documents in the National Archives reveal stories of friendship and betrayal, and competence and ineptitude, as the two sides sought out the best men to lead.

Clockwise, from top left: Lt. Gen. Ulysses S. Grant, ca. 1865 [111-B-4503]; Gen. Joseph E. Johnston, ca. 1865 [111-B-1782]; Maj. Gen. James E. B. Stuart, 1863 [64-M-9]; Maj. Gen. William T. Sherman, ca. 1865 [111-B-1769].

Rear Adm. Raphael Semmes, ca. 1865

U.S. Naval Historical Center

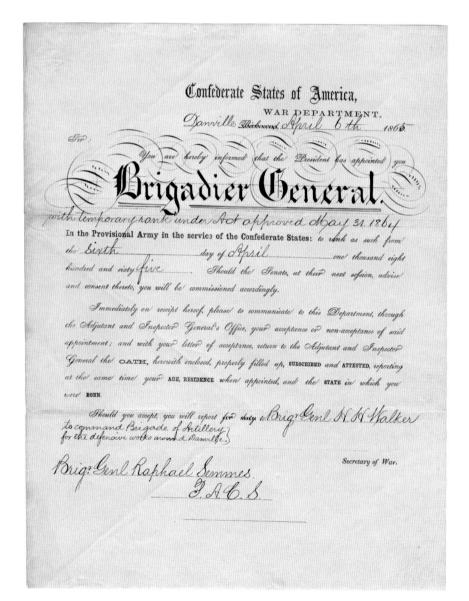

FROM UNION TO CONFEDERATE OFFICER

When the Civil War began, Maryland-born Raphael Semmes was an officer in the U.S. Navy. He resigned and offered his services to the Confederacy, where he commanded the Confederate raiders CSS *Florida* and CSS *Alabama*. He was not alone. Hundreds of officers in the U.S. Army, Navy, and Marine Corps—including Robert E. Lee—resigned their commissions when their home or adopted states seceded.

Late in the war, when the Confederacy had few ships left and needed experienced senior officers, Semmes was appointed a brigadier general in the Provisional Army of the Confederate States. This is his commission. The Confederate government had evacuated Richmond, however, and his appointment was never signed.

National Archives, War Department Collection of Confederate Records

Lt. Gen. Ulysses S. Grant, ca. 1865

National Achives, Records of the Office of the Chief Signal Officer [111-B-4503]

FROM LEATHER MERCHANT TO PRESIDENT

In 1860 a census taker in Galena, Illinois, recorded a family headed by a leather merchant named W. L. Grant. Although Grant's estate was worth only $200, this page from the census shows that he had a house servant.

Today W. L. Grant is better known as Ulysses S. Grant. By the time of the 1870 census he had risen from obscurity to General-in-Chief of the Union Army and from there to President of the United States.

National Archives, Records of the Bureau of the Census

Gen. Joseph E. Johnston, ca. 1865

National Archives,
Records of the Office of the
Chief Signal Officer [111-B-1782]

THE SOUTHERN TELEGRAPH COMPANIES.

Terms and Conditions on which Messages are Received by these Companies for Transmission.

The public are notified that in order to guard against mistakes in the transmission of messages, every message of importance ought to be repeated by being sent back from the station at which it is to be received to the station from which it is originally sent. Half the usual price for transmission will be charged for repeating the message, and while these Companies will as heretofore use every precaution to insure correctness, they will not be responsible for mistakes or delays in the transmission or delivery of repeated messages beyond five hundred times the amount paid for sending the message, nor will they be responsible for mistakes or delays in the transmission of unrepeated messages, from whatever cause they may arise, nor the delays arising from interruptions in the workings of their Telegraphs, nor for any mistakes or omissions of any other Company over whose lines a message is to be sent to reach the place of destination. All messages will hereafter be received by these Companies for transmission subject to the above conditions

J. R. DOWELL, Gen'l Sup't, Richmond, Va.   **W. S. MORRIS, Pres't, Richmond, Va.**

Received at .... July 18 1864 at .... o'clock, ... minutes,

By telegraph from Near Atlanta 18.   To Gen S Cooper

Your dispatch of yesterday received and obeyed —
Command of the army & dept of Tennessee has
been transferred to Gen Hood — As for the alleged
causes of my removal I assert that shermans army
is much stronger compared with that of Tennessee
than Grants compared with that of Northern Virginia
yet the enemy has been compelled to advance

GENERAL JOHNSTON REPLACED

Confederate President Jefferson Davis had a difficult relationship with his former West Point schoolmate, Gen. Joseph E. Johnston, commander of the Department and Army of Tennessee. In mid-1864 Johnston failed to halt Sherman's march on Atlanta, and Davis replaced Johnston with Lt. Gen. John B. Hood. Confederate Adj. Gen. Samuel Cooper conveyed the news to Johnston. In this telegram of July 18, 1864, Johnston acknowledged Cooper's order and turned over command of the Department and Army of Tennessee to General Hood—but with little grace. Hood made poor decisions during the seven months he commanded the Army of Tennessee. He resigned on January 13, 1865. Despite their earlier conflicts, President Davis selected General Johnston to once again command the Army of Tennessee.

National Archives, War Department Collection of Confederate Records

> *"Confident language by a military commander is not usually regarded as evidence of competency."*

GEN. JOSEPH E. JOHNSTON, COMMANDER OF THE DEPARTMENT AND ARMY OF TENNESSEE

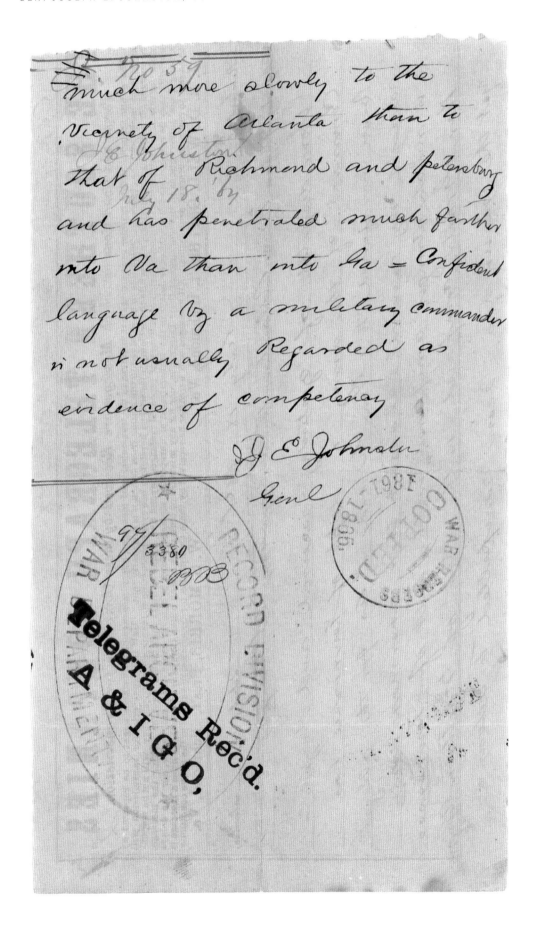

No.	NAMES. PRESENT AND ABSENT.	RANK.	DATE OF COMMISSION, OR REGIMENTAL APPOINTMENT.	STATION.	MUSTERED INTO SERVICE.			LAST PAID.		NAMES. PRESENT.
					WHEN.	WHERE.	BY WHOM.	BY PAYMASTER.	TO WHAT TIME.	
1	Albert S. Johnston	Col.	March 3, 55	Camp Cooper Texas						
2	Robert E. Lee	Lieut Col.	March 3ᵈ 55	Do Do Do						
3	George H. Thomas	Major	May 12, 55	"						George H. Thomas.
4	Earl van Dorn	Do	June 28, 60	"						
5	William W. Lowe	Adjutant	May 1, 1858	"						
6	Joseph F. Minter	Regt. QM	Oct. 1, 1856	"						Joseph F. Minter

MUSTER ROLL of the Field and Staff of the Second Regiment of Cavalry Volunteers, in the service ... , from the Thirty-first day of August , 1860, when last mustered, to the Thir...

STACKING THE DECK DETAIL

In 1855, Secretary of War Jefferson Davis handpicked Albert S. Johnston, Robert E. Lee, and William J. Hardee to lead the newly constituted 2nd Cavalry Regiment. Eighteen of the regiment's 34 officers resigned to serve the Confederacy.

National Archives, Records of the Adjutant General's Office, 1780's–1917

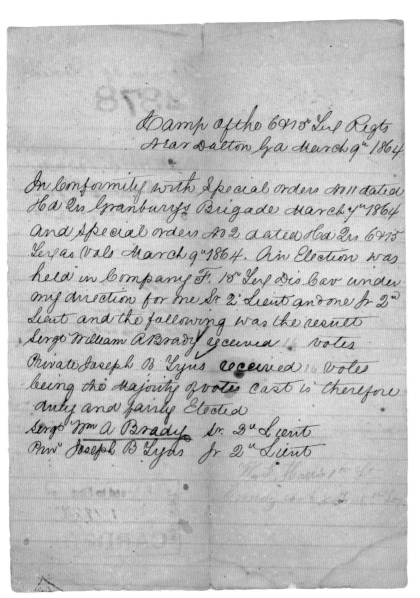

PROMOTED BY ELECTION

Electing junior officers such as lieutenants and captains was common among state troops of both the North and South. This report from Confederate 1st Lt. W. L. Harris of the 15th Texas Dismounted Cavalry certified the results of an election held on March 9, 1864, to fill two vacancies in Company F. The men elected Sgt. William A. Brady and Pvt. Joseph B. Lyas to be lieutenants.

National Archives, War Department Collection of Confederate Records

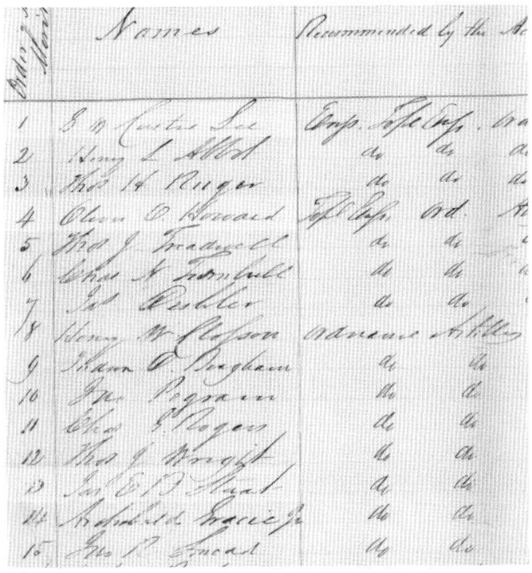

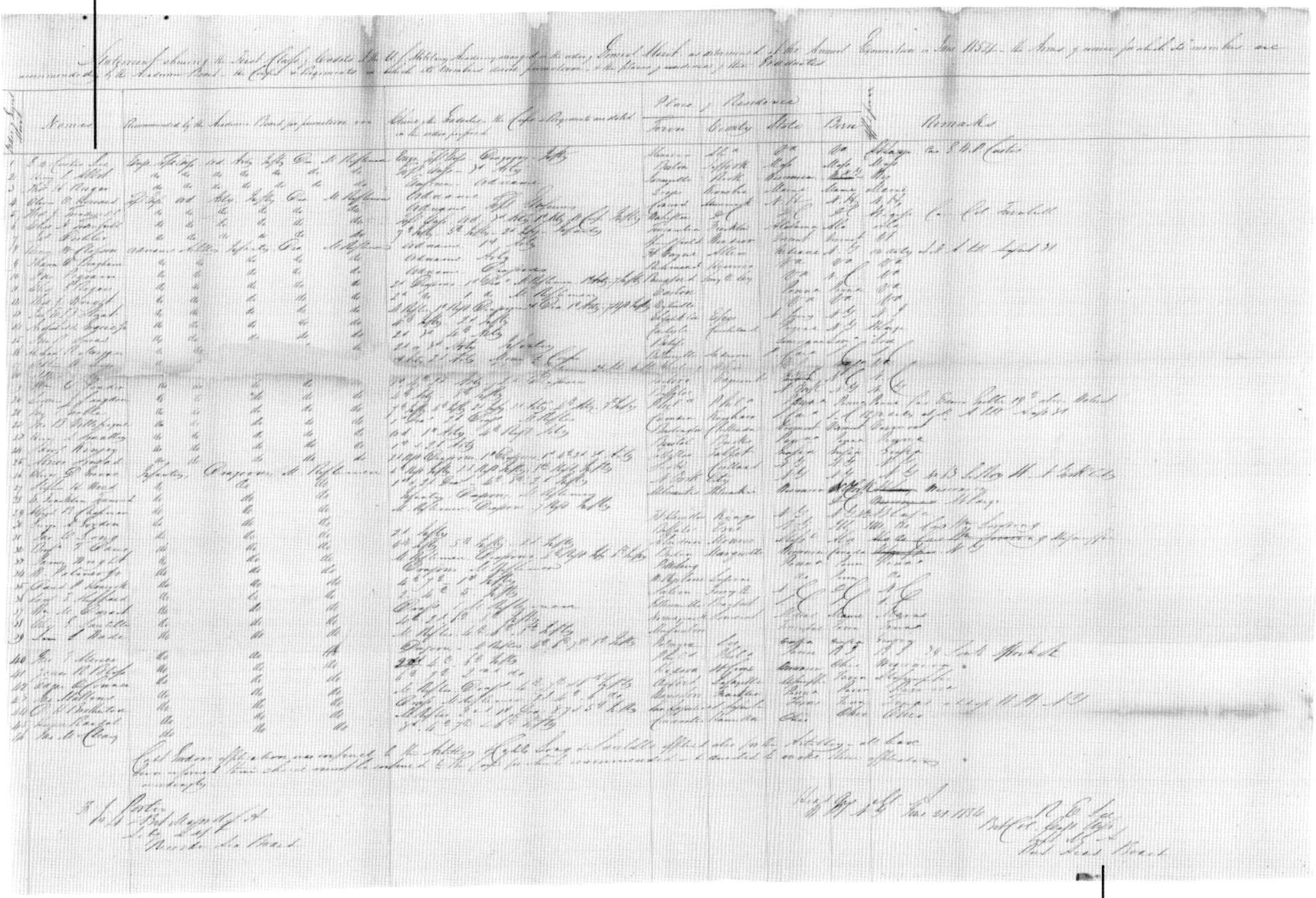

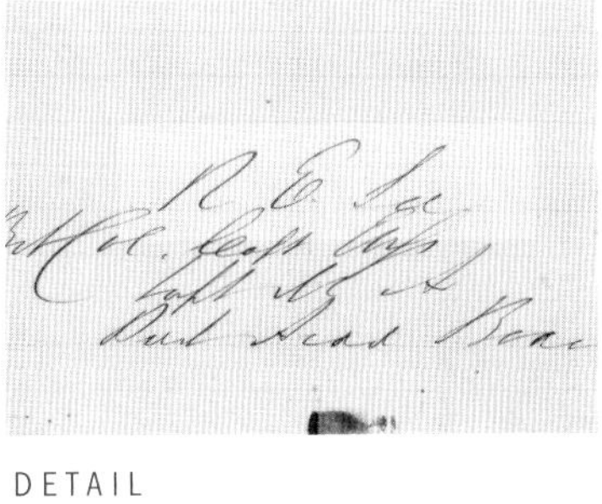

DETAIL

DREAM SHEET

As West Point cadets neared graduation, they were allowed to state their preference for branch of service and regiment in which they hoped to serve. The cadets were ranked in order of merit, and the academic board made its recommendations known. The academy's superintendent, Robert E. Lee, signed this record in June 1854. His son's name topped the list, which also included James E.B. Stuart and Oliver O. Howard.

National Archives, Records of the Adjutant General's Office, 1780's–1917

DETAIL

Maj. Gen. James E. B. Stuart, 1863

*National Archives, Records of the
National Archives and Records
Administration* [64-M-9]

STUART RECOMMENDED
FOR PROMOTION

Over three days in June 1862, Confederate
Brig. Gen. J.E.B. Stuart and 1,200 cavalrymen
rode completely around Union Maj. Gen.
George B. McClellan's Army of the Potomac.
Stuart's superior, Gen. Robert E. Lee, put the
information gained to good use.

Virginia Governor John Letcher wrote this letter
to President Jefferson Davis recommending
Stuart for promotion. During his "Ride around
McClellan," Stuart outwitted Union troops
commanded by his father-in-law, Maj. Gen.
Philip St. George Cooke.

*National Archives, War Department
Collection of Confederate Records*

Maj. Gen. William T. Sherman, ca. 1865

National Archives, Records of the Office of the Chief Signal Officer [111-B-1769]

Maj. Gen. Winfield S. Hancock, ca. 1865

National Archives, Records of the Office of the Chief Signal Officer [111-B-4165]

Maj. Gen. Philip Sheridan, ca. 1865

National Archives, Records of the Office of the Chief Signal Officer [111-B-7205]

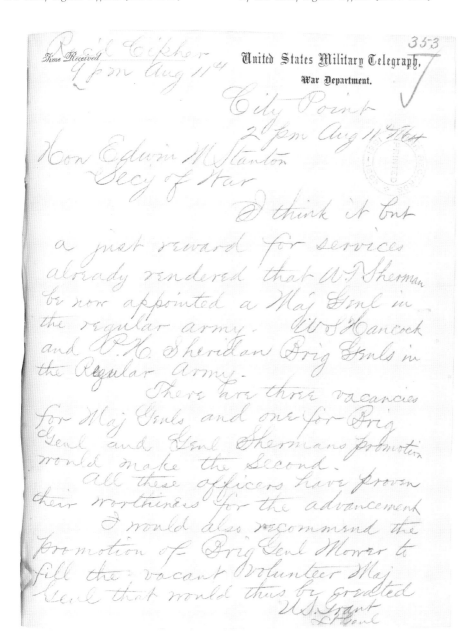

REWARDING JOBS WELL DONE

Lt. Gen. Ulysses Grant sent this telegram to U.S. Secretary of War E. M. Stanton on August 11, 1864. It recommends promoting William T. Sherman to the rank of major general, and Winfield S. Hancock and Philip H. Sheridan to the rank of brigadier general, for their accomplishments during the war.

National Archives, Records of the Office of the Secretary of War

Stacks in the National Archives
Building, Washington, DC

*National Archives photograph
by Earl McDonald*

Behind the Scenes: The Stacks

Within the National Archives Building is an area known as "the stacks" that holds about a billion records—the evidence of our nation's story. Beyond staff, relatively few people have an opportunity to visit and explore this very special space.

There are 21 tiers of stacks. Because no building in Washington, DC, can reach higher than the Capitol building (12 floors), the tiers are only seven feet high. The overhead is packed with conduits, pipes, and exit signs. Many staff have to duck as they work their way through the space.

Both the temperature and the humidity in the stacks are controlled. Temperatures tend to be on the cool side. Staff members keep sweaters at their desks to put on when they work in the stacks. Because of the constant blowing of fans, the space is noisy as well as cold.

Locations of specific records are denoted by an arcane alphanumeric code that leads staff to the correct tier, building side, stack, row, compartment, and shelf. Upon entering a stack, a researcher finds the correct row and hits a light switch that controls a timed fluorescent light. Rows are narrow—just wide enough for a cart and one person. Each row is separated into compartments about four feet wide, and each compartment is lined with shelves that reach from floor to ceiling. On these shelves are the archival boxes and volumes containing the records of America's history.

One chapter of that national story is the Civil War. These boxes and volumes hold such treasures as Jefferson Davis's correspondence, telegrams sent and received by Ulysses S. Grant, and the engrossed bills of the Confederate States of America. They hold the communications of naval vessels, diplomats, and army officers . . . the records of drafts and substitutes . . . photographs by the Mathew Brady Studio . . . and many millions of other historic documents that enable us to piece together and better understand our past.

FINDING LEADERS
William J. Sandoval

Research on the leaders who served in the Union and Confederate armies leads to the development of a fascinating web of relationships and new kind of computer interactive.

About 20 years ago, I read James McPherson's one-volume history of the Civil War era, *Battle Cry of Freedom*. Since then, I have gone back to that book to re-read the lines that comprise the second-to-last paragraph of the well-written prologue. In those lines, McPherson provides details of the relationships among men who fought closely together in the Mexican War and who then went on to fight against each other in the Civil War. I continue to ponder the irony that the men who led the armies and governments of both sides in the Civil War were not strangers to each other. On the contrary.

America's mid-19th-century professional army, including the officer corps, was small—with only 16,367 officers and men on the eve of the Civil War. The officers all knew each other, most of them quite well. Their relationships formed over time, usually beginning on the plain at the United States Military Academy at West Point, New York. They roomed together, attended classes together, and graduated together. Over the years they met the men of the classes above and below them. They were influenced by their professors, instructors, and Academy leaders. They went on to court the same women and fight side by side in Florida, Mexico, or on the Great Plains.

They built lighthouses along America's shorelines and explored the nation's interior. They lent each other money and married each other's sisters and cousins.

Then they spent four years trying to kill each other.

Web of Relationships

As the National Archives began planning this exhibit on the Civil War, I researched the leaders who guided the armies of the North and South through the most horrible four years of this nation's history. I wanted to give visitors a sense of the Herculean task both sides faced in raising, and finding leaders for, the huge armies that fought across the country. As I conducted this research, I came across anecdotes and stories of the relationships these men shared. I started recording these linkages on pieces of scrap paper and notebooks. Eventually this project became an animated presentation.

As the men populated the screen—and as lines linked those who were in the same class at West Point, who served together during the Mexican War, or who were related to each other—a virtual spider web appeared. When I shared that presentation

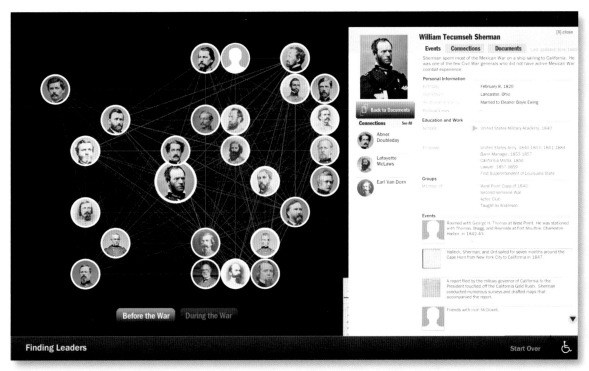

This screenshot from an interactive featured in the "Discovering the Civil War" exhibition uses social media tools to illustrate the intricate and unexpected pre-war relationships between major leaders on both sides of the Civil War.

Courtesy of Cortina Productions, Inc.

Many of the cadets on this 1838 roster of the United States Military Academy, such as those highlighted above, served together in Mexico or were stationed together on the Great Plains. *National Archives, Records of the Adjutant General's Office 1780's–1917*

Head Q'rs Prov'l A.C.S.
Charleston S.C. April 16. 1861.

Sir,

I have the honor to submit the following summary statement of the circumstances of the surrender of Fort Sumpter.

On the refusal of Major Anderson to engage, in compliance with my demand, to designate the time when he would evacuate Fort Sumpter, and to agree meanwhile not to use his guns against us; at twenty minutes past three o'clock in the morning of the 12 inst I gave him formal notice that, within one hour my batteries would open on him. In consequence of some circumstance of delay, the bombardment was not begun precisely at the appointed moment, but, at thirty minutes past four o'clock the signal gun was fired, and within twenty minutes all our batteries were in full play. There was no response from Fort Sumpter until about seven o'clock, when the first shot from the enemy was discharged against our batteries on Cumming's Point. By eight o'clock the action became general, and throughout the day was maintained with spirit on both sides. Our guns were served with skill and energy. The effect was visible in the impressions made on the walls of Fort Sumpter.

and to my Staff, regular and volunteer, I am much indebted for the prompt and complete execution of my orders, which had to be communicated in open boats during the bombardment, to the different batteries then engaged. I remain Sir Very Resp'y

Your Ob. Serv't

G.T. Beauregard
Brig. Gen. Com'd'g

Hon. L.P. Walker
Sec'y of War
Montgomery – Ala –

Brig. Gen. P.G.T. Beauregard sent this report to the Confederate Secretary of War in Montgomery, Alabama, on April 16, 1861. Four days earlier he had opened fire on Fort Sumter, which was under the command of his former West Point instructor, Maj. Robert Anderson.

National Archives, War Department Collection of Confederate Records

List of Officers as reported for duty .....

June 2 1846. W. H. Macomb — — .... Act. Master .
"   "   J. W. A. Nicholson .... Passed Midshipmen
"   3   "   J. J. Abernethey .... Pass. Ass. Surgeon
"   6   "   W. B. Muse .... Passed Midshipmen
"   3   "   A. S. Myers .... Capt. Clerk
June   J. H. Spotts .... Passed Midshipmen
Joseph. Wilson Esq. .. .. Purser.

List of Officers of the U.S. Army on board U.S. Iron Ship Lexington

C. 2. Tompkins, Comp. F. 3 Arty.   Captain
E. O. C. Ord   "   "   "   1st Lieutenant,
W. T. Sherman   "   "   "   "   "
L. Loeser   "   "   "   2nd   "
C. J. Minor   "   "   "   Bvt 2d "

H. W. Halleck, 1st Lieut Corps of Engineers.   Jas L. Ord, Medical Staff

This 1847 logbook reveals that Sherman, Ord, and Halleck spent seven months of the Mexican War together aboard the USS _Lexington_ as she sailed from New York City, around Cape Horn, and to San Francisco, California.

National Archives, Records of the Bureau of Naval Personnel

with other members of the team, they, too, expressed surprise that these men's lives were so intertwined.

That presentation turned into one of the richest computer interactives on which I've ever worked.

An Interactive Takes Shape

The exhibit team decided to create a records-based interface that would look familiar to many social network users. We started with one document—the Catalogue of the Cadets of the U.S. Military Academy, dated September 1, 1838. This document contains the names of dozens of Civil War officers. We decided to focus on several who had a larger impact on the war—Henry W. Halleck, Edward O. C. Ord, William T. Sherman, George H. Thomas, Richard S. Ewell, Richard B. Garnett, John F. Reynolds, Don Carlos Buell, Abner Doubleday, Daniel H. Hill, James Longstreet, Lafayette McLaws, John Pope, Earl Van Dorn, and William S. Rosecrans.

As visitors explore the document, photographs of these men float off the page, and lines indicate their connections to each other. As more documents—or pages within a document—are explored, new faces and linkages appear. Existing linkages get bolder to represent stronger ties.

Visitors can select a photograph to explore an officer in depth. The initial biographical page contains a photograph, short biography, birth date and place, political leanings, schools, and photographs of other officers with whom the officer shared a common history. Visitors learn that some men were congressmen, others inventors. Still others left the army for greener pastures. Visitors can find out who dated the same woman or married a friend's sister or cousin. They can even look at all of the records in which an officer's name appears and all of the officers to which he is linked.

Difficult Choices

I had researched 52 of the better-known Civil War leaders and presented that as the universe from which to draw. But how many men should we include? Too many could overwhelm the visitor. The lines connecting them would be impossible to untangle. Too few and we would not make the point that they *all* knew each other. Could we achieve our goal with just 20 men? Did we need all 52?

In the end, we decided to include 48 officers. Dozens of records from the National Archives allow visitors to explore each of the records in as much, or as little, detail as he or she wants. Visitors can enlarge each record, move it around on the desktop, and flip through multiple pages. Highlighting helps the visitor focus on the connections and other interesting information. Handwritten text is transcribed so that visitors can easily read it.

Relationships Revealed

So what can visitors discover? Here are just a few examples of the connections that emerge.

- **Lewis Addison Armistead,** the Confederate brigadier general who led his troops to breach the Union line on Cemetery Ridge at Gettysburg, resigned from West Point to avoid a court martial for breaking a plate over the head of fellow cadet and future Confederate lieutenant general and corps commander Jubal A. Early.

- **Pierre Gustave Toutant Beauregard** fired on Fort Sumter to start the war. The fort was commanded by his former West Point artillery instructor, Robert Anderson.

- **Henry Halleck, Edward O. C. Ord, and William T. Sherman** —all future Union Army commanders—spent the Mexican War on a ship headed for California. By the time they arrived, the war in California was over.

- **George H. Thomas, Braxton Bragg, William T. Sherman, and John F. Reynolds** were all stationed at Fort Moultrie, Charleston, South Carolina, in 1842 and 1843.

- **Lafayette McLaws's** wife was a cousin of Jefferson Davis.

- **Ulysses S. Grant** married Julia Dent, the sister of his West Point classmate, Frederick Dent. Julia was a cousin of Mary Ann Dent, mother of James Longstreet.

Creating the Finding Leaders interactive was like participating in a huge scavenger hunt in which no one knew what would be found. We hope that visitors will walk away not only understanding that these men knew each other, but wondering how that intimate knowledge of allies and foes shaped the course and outcome of the war.

NOTE ON SOURCES

It would be impossible to include a list of all of the sources that provided information about all of these men. Major sources include John C. Waugh's *The Class of 1846* (New York: 1994) and Martin Dugard's *The Training Ground* (New York: 2008). Both offer great insight into the relationships these men shared and forged during their time at West Point and in Mexico. Of course, Shelby Foote's massive *The Civil War* (New York: 1963) and James McPherson's *Battle Cry of Freedom* (New York: 1988) provided additional material and the impetus for this undertaking. The Internet was a great source of material that required fact checking but, when confirmed, added to the interactive's depth and breadth. Biographies of the men proved invaluable in confirming items hinted at elsewhere and in providing context and understanding. Primary source material included Maj. Gen. Winfield Scott's letter to Secretary of War William L. Marcy recounting the campaign to capture Mexico City. It is found in The Secretary of War, Letters Received, 1847, Records of the Adjutant General's Office, 1780's-1917, Record Group (RG) 94. Other great sources are also found in Entry 227 of RG 94. The results of the semiannual examinations and muster rolls of the United States Military Academy are found there. These list the cadets in order of merit as determined by the most recent semiannual examination or muster.

CHAPTER 4

WE WERE THERE

The Civil War transformed the lives of all who were swept up in it—whether on a battlefield or in a hospital, on a farm, or in a factory.

- Who were the men and women in blue and gray?
- Who tended to them when they were sick or wounded?
- Who took care of the farms and homes left behind?
- Who worked in the arsenals, built the forts, and provided supplies?

As you'll see here, records preserved in the National Archives contain remarkable stories of ordinary people as well as generals and statesmen.

Men on the deck of the USS *Monitor,* 1862   DETAIL

National Archives, Records of the Office of the Chief Signal Officer [111-B-246]

Pay Roll of Slaves employed at the C. S. Armory, Macon, Ga.

Carpenters

BOUND TO THE CONFEDERATE EFFORT

This ledger sheet lists slaves employed at the Confederate States Armory in Macon, Georgia, in December 1862. You can find the names and occupations of each slave and the amount paid to the owner. It was not uncommon for slaves to be employed or contracted out to support the Confederate war effort. They were used in essential civilian jobs to free white males for service in the Confederate Army.

National Archives, Records of the War Department Collection of Confederate Records

Confederate pickets
on duty, ca. 1862

*National Archives,
Records of the Office of
the Chief Signal Officer*

[111-B-3368]

Descriptive Roll of Company K. Capt Thos Hanna

Names	age	Enlistment date	period	Height feet	in	Complexion	Hair	Eyes	occupation	where born county	State
Thos Hanna	33	Oct 19	12	5	10	fair	Light	Blue	Farmer	Giles	Tenn
Wm W. Brownlow	27	" 19	12	6	1	fair	light	Blue	Farmer	Giles	Tenn
E. A. Beasley	40	" 19	12	6	0	fair	Sandy	Blue	Farmer	Giles	Tenn
John L. Brownlow	35	" 19	12	5	10	fair	light	Blue	Farmer	Rutherford	Tenn
John M. Crook	32	" 19	12	5	8	dark	dark	dark	Farmer	Rutherford	Tenn
D. M. Jones	23	" 19	12	6	0	fair	Sandy	Blue	Farmer	Giles	Tenn
John M. Faulch	25	" 19	12	5	6	fair	black	Blue	merchant	Giles	Tenn
Wm L. Robison	22	" 19	12	5	8	fair	light	Blue	Farmer	Giles	Tenn
Jas M. Howard	20	" 19	12	6	0	fair	light	Blue	Farmer	Giles	Tenn
T. C. Griffin	22	" 19	12	6	0	fair	light	Blue	Farmer	Giles	Tenn
Jas F. Thomas	28	" 19	12	6	0	fair	light	Blue	Farmer	Newbury	North Carolina
John M. Paisley	20	" 19	12	6	2	fair	dark	Blue	Farmer	Giles	Tenn
Edw M. Williams	24	" 19	12	6	0	dark	dark	Blue	Farmer	Giles	Tenn
Wm W. Ashford	20	" 19	12	5	5	light	light	Blue	Farmer	Giles	Tenn
Amos A. Appleton	14	" 19	12	5	2	fair	light	Blue	Farmer	Giles	Tenn
Thos J. Appleton	18	" 19	12	5	4	dark	dark	Blue	Farmer	Lawrence	Tenn
Joseph C. Anthony	18	" 19	12	5	10	fair	dark	Blue	Farmer	Limestone	Alabama
Jesse L. Brunson	25	" 19	12	6	10	dark	black	Black	preacher	Giles	Tenn
Robt J. Brunson	19	" 19	12	6	8	dark	Black	dark	Farmer	Giles	Tenn
Jas C. Brownlow	24	Dec 4	12	5	10	fair	light	Blue	Farmer	Giles	Tenn
E. M. Booth	18	" 19	12	5	8	fair	light	Blue	Farmer	Limestone	Alabama
Ephraim Barr	28	" 19	12	5	8	dark	dark	Blue	Farmer	Lauderdale	Alabama
David Bodenhamer	18	" 19	12	5	7	fair	light	Blue	Farmer	Giles	Tenn
Wm D. Bradley	18	" 19	12	5	7	fair	light	Blue	Farmer	Giles	Tenn
Theo Burge	32	" 19	12	5	10	dark	dark	Black	Farmer	Giles	Tenn
John L. Bodenhamer	24	Nov 6	12	6	0	fair	light	dark	Farmer	Giles	Tenn
Jas Cox	19	" 19	12	5	8	fair	dark	Blue	Farmer	Giles	Tenn
S. G. Case	44	" 19	12	5	6	dark	dark	dark	Farmer		South Carolina
John L. Ezell	24	" 19	12	5	2	dark	dark	Black	Farmer	Lawrence	Tenn
Allen Ezell	20	" 19	12	5	3	dark	dark	Blue	Farmer	Lawrence	Tenn
Theo Ezell	20	" 19	12	5	0	dark	dark	Black	Farmer	"	Tenn
Robt Ezell	28	" 19	12	5	8	dark	dark	Blue	Farmer	Giles	Tenn
John R. Eubanks	22	" 19	12	5	6	fair	Sandy	Blue	Farmer	Giles	Tenn
Wm B. Eubanks	32	" 19	12	5	8	dark	Black	Black	merchant	Giles	Tenn
Jas R. Foag	33	" 19	12	6	1	dark	dark	Black	carpenter	Giles	Tenn
John J. Scott	20	" 19	12	5	0	dark	dark	Blue	Farmer	Giles	Tenn
Jas H. Graves	39	" 19	12	6	0	fair	dark	Blue	brick mason	Carroll	South Carolina
N. J. B. Graves	23	" 19	12	6	1	dark	dark	Blue	Farmer	Giles	Tenn
Wm L. Graves	32	" 19	12	6	0	fair	light	Blue	Farmer	Giles	Tenn
George M. Glover	25	" 19	12	5	6	fair	Sandy	Blue	Carpenter	Giles	Tenn
Jas C. Griffin	18	19	12	5	0	fair	light	Blue	Farmer	Giles	Tenn
John J. Gibbins	32	" 19	12	6	0	dark	Black	dark	Farmer	Lawrence	Tenn

TREASURE TROVE OF DETAIL

This descriptive roll was recorded at the time of enlistment for Company K of the 32nd Tennessee Volunteers. Records such as these are valuable resources for researchers because they include information about each individual soldier. By examining just this one page, you can learn a lot about the soldiers' ages, physical characteristics, birthplaces, and occupations.

National Archives, Records of the War Department Collection of Confederate Records

*"I would have rather been shot dead,
than to have been known to be a woman."*

SARAH EMMA EDMONDS SEELYE

Sarah Edmonds in male attire, ca. 1862

Courtesy of the State Archives of Michigan

Sarah Edmonds in female attire, 1867

Courtesy of the State Archives of Michigan

Passing as a Man

Neither the Union nor the Confederate Army allowed women to enlist. However, hundreds of women served by passing as men. Sarah Emma Edmonds, alias Frank Thompson, passed as a man for two years with Company F, 2nd Michigan Infantry Volunteers. She deserted after contracting malaria and fearing she would be discovered.

Edmonds returned to civilian life as a woman, married, and focused on raising her family. However, she suffered a lifelong disability as a result of her service and eventually applied for a pension because her family needed the income. The Bureau of Pensions denied her pension application, but in 1884 Congress passed a private bill granting her pension.

PROOF OF ORIGIN OF DISABILITY.

NOTE.—This affidavit must be executed by a Commissioned Officer, if possible; but if not possible to secure such evidence, then two of the soldier's comrades should testify.

State of _Michigan_, County of _Jackson_, ss:

ON THIS _13_ day of _September_, A.D. 18_97_, personally appeared before me, a _Notary Public_ in and for the aforesaid County, duly authorized to administer oaths, _R. M. Talcott_, aged _59_ years, a resident of _Concord_, in the County of _Jackson_ and State of _Mich_ who, being duly sworn according to law, state that _he is_ acquainted with _S Emma E. Seelye_, applicant for Invalid Pension; and know the said _S Emma E Seelye_ to be the identical person of that name who enlisted or volunteered as a _Private_ in Company _F_ _2_ Regiment of _Mich Infy_ Vols., and who _____ [Died or was discharged.]
at _____ on or about the _____ day of _____, 186_
by reason of _____ [Here insert the reason of the soldier's discharge, if known; if not known, so state, or, if he died, so state.]

That the said _Seelye known as Frank Thompson_ while in the line of his duty, at or near _Centerville Va_ in the State of _Virginia_, did, on or about the _2ᵈ Battle_ day of _Bull Run_, 186_, become disabled in the following manner, viz. _She was mail carrier & came on one of her trips with_ [Here state the time and place and manner in which the wound or other injury was received. Describe the wound or injury, the] _the mail badly hurt & was not able to git around much_ part of the body wounded or injured, and all the circumstances attending it. If sick, was, state time and place when contracted, what _for several days She (or he as then known) was my_ caused it, the name of the sickness, and how it affected him. _but I never knew that she was a woman_ _Bunk mate considerable of the time, she was so_ _badly hurt that I had to assist her in distrib_ _uting the mail while she lay on the ground_

That the facts stated are personally known to the affiant by reason of [Here state whether affiant was with]
on a blanket & she had her rations cooked
the command at the time the claimant contracted his disability, or whether his knowledge was otherwise obtained. All the facts
and brought to her. She carried the mail
known to affiant relative to the soldier's medical treatment for his disability while in the service should be stated, giving time and
on a mule I helped her care for her mule
place, if possible.]
while she was so badly laid up until she
got able to take care of it herself She said
her mule fell and hurt her coming to the
regiment with the mail from Washington D.C.

When Sarah Emma Edmonds filed for an invalid pension under her married name of Seelye, one of her fellow soldiers provided this testimony regarding her service.

National Archives, Records of the Department of Veterans Affairs

DETAIL

This bill granted Sarah Emma Edmonds Seelye a pension. It includes the amount she received each month—"twelve dollars."

National Archives, Records of the Department of Veterans Affairs

[Printer's No., 5765.

48TH CONGRESS, 1ST SESSION.

H. R. 5335.

IN THE HOUSE OF REPRESENTATIVES.

FEBRUARY 25, 1884.

Read twice, referred to the Committee on Invalid Pensions, and ordered to be printed.

Mr. CUTCHEON introduced the following bill:

A BILL

Granting a pension to Mrs. Sarah E. E. Seelye, alias Franklin Thompson.

1   *Be it enacted by the Senate and House of Representa-*
2   *tives of the United States of America in Congress assembled,*
3   That the Secretary of the Interior is hereby authorized and
4   directed to place on the pension-roll the name of Sarah E.
5   E. Seelye, alias Franklin Thompson, who was late a private
6   in Company F, Second Regiment of Michigan Infantry Vol-
7   unteers, at the rate of twelve dollars per month.

WHERE TO GO?

Civilians from both sides often found themselves refugees—caught between Confederate and Union forces.

National Archives, Donated Materials in the National Archives [200-CC-306]

NATIVE AMERICANS SIGN UP

Antoine Scott, a Chippewa Indian, was one of more than 20,000 Native Americans who served in the Civil War. He enlisted on July 4, 1863, with Company K of the 1st Michigan Sharpshooters—one of the largest units of Native Americans serving the Union east of the Mississippi. Native Americans fought in both armies.

Private Scott was recommended for a Medal of Honor for "conspicuous gallantry" at the Battle of the Crater on July 30, 1864. The nomination described how he "deliberately fired his piece until the enemy was close . . . instead of surrendering, he ran the gauntlet of shot and shell and escaped." Scott did not receive the medal.

National Archives, Records of the Adjutant General's Office, 1780's–1917

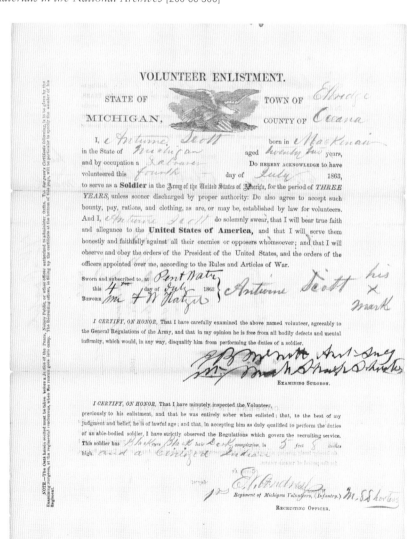

IN THE TRENCHES

Soldiers in trenches two miles south of Fredericksburg, on the eve of the Battle of Chancellorsville, April 1863

National Archives, Records of the Office of the Chief Signal Officer [111-B-157]

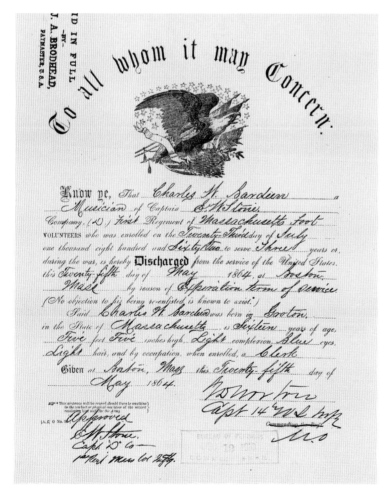

DETAIL

DISCHARGED AS A TEENAGER

When Charles Bardeen enlisted in the Union Army, he was 14 years old. He went on to witness the Battles of Fredericksburg, Chancellorsville, Gettysburg, and the Wilderness before being discharged at the age of 16. This certificate records his discharge in Boston, Massachusetts, on May 25, 1864.

National Archives, Records of the Department of Veterans Affairs

THE CORPS D'AFRIQUE

Union General Nathaniel Banks organized the Corps d'Afrique in the spring of 1863. The unit was made up largely of former slaves from southern Louisiana. The officers were all white. Some of the officers and men were drawn from Louisiana's Afro-Creole community and had earlier served in a Confederate unit known as the Louisiana Native Guards. This photograph was taken in Port Hudson, Louisiana, around 1864.

National Archives, Records of the War Department General and Special Staffs [165-JT-433B]

FREE TO FIGHT

Until January 28, 1865, Jacob "Charles" Lingo was a slave in Delaware. Then he enlisted with the 25th United States Colored Infantry. His owner, Coard Warrington, received $300—and Lingo received his freedom.

This deed of manumission provides a record of the transaction. Delaware was a border state that allowed slavery and had strong Confederate ties. Nevertheless it remained loyal to the Union and rejected secession in early 1861.

National Archives, Records of the Adjutant General's Office, 1780's–1917

E.

DEED OF MANUMISSION AND RELEASE OF SERVICE.

Whereas my slave *Jacob Lingo* has enlisted in the service of the United States: now, in consideration thereof, I, *Coard Warrington*, of *Sussex* county, State of *Delaware*, do hereby, in consideration of said enlistment, manumit, set free, and release the above-named *Jacob Lingo* from all service due me; his freedom to commence from the *28th* day of *January* 1864, the date of his enlistment as aforesaid in the *25th* Regiment of Colored Troops, in the service of the United States.

Witness my hand and seal, this *Sixteenth* day of *January*, 1865.

Coard Warrington

SEAL.

Witness:
L H King
James G Fenwick
Robert L Lacey

Sussex County, ss
State of *Delaware*, 1865.

Before me appeared this day *Coard Warrington*, and acknowledged the above Deed of Manumission and Release of Service to be his free act and deed.

Robert L Lacey Notary Public

"He was truly a brave and good soldier..."

ROBERT J. BELL, CONFEDERATE SURGEON

SEAMSTRESSES PROTEST AN INJUSTICE SELECTED PAGE

A group of seamstresses working at the U.S. Arsenal in Philadelphia wrote this letter to the Secretary of War in 1862 to "most respectfully remonstrate" about work that had been taken from them and given to a contractor. The contractor paid only about half what the women previously received. Since many of the women had husbands, fathers, and sons in the Army, their wages were their sole means of livelihood.

National Archives, Records of the Office of the Quartermaster General

"MY DEAR WIFE"

Behind Union lines, under a "flag of truce," Confederate surgeon Robert J. Bell wrote to his wife of the death of her "gallant brother" Sylvester at the Battle of Helena in Arkansas. His wife never received the letter. It was found among other letters confiscated by Union authorities from a Confederate sympathizer in Missouri.

National Archives, Records of U.S. Army Continental Commands, 1821–1920

MATHEW BRADY'S WAR PHOTOGRAPHS

Mathew Brady had established himself as a photographer before the Civil War began, with studios in New York and Washington, DC. Throughout the war Brady and a team of photographers followed the Union and Confederate armies and documented their activities—sometimes at risk to their own lives. Photographs like the ones on these pages brought the war into everyone's home. The National Archives holds a treasured set of Mathew Brady's original glass plate negatives.

Guard boat of the Port of Alexandria, Virginia, ca. 1861–65. DETAIL
National Archives, Records of the Office of the Chief Signal Officer [111-B-513]

Zouave soldier, ca. 1861–65

National Archives, Records of the Office of the Chief Signal Officer [111-B-6343]

Union soldiers, ca. 1861–65 DETAIL

National Archives, Records of the Office of the Chief Signal Officer [111-B-5343]

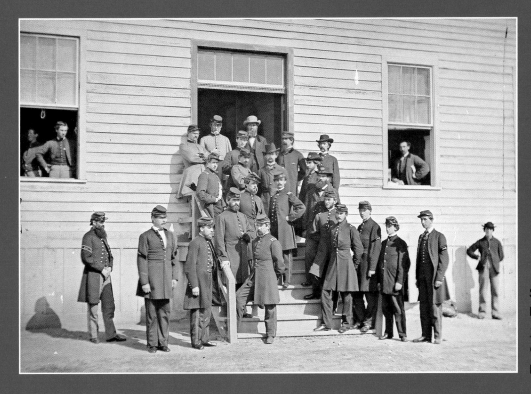

Surgeons of Harewood
Hospital, Washington, DC. DETAIL
*National Archives, Records of the
Office of the Chief Signal Officer*
[111-B-327]

Camp scene, showing company kitchen,
ca. 1861–65. DETAIL
*National Archives, Records of the
Office of the Chief Signal Officer*
[111-B-252]

Company of Infantry on Parade near
Harpers Ferry, Virginia,
ca. 1860–65. DETAIL
*National Archives, Records of the
Office of the Chief Signal Officer*
[111-B-189]

LETTER FROM A CIVIL WAR SOLDIER'S PENSION FILE

Bruce I. Bustard

Letters written by a homesick teenage soldier to his mother and family lead to the story of his wartime experiences and how those experiences affected his entire family.

June 15, 1862: A teenage soldier sits "in camp" writing to his mother. On this "sabeth day" Cpl. Benjamin Chase of the 5th New Hampshire Volunteers has been in the U.S. Army for seven months. The day before he had received a letter from his sisters, and this touch of home lifted his spirits. "[I] feel well and smart this pleasent morning," he writes. "[I] feel better this morning than i have for the last month."

December 13, 1862: The teenager, recently promoted to sergeant, stands with his regiment on a street in Fredericksburg, Virginia. They are about to march 700 yards across an open field and assault Marye's Heights, a well-protected Confederate position. From the sounds and smells of the battle, the men of the 5th know they will face murderous fire. Their commander offers only the briefest advice: "stand firm and fire low."

October 31, 1882: A 68-year-old mother and her 45-year-old daughter fill out government forms hoping for a bit of financial relief. The mother was once "cheerful and singing around the house," but the war had "a great effect" and she was now "sad and dejected and has never been heard to sing a word."

April 23, 2007: A 53-year-old historian opens Benjamin Chase's Civil War pension file in the National Archives. The file smells not just of age but of bureaucracy. He reads letters from lawyers, physicians, and claimants and thumbs through "depositions," "affidavits," and "notices." In the midst of this routine paper work, he discovers 11 original letters from Chase to his family. He wonders: Who was Benjamin Chase? Why would his family part with the letters he sent home? What happened to him?

Born in New Hampshire

Benjamin Chase's story begins in the village of Meredith, New Hampshire. In 1860, Meredith was a farming town of 1,944 residents located in the center of the state on Lake Winnipesauke. Benjamin's father, 50-year-old Madison Chase, was a carpenter who supplemented his income by farming two acres. Benjamin was the sixth of 11 children. His siblings ranged in age from 23-year-old Melissa, known as "Vittie," to 2-year-old Lizzie. Four older siblings—Freeman, Melvin, George, and Sarah—had married and left home. Nancy Chase, Benjamin's mother, was 46 in 1860 and had given birth to her 11 children over 21 years.

Line 37 on this page of the 1860 census for Meredith, New Hampshire, recorded Benjamin Chase's age as 14. DETAIL

National Archives, Records of the Bureau of the Census

Benjamin Chase described the Battle of Fair Oaks, as "a dreadfull battle."

Courtesy of the Library of Congress

When war came in 1861, Benjamin Chase may have had patriotic reasons to join the fight, but he certainly had financial ones. His parents were in debt. The Chases had run up such a large bill at the local store that Madison, who had been injured, was forced to mortgage his land to its owner. Whatever his motivations, on September 19, 1861, Benjamin enlisted in the 5th Regiment, New Hampshire volunteers. His enlistment form says he was 18, but the 1860 census lists him as 14. It was not unusual for boys younger than 18 to serve. The promise of $13 a month plus a cash bounty for enlisting probably persuaded his parents—whose two older sons were already in the Army—to allow him to join up.

First Combat

Benjamin and the rest of the 5th New Hampshire were drilled, paraded, and exhorted by politicians. They then traveled hundreds of miles by train, wagon, and ferry from New Hampshire to a camp near Yorktown, Virginia. On June 1, 1862, Benjamin experienced combat for the first time. During the Battle of Fair Oaks, his company was only 30 yards away from Confederate lines when it received its first taste of enemy fire. Two weeks later Benjamin recalled "a dreadfull battle" where "it was a wonder that I dident get killed for i was right among them all. the boys got killed and wounded that stood right beside of me." He had seen things that no one—especially a teenager—should. "[I]t was a hard sight to see the dead and wounded lay on the battle ground."

Refusing to dwell on the battle, Benjamin writes about how much he misses home, complains about soldiering, and seeks to reassure his mother. "I only do wish I could be at home" he writes. There he could taste "good green peas," and "a piece of brown bread would taste like honey to me." He now knows "what hard living is." But when he enlisted, there had

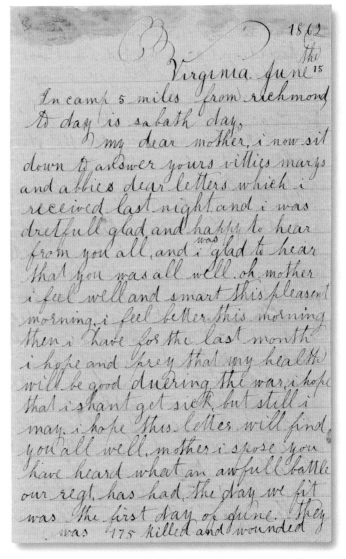

SELECTED PAGE   Benjamin Chase wrote this letter to his family in Meredith, New Hampshire, shortly after the Battle of Fair Oaks.

National Archives, Records of the Department of Veterans Affairs

AFFIDAVIT FOR
Neighbors' and General Purpose.

STATE OF _NewHampshire_   COUNTY OF _Belknap_   SS.

In the matter of _Pension Claim No 264016, of Nancy Chase, as mother of_ _Benj F Chase, of Co E. 5ᵗʰ N.H. Vols._

ON THIS _31st_ day of _October_ A. D., 188_2_, personally appeared before me, a _Justice of the Peace_ in and for the aforesaid county, duly authorized to administer oaths, _Vittie M. Chase_ aged _45_ years, a resident of _Meredith N.H._

aged _____ years, a resident of _____

well known to me to be reputable and entitled to credit, and who being duly sworn, declare in relation to aforesaid case as follows:

That I am daughter of Madison and Nancy Chase. That the anxiety attending the enlistment and service of three, and the death of one, of her sons in the war, had a great effect upon my mother already enfeebled with raising a large family; that before the war she was cheerful and singing about the house but afterward sad and dejected and has never been heard to sing a word since the death of Benjamin F.; that as a consequence my help has been needed in the family to do the hardest of the work, that in 1862 1863 1864 1865 1866 1867 1868 1869 1870 1871 1872 1873 1874 1875 1876 1877 1878 1879 and 1880 I did such work without pay or remuneration, that as I received no pay I kept no account of my labor and cannot state its value, but, according to the best of my judgment and belief, the amount of service I rendered my parents could not have been hired for less than from forty to sixty dollars in each of said years. That I have loaned my father money earned in the employment of others, and that I now hold a note against him for such money to the sum of fifty dollars and interest two years. That the said Benj F Chase was not married and left no widow at his decease.

Post Office address is _Meredith Village, N.H._

I further declare that _I have_ no interest in said case, and _am_ not concerned in its prosecution.

Vittie M. Chase
(Affiants' Signature.)

(If Affiants sign by mark, two persons who can write sign here.)

IMPORTANT.—If testimony is given as to physical condition of claimant, it should be stated how long you have known him. If before his enlistment, was he sound and free from his present disability; and what his physical condition was when you first saw him after his discharge; what he complained of, and about to what extent (⅛,¼,⅜,½,¾,) or how much it has disabled him yearly during your knowledge of his case; also state how you know the facts to which you testify.

Benjamin Chase's sister Vittie filled out this affidavit in an effort to have her mother receive a pension.

National Archives, Records of the Department of Veterans Affairs

been few alternatives: "they wasent anything that i could get to do and so i thought i would enlist all the other boys was going to and i wanted to see a little of the world to." If he had to do it over, "i should never enlist again." He did not believe that he would die but tells his mother: "i may live to get home again and may not. if i get killed out hear it will be the last of me, but i have a great mind of getting home again." As he does in many of his letters, he assures his father that he will send part of his pay home.

Homesick

Over the next few months, Benjamin's letters home are filled with many of the same themes as his June 15 letter. He is homesick and wants packages. His family shouldn't worry. He will send money. On June 24, 1862, he writes that "i never want to be in another battle but if we have to fight i shall fight again." The 5th does fight again, at Malvern Hill and, most notably, at Antietam on September 17, 1862. There, according to Chase, the regiment lost 118 men at the Cornfield, Sunken Lane, and Burnside's Bridge. In the last letter in his file, Chase's mood is low: "I hate this foolish war more and more everyday." Benjamin's war would last only a few months longer. On December 13, at Fredericksburg, the 5th bravely attacked Marye's Heights but was annihilated. The frontal attack "into the blaze of the enemy's fire" cost 8,000 Union dead or wounded. The 5th had begun the day with 266 officers and men. At day's end, 193 were killed, wounded, captured, or missing. "We were most all cut down," recalled a corporal.

Benjamin Chase was one of the slaughtered.

Family Crisis

The deadly cost of the assault on Marye's Heights must have caused an outpouring of sadness across central New Hampshire. At the Chase farm in Meredith, Benjamin's death provoked not only grief but a family crisis whose consequences would last for decades. Madison and Nancy Chase had become increasingly dependent on "our darling Bennie" for support. Madison suffered from "heart trouble and a rupture" and was frequently unable to work. They had four children under the age of 13. The summer before Benjamin's death, their eldest son, George, had died of consumption. Much of the burden for supporting the family after 1862 would fall on the oldest daughter, "Vittie," who was 25 years old when her brother was killed. Benjamin's death would shape her life in several dramatic ways. She never married or had children. She supported her mother and father for the rest of their lives. She even loaned her father money.

Fortunately for the Chase family, Congress had provided pensions for mothers of fallen soldiers. But qualifying for a pension required proving that a family had been, at least in part, dependent on the soldier for support. Nancy Chase's pension application is filled with depositions and affidavits seeking to establish this point. Vittie Chase stated that she had shouldered the burden of supporting her parents: "My help has been needed in the family to do the hardest of the work." Neighbors added their recollections that Bennie had been "a good boy" who had worked for them and who signed his pay over to his father.

Madison Chase's statement notes that he had paid off some of his debts using the money sent by his son: "in his letters now on file in this case in the Pension Office, [Benjamin] directed me to pay with the money which he from time to time sent me." In other words, the letters sent home by this young soldier were included as evidence for his support of his family. The strategy succeeded. Nancy Chase eventually received a pension of $12 a month.

November 11, 2007: The historian visits Fredericksburg National Cemetery and asks if Benjamin Chase is buried there. There is no record of his burial. The historian learns that the names of most of the soldiers interred there are unknown. What became of Bennie's remains? Was he buried unknown, "on the field?" Or was he returned to Meredith?

Back at the National Archives, the historian examines War Department records documenting headstone applications for deceased Civil War soldiers. These provide one more answer. Benjamin Chase was buried in Meredith Village Cemetery. The homesick teenager who sent his pay to his father, asked for care packages, and longed to eat his Mother's brown bread had finally come home.

NOTE ON SOURCES

Benjamin Chase's compiled military service record in Records of the Adjutant General's Office, 1780's-1917, Record Group (RG) 94, gives the outline of his time in the U.S. Army. His mother's pension file, containing his letters home, in Records of the Department of Veterans Affairs, RG 15, is much more revealing about his life and his family's. The Chase family is listed in the 1860 census schedules for Meredith, New Hampshire. Mike Pride and Mark Travis's My Brave Boys: To War With Colonel Cross & the Fighting Fifth (2001) is a good modern history of the Fifth New Hampshire that draws on original sources including Benjamin's letters. The regimental history, A History of the Fifth Regiment New Hampshire Volunteers in the American Civil War, 1861-1865 (1893) was written by its regimental surgeon, William Child, and contains narratives, reminiscences, and other accounts by its members. George C. Rable's Fredericksburg! Fredericksburg! (2002) not only details the battle itself in vivid detail but places it in the political and military context of the War.

PARTISAN RANGERS!

I have just returned from our army in

Mississippi, where, after a stay of some months, I received authority from General Price to raise and organize a squadron of Independent Rangers to serve under his orders, after his return to the west of the Mississippi River. The necessity of constant activity in this kind of service will be congenial to the chivalrous character of Texans, and also promotive of a degree of good health rarely found in the midst of large armies, or in the ordinary service. This band will be organized strictly under the law of Congress legalizing Partizan warfare. and will be subject to no orders except those of the Major General. As it will be composed principally of men not subject to conscription, but whose patriotic spirit alone enlists their efforts in our country's cause at this crisis, the General will expect from it the most important and valuable services in hovering around the enemy in his marches through our country, killing off his pickets, cutting off his trains and capturing his property, in short, in being a terror to him by day and by night, wherever he may be.

It presents a wide field for the exercise of individual prowess and skill, and all instances of personal daring and courage will be most amply rewarded. Every member must furnish his own horse and arms, for which full payment will be made if lost in battle. The pay, per month, for man and horse, the same as in the regular service. On being mustered into service, every man will receive a bounty of Fifty Dollars. When a sufficient number are enrolled to compose a Squadron---two companies---some central place will be selected at which to rendezvous and organise by the election of officers &c.

Transportation, subsistence &c. will be furnished by the Government. Address me at Alto, Cherokee County, Texas, or R. G. Ash, Houston, Texas.

ALTO, Texas, July 9, 1862.   WM. F. REESE.

CHAPTER 5

A LOCAL FIGHT

For many people the Civil War conjures up images of huge armies colliding on legendary battlefields such as Gettysburg, Antietam, and Shiloh. Those battles were significant, but the Civil War also included many smaller clashes that bitterly divided neighbors in places such as Pilot Knob, Missouri; Lawrence, Kansas; and Goodson, Virginia.

- Who was involved in these fights?
- How did they start?
- And how did they help shape the war?

Records from the National Archives document it all—the major battles as well as the skirmishes, guerrilla raids, and occupations in communities with divided loyalties.

PARTISANS? GUERRILLAS? BANDITS?

This broadside from Texas recruited men for an irregular Confederate unit. Confederates organized partisan units to harass Union forces through small raids and ambushes—disrupting Union supply lines and forcing the U.S. Army to use valuable manpower to protect civilian lives. This type of warfare sometimes turned ugly and led to reprisals against civilians, violence against prisoners, and even atrocities. It became difficult to distinguish soldiers from bands of thieves, murderers, or vigilantes.

National Archives, War Department Collection of Confederate Records

HARPER'S WEEKLY.
A JOURNAL OF CIVILIZATION

VOL. VII.—No. 349.]   NEW YORK, SATURDAY, SEPTEMBER 5, 1863.   [SINGLE COPIES SIX CENTS.
[$3.00 PER YEAR IN ADVANCE.

Entered according to Act of Congress, in the Year 1863, by Harper & Brothers, in the Clerk's Office of the District Court for the Southern District of New York.

MOSEBY'S GUERRILLAS DESTROYING SUTLERS' TRAIN.—[SEE PAGE 567.]

PARTISAN AMBUSH

This illustration shows an attack on a Union supply train by one of the Confederacy's most daring partisan
commanders, John Singleton Mosby and his cavalry—Mosby's Rangers. They were seen as "partisans" and
not "guerrillas" because they wore Confederate uniforms and were authorized by the Confederate government.
Mosby himself was known as the "Gray Ghost" for his ability to suddenly appear, fight, and then just as quickly
disappear into the surrounding countryside.

From Harper's Weekly, *September 5, 1863*
Courtesy of the Library of Congress

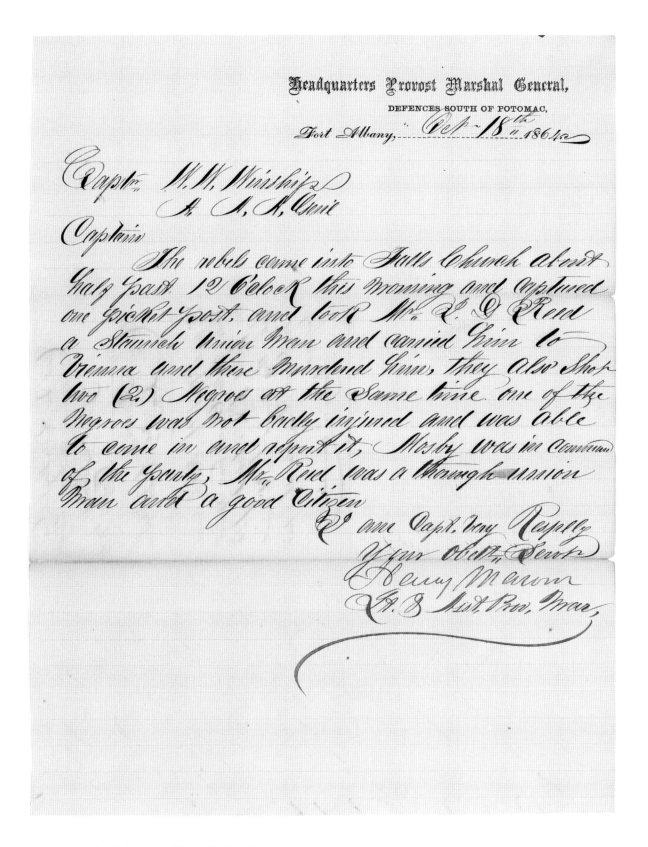

Headquarters Provost Marshal General,

DEFENCES SOUTH OF POTOMAC,

Fort Albany, _____ Oct 18th 1864

Captn. W. W. Winship
      A. A. A. Genl

Captain

    The rebels came into Falls Church about half past 12 O'clock this morning and captured one picket post, and took Mr. L. D. Read a staunch Union man and carried him to Vienna and there Murdered him, they also Shot two (2) Negroes at the same time. one of the Negroes was not badly injured and was able to come in and report it, Mosby was in Command of the party, Mr. Read was a through union Man and a good Citizen

      I am Capt. Very Respfly
      Your Obdt. Servt
      Henry Marom
      Lt. & Asst Prov. Marr,

MOSBY RAIDS VIRGINIA

This letter describes a raid on Falls Church, Virginia, by John Singleton Mosby and his cavalry. Mosby's Rangers operated behind Union lines in Northern Virginia, seizing supplies and capturing prisoners. This letter describes how the rebels "captured one picket post," carried one "staunch Union man" to Vienna and murdered him here, and also "shot two (2) Negroes at the same time."

National Archives, Records of U.S. Army Continental Commands, 1821–1920

RAIDERS FROM TENNESSEE

DETAIL

Virginia and Tennessee both joined the Confederacy. And both states held sizable numbers of Union supporters, especially in the mountains of eastern Tennessee and western Virginia. In this petition, Confederates from a town in southwestern Virginia asked Governor John Letcher to arm their home guard against Union raiders from eastern Tennessee who were "hostile to the cause of Southern Independence."

National Archives, War Department Collection of Confederate Records

UNION SYMPATHIZERS IN A CONFEDERATE STATE

These Tennessee Unionists met secretly in 1862, vowing to stand with the United States even though Tennessee had joined the Confederacy. In addition to the 150,000 black Southerners who served in the Union Army, at least 100,000 white Southerners served as well. Confederate deserters and draft dodgers sometimes formed guerrilla units that operated throughout the South, especially in the southern Appalachian Mountains.

From Harper's Weekly, *March 29, 1862*
Courtesy of the Library of Congress

A THRILLING SCENE IN EAST TENNESSEE—COLONEL FRY AND THE UNION MEN SWEARING BY THE FLAG.—[See Page 203.]

"immediately arrest at least five of the most prominent and active rebel sympathizers"

GOVERNOR THOMAS BRAMLETTE

PROCLAMATION BY THE GOVERNOR.

EXECUTIVE DEPARTMENT,
FRANKFORT, KY., January 4th, 1864.

The frequent outrages perpetrated in various parts of the State by lawless bands of marauders, can in a large degree be traced to the active aid of rebel sympathizers in our midst, or their neglect to furnish to Military Commandants the information, in their possession, which would lead to the defeat and capture of such marauders.

Sympathizers with the rebellion who, while enjoying protection from the Government, abuse the leniency extended to them by concealing the movements of rebel guerrillas, by giving them information, affording them shelter, supplying them with provisions, and otherwise encouraging and fomenting private raids, are in criminal complicity with all the outrages perpetrated by the marauders whom they secretly countenance.

It is in the power of persons whose sympathies are with the rebellion to prevent guerrilla raids, almost invariably, by furnishing to Military Officers of the United States or State of Kentucky, the information which experience has proved them to be, as a general thing, possessed of.

If all would unite, as is their duty, in putting down guerrillas, we should soon cease to be troubled with their raids. A neglect to afford all assistance and information which may aid in defeating the designs of marauding parties, can but be construed as a culpable and active assistance to our enemies.

I, therefore, request that the various Military Commandants in the State of Kentucky will, in every instance where a loyal citizen is taken off by bands of guerrillas, immediately arrest at least five of the most prominent and active rebel sympathizers in the vicinity of such outrage for every loyal man taken by guerrillas. These sympathizers should be held as hostages for the safe and speedy return of the loyal citizens. Where there are disloyal relatives of guerrillas, they should be the chief sufferers. Let them learn that if they refuse to exert themselves actively for the assistance and protection of the loyal, they must expect to reap the just fruits of their complicity with the enemies of our State and people.

THO. E. BRAMLETTE.

HOSTAGES IN KENTUCKY

Kentucky never formally left the Union, but its population was deeply split. The state declared itself neutral until Confederate forces invaded in 1861. Kentucky was accepted into the Confederacy and given a star on the Confederate flag.

By 1864 intense Confederate guerrilla activity led Governor Thomas Bramlette to issue this proclamation ordering the arrest of Confederate sympathizers, who were held as hostages in retaliation for the kidnapping of Unionists. Bramlette requested that military commanders "immediately arrest at least five of the most prominent and active rebel sympathizers in the vicinity of such outrage for every loyal man taken by guerrillas."

National Archives, Records of U.S. Army Continental Commands, 1821–1920

FLAG INSULTED IN MISSOURI

Towns in Missouri were often divided between Union and Confederate supporters. In this special order, the local Union commander describes the insult that anti-Union members recently inflicted on the U.S. flag displayed behind the pulpit of a church in New Harmony, Missouri. The flag was "forcibly taken from over the Pulpit of the Church . . . and thrown out of doors." The commander threatened to close the church and arrest its parishioners if they did not restore the American flag to its honored place.

National Archives, Records of U.S. Army Continental Commands, 1821–1920

KANSAS INVADED

Lawrence, Kansas, served as a base for Union raids into Confederate parts of Missouri and also as a center for recruiting African American troops. On August 21, 1863, Confederate guerrilla leader William Quantrill and 450 of his men attacked the town. They burned much of it, robbed stores, and killed hundreds of civilians. Kansas Governor Thomas Kearney sent this telegram to the Secretary of War asking for arms to protect Lawrence.

National Archives, Records of the Secretary of War

SELECTED PAGE

NATIVE AMERICANS
TRAPPED IN THE MIDDLE

Native Americans were caught between the Union and the Confederacy, and several tribes were split in their loyalties. In this letter, U.S. Commissioner of Indian Affairs William P. Dole described the plight of a group of Creek Indians. Loyal to the Union, they were driven from their lands by Confederate forces and other Creeks sympathetic to the Confederacy. The refugees eventually fought their way to Kansas, where they faced starvation and harsh winter conditions.

National Archives, Records of the Office of the Secretary of the Interior

Rebels Invade Vermont from Canada

On October 19, 1864, 22 Confederate agents, led by Kentuckian Bennett H. Young, raided the small town of St. Albans, Vermont. Most of the raiders had been Confederate prisoners of war who had escaped to Canada. Arriving in St. Albans, the group initially posed as hunters on holiday, but once registered at their hotel, they changed into their uniforms. They then entered the town's three banks and announced they were Confederate soldiers. They robbed the banks of over $200,000, killed a civilian, stole horses, and destroyed property. An attempt to burn down the town failed when the raider's "Greek Fire" incendiary device failed to ignite.

Vermont's Governor, J. Gregory Smith, sent a telegram to Maj. Gen. John A. Dix describing the damage that had been done and asking Dix to send "such force as you can to help us." A posse from St. Albans pursued the rebels and captured some of them across the border, where they were turned over to Canadian authorities. The United States asked that the raiders be extradited, but Canadian courts ruled that the raiders were soldiers and could not be returned to the United States.

Eventually Canada reimbursed the St. Albans banks, but tensions remained high along the border for the rest of the war.

"REBELS FROM CANADA HAVE INVADED THE STATE . . . ."

Vermont Governor J. Gregory Smith, sent this appeal for help to Maj. Gen. John A. Dix.

National Archives, Records of the Office of the Secretary of War

SAVING MAJOR WOLF
Bruce I. Bustard

The serendipitous discovery of a record reporting the execution of six Confederate soldiers led to the unfolding of the dramatic story of how President Lincoln helped stay the execution of Union Maj. Enoch Wolf.

Room 200 in the National Archives Building—the Archives' Central Research Room—is probably not most people's idea of an exciting place. It is dimly lit and wood paneled with a high, ornately carved ceiling. Visitors and staff speak in whispers amidst the hum of copiers and the clicking of laptop computers. For researchers, however, Room 200 is a special place where you go to solve mysteries and make discoveries. It is where you meet the past close up.

You may have read books and articles about your subject. You may have studied printed reports and memoirs. But in the Central Research Room you can open boxes or crack volumes and look at original documents—the evidence left by actual participants in historic events. You wait for your cart of records to arrive with a tingle of anticipation. When you open the boxes, you are often surprised by the stories you find inside. And the documents lead to new questions about the history you thought you knew.

An Accidental Discovery

Just such a moment happened to me in Room 200 one winter afternoon when I was conducting research for the Civil War exhibit. I was reading letters received by the Union Provost Marshal's office in Missouri in 1864.

Like many Civil War records, each letter in my box was wrapped by a sheet of paper that quickly tells you the subject of the correspondence. The records I was reading had headings such as "Reports on Enlistments," "Letter regarding saloons," and "Arrest for curfew violation." Then I came upon one that stopped me short: "Reports the execution of the six rebel soldiers held as hostages for Major Wilson and men." Opening the letter, I found this brief note, dated October 30, 1864, from Lt. Col. Gustav Heinrichs to Acting Provost Marshal Col. Joseph Darr:

I have the honor to report that the execution of the six rebel prisoners of war mentioned in Special Order Nos 279 and 280 current series from your Office took place near Fort No 4 in this City at the specified time, and was performed to my entire satisfaction by the detail of the Provost guard in command of Capt. Jones, consisting of 44 men of the 10th Kansas and 10 men of the 41st Mo. Inf.

The men fired at a distance of fifteen paces and five of the six were shot through the heart, and they were all instantly killed. I desire to call your attention, Colonel to the good conduct of the officers and men detailed for this unpleasant duty, and remain your obedient serv't.

DETAIL

This October 30, 1864, report from Lt. Col. Gustav Heinrichs to Col. Joseph Darr gave the grim details of the execution of six Confederate enlisted men in retaliation for the killing of Maj. James Wilson and his men in a matter-of-fact fashion. *National Archives, Records of U.S. Army Continental Commands, 1821–1920*

Missouri was badly divided during the Civil War and saw some of the most intense guerrilla fighting of the war.

Pilot Knob ⚓ is located in the southeastern part of the state, in Iron County.

National Archives, Records of the Office of the Corps of Engineers (Civil War Map File, Q 82)

What was this? Why had "six rebel prisoners of war" been held hostage and then executed? Who were these men? And who was Major Wilson? The execution was at odds with the Civil War images I'd carried with me since childhood: images of epic battles fought by gallant soldiers who followed a strict code of principled, old-fashioned morality. This report seemed to tell a very different story.

The War in Missouri

The population of Missouri, where the executions took place, was split between supporters of the Union and the Confederacy. Confederates raised irregular or "partizan" units to resist the "occupation" of their state. At first these groups wore uniforms and followed a formal command structure designed to keep abuses in check. Soon, however, the lines between authorized irregular warfare and criminal behavior blurred. Missouri's Civil War devolved into a brutal guerrilla conflict.

U.S. forces used increasingly harsh counterinsurgency tactics, and civilian Union supporters raised their own informal armed groups. By 1864 it was common in Missouri for roving bandits of armed men to burn homes; murder civilians who supported the other side; and steal food, clothing, and horses. Neighbors turned on neighbors—often for reasons that had little to do with the war. And those who were captured by guerrillas, like Major Wilson, could expect the worst.

An Eye for an Eye

While the report in the Provost Marshal's file was mysterious, it also gave me several leads. The first was the reference to "Major Wilson and men." If I could work out who this Major Wilson was, I could probably find his military service record—and possibly his pension record—in the Archives. The second clue was Heinrichs's reference to Special Orders 279 and 280. Finally, the knowledge that

Heinrichs wrote from St. Louis, Missouri, on October 30, 1864, helped narrow things down.

I quickly located printed versions of Special Orders 279 and 280 in *The War of the Rebellion: A Compilation of the Official Records of the Union and Confederate Armies*. These and other related transcripts of documents provided the basic facts. In the fall of 1864, Maj. James Wilson and six of his men of the 3rd Missouri State Militia Cavalry were captured at Pilot Knob, Missouri. A Confederate officer handed the prisoners over to the guerrilla fighter, Tim Reves, near Union, Missouri. The "blood stained outlaw" then "brutally murdered" Wilson and his men. In retaliation, Provost Marshal Joseph Darr chose six Confederate prisoners of war to be "shot to death by musketry." It is these men whose deaths were noted in Heinrichs's October 30 report.

But executing six enlisted men did not, in the minds of Union authorities, amount to "an eye for an eye." James Wilson was an officer. Retribution for his execution demanded that a Confederate major die as well. An order was issued that "the first captured Confederate Major" be sent to the Union prison in St. Louis to face a firing squad. The unlucky Confederate was Major Enoch Wolf, of Major Ford's Arkansas Battalion. He was captured in Kansas on October 26, 1864. My next step was to read Wolf's Confederate service record in the holdings of the War Department Collection of Confederate Records.

Wolf's Ordeal

The uncomprehending Wolf was attached to an iron ball and anvil at the Gratiot Street Prison in St. Louis and told that he was to be "shot to death by musketry on Friday next between the hours of nine and eleven o'clock." On November 8, the day he was informed of his execution, Major Wolf wrote to Gen. William S. Rosecrans, who commanded the Department of Missouri. Wolf asked Rosecrans to demand that his Confederate counterpart, General Price, turn over "the notorious bushwacker Tim Reves to be executed."

Rosecrans did not reply. On November 10, the day before Wolf was to be executed, he wrote to Rosecrans again. This time he requested a delay "of a few days" so he could "prepare for death." The General agreed. Soon after, according to some accounts, Wolf seems to have been visited by a minister, to whom Wolf gave a last letter to his wife. The letter contained a line asking Wolf's wife to say good-bye to his Masonic friends. After reading this line, and confirming that the major was a Mason, the minister rushed from his cell.

Wolf's fate became a public cause. Within less than a day several groups—including the "Union ladies of the City of St. Louis" and "faithful supporters of the Federal Government"—sent petitions and letters to Rosecrans asking that he stay the execution until he had at least determined that General Price was not going to turn over Reves. At the same time, two St. Louis civilians telegrammed President Lincoln asking for Presidential clemency.

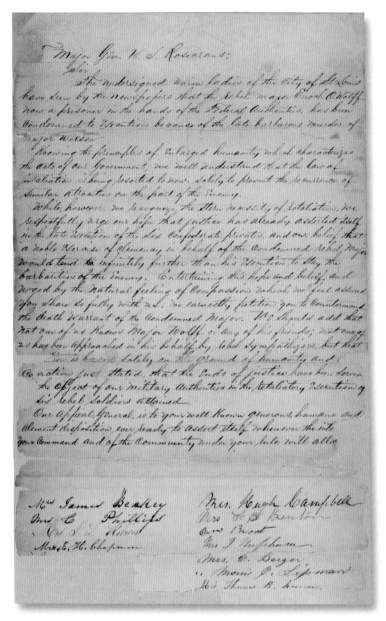

Loyal Unionists like these mounted a campaign to spare Maj. Enoch Wolf from the firing squad. DETAIL

National Archives, War Department Collection of Confederate Records

Later on November 10, in response to the petitions, Rosecrans again delayed the execution—this time until November 25. That same day Lincoln telegrammed Rosecrans: "Suspend execution of Major Wolf until further order." Lincoln also asked the general to explain his actions.

As ordered, Rosecrans suspended Wolf's execution. But he wrote the President a long letter defending his actions and chafing at being contradicted by someone almost 900 miles away who did not understand the war in Missouri. His order to execute Wolf had one goal: "to secure our prisoners from murder." Wilson's death had been "cold blooded murder." Rosecrans had the "right, and even duty" to "hold any organized body of men responsible for the actions of their organization." War, he reminded his commander-in-chief, required the deaths of "men who have done no wrong." Price had not prevented the "official murder" of U.S. soldiers. Only a threatened "sense of personal security" would make the point.

President Lincoln's telegram to General Rosecrans suspended Enoch Wolf's execution only hours before the major was to die.

National Archives, Records of the Office of the Secretary of War

More Questions

We do not know what Lincoln thought of Rosecran's justification, but the President's telegram did save Major Wolf. Although it stopped Wolf's execution only temporarily, Wolf never faced a firing squad—probably because Rosecrans was relieved of his command in January 1865. The new general, Grenville Dodge, took no further action. Wolf was transferred to the Union prisoner-of-war camp on Johnson's Island, Ohio. On February 24, 1865, he was exchanged for other prisoners at City Point, Virginia. There is no record that Tim Reves was ever held responsible for the deaths of Major Wilson and his men. Enoch Wolf died at the age of 83 on October 20, 1910, in Myrone, Arkansas.

The murder of Major Wilson and his men, the execution of six innocent Confederate enlisted men, and the saving of Major Wolf raise several weighty questions:

- Was Major Wolf simply the lucky beneficiary of Lincoln's compassion?
- What role did Wolf's status as an officer play in how military justice played out?
- Was the vicious guerrilla war in Missouri exceptional? Or does it point to new directions for Civil War historians?

Whatever the answers to these questions, the records brought to Room 200 in the National Archives Building will undoubtedly be essential to discovering them.

NOTE ON SOURCES

The report on the execution of the six Confederate enlisted men can be found in Department of the Missouri, Letters Received, Entry 2786 part 1, Records of U.S. Army Continental Commands, 1821-1920, Record Group (RG) 393. Maj. James Wilson's service record is held in Records of the Adjutant General's Office, 1780's-1917, RG 94. Enoch Wolf's service record is in War Department Collection of Confederate Records, RG 109. Telegrams to and from President Lincoln are in Records of the Secretary of War, RG 107. General Rosecrans's response to Lincoln is among letters sent from the Department of the Missouri in entry 2571, RG 94. The most comprehensive study of the war in Missouri remains Michael Fellman's *Inside War: The Guerrilla Conflict in Missouri During the American Civil War* (1989). Daniel E. Sutherland's *A Savage Conflict: The Decisive Role of Guerrillas in the American Civil War* (2009) is a broader, more recent study.

照會事本大臣現奉到

上諭選派本國賢明人姓榮日德名約瑟來到汕頭港口管理通商事

缺業已赴任理合照知

貴親王轉為行知汕頭地方官以便文書往來和衷辦事須至照

會

右

大清欽命總理各國事務和碩恭親王

甲子年正月 十七 日

No. 409
A. Burlingame
to Prince Kung
March 8. 1864

大亞美理駕合眾國欽命辭劄中華便宜行事全權大臣蒲

照會事現在美國有一要事照請

貴國得知曩者本國南方逆命與兵征勦現時三年之久已得克

本國官軍水陸圍困希於此年內將能折服南方但先時南逆設

船幾隻安置軍火要出大洋肆掠北方貨船該南逆無港口出入

船亦不能拖帶入內地于別國亦不准其拖入因其背理亦違萬

在大洋將船連貨燒燬現時本國兵船追勦此數南逆火輪船實

亞勒巴麻逃走將到中國沿海現已聞在南洋燒燬北方貨船數

大臣先為預防之故請

CHAPTER 6

GLOBAL WAR

Through diplomatic negotiations and naval conflicts, the Civil War's impact extended far beyond U.S. borders—to London and Beijing, Cape Town and Rio de Janeiro. While Union and Confederate troops battled on American soil, a global diplomatic battle ensued.

- Why did the Confederacy seek recognition abroad?
- How did the U.S. Government react to Confederate efforts to gain recognition?
- Did Confederate and Union ships battle beyond North American waters?

The documents reproduced on the following pages provide a glimpse of the Civil War's global reach.

DIPLOMATIC AGREEMENT WITH CHINA DETAIL

In this letter dated March 8, 1864, U.S. Minister Anson Burlingame informed Chinese Foreign Minister Prince Kung that the Confederate ship *Alabama* had been attacking U.S. merchant ships. He asked Kung to consider China's treaty obligations and the interest of international commerce and to deny the *Alabama* or any other Confederate ship entrance to Chinese waters. Kung agreed. Burlingame maintained this Chinese-language copy of the letter in his files.

National Archives, General Records of the Department of State

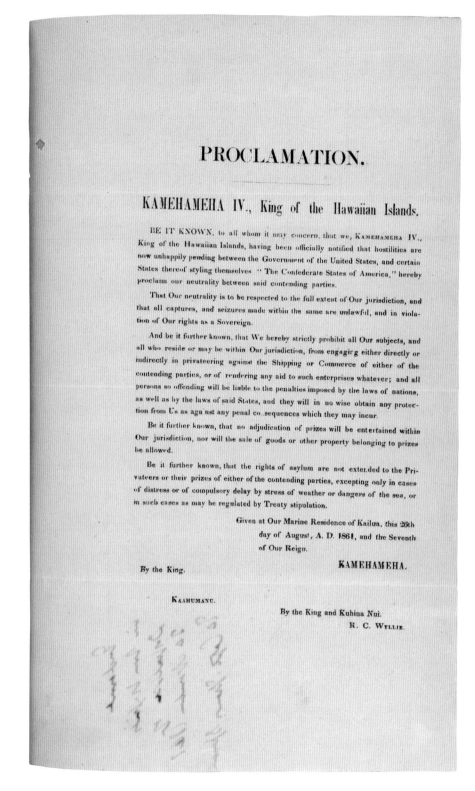

PROCLAMATION.

KAMEHAMEHA IV., King of the Hawaiian Islands.

BE IT KNOWN, to all whom it may concern, that we, KAMEHAMEHA IV., King of the Hawaiian Islands, having been officially notified that hostilities are now unhappily pending between the Government of the United States, and certain States thereof styling themselves "The Confederate States of America," hereby proclaim our neutrality between said contending parties.

That Our neutrality is to be respected to the full extent of Our jurisdiction, and that all captures, and seizures made within the same are unlawful, and in violation of Our rights as a Sovereign.

And be it further known, that We hereby strictly prohibit all Our subjects, and all who reside or may be within Our jurisdiction, from engaging either directly or indirectly in privateering against the Shipping or Commerce of either of the contending parties, or of rendering any aid to such enterprises whatever; and all persons so offending will be liable to the penalties imposed by the laws of nations, as well as by the laws of said States, and they will in no wise obtain any protection from Us against any penal consequences which they may incur.

Be it further known, that no adjudication of prizes will be entertained within Our jurisdiction, nor will the sale of goods or other property belonging to prizes be allowed.

Be it further known, that the rights of asylum are not extended to the Privateers or their prizes of either of the contending parties, excepting only in cases of distress or of compulsory delay by stress of weather or dangers of the sea, or in such cases as may be regulated by Treaty stipulation.

Given at Our Marine Residence of Kailua, this 26th day of August, A. D. 1861, and the Seventh of Our Reign.

KAMEHAMEHA.

By the King.

KAAHUMANU.

By the King and Kuhina Nui.
R. C. WYLLIE.

PROCLAMATION FROM THE PACIFIC

In August 1861 King Kamehameha IV proclaimed that the Hawaiian Islands would remain neutral in the conflict between the United States and "certain States therof styling themselves 'The Confederate States of America.'" The King prohibited his subjects from helping either side raid commercial vessels. Since commercial raiding was a key component of the Confederacy's naval strategy, that prohibition affected the South more than it did the North.

National Archives, General Records of the Department of State.

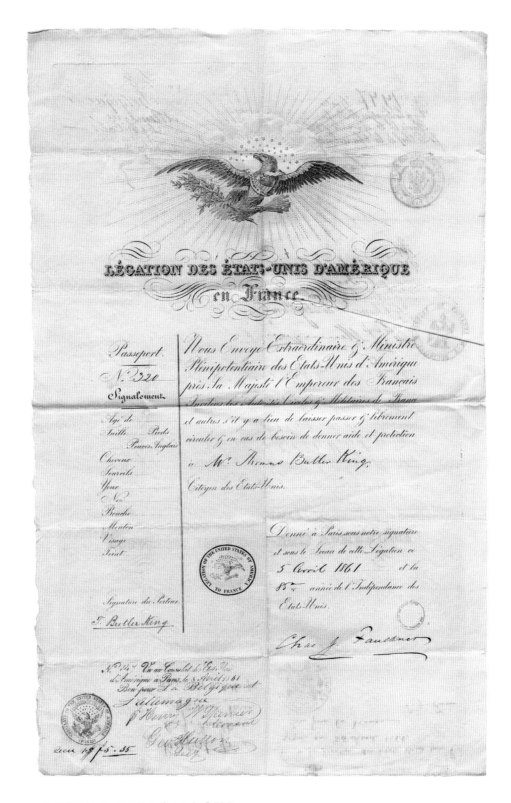

ACT OF DIPLOMACY?

On April 5, 1861, U.S. Ambassador to France Charles Faulkner issued this passport to Thomas Butler King, a Confederate emissary. At the request of Joseph Brown, Governor of Georgia, King planned to purchase muskets in Europe. The previous year, Faulkner himself had tried to purchase French arms for Virginia.

Just two weeks after taking office, President Lincoln replaced Faulkner with William Dayton. Faulkner was imprisoned but later exchanged for a Union prisoner.

National Archives, General Records of the Department of State

This map shows the proposed Pacific Telegraph from San Francisco to Moscow. It was submitted to the Committee on Commerce with a petition for a survey related to a telegraphic line from the Amoor River to "Russian America" (Alaska) around 1862.

National Archives, Records of the U.S. House of Representatives

A.

List of the Diplomatic Agents of the Confederate States, and their Secretaries, in Foreign Countries

Name	Office	Countries to which they were sent	When appointed	Salary
Pierre A. Rost [a]	Commissioner	Great Britain, France, Belgium & Russia	March 16, 1861	$ 12,000
A. Dudley Mann [b]	do.	"	"	12,000
Walker Fearn [c]	Secretary	"	"	3,600
James M. Mason	Commissioner	Great Britain	Aug. 24, 1861	12,000
James E. Macfarland	Secretary	"	"	3,600
John Slidell	Commissioner	France	"	12,000
George Eustis	Secretary	"	"	3,600

(a) Assigned to Spain August 24, 1861. Resigned May 28, 1862.
(b) Assigned to Belgium Sept. 23, 1861.
(c) Assigned to Spain Sept. 23, 1861.

CONFEDERATE AGENTS ABROAD

This list reveals Confederate diplomatic agents and their secretaries around 1862. The agents served throughout Europe—including Belgium, France, Great Britain, Russia, and Spain.

National Archives, War Department Collection of Confederate Records

JAMES M. MASON

Formerly a U.S. Senator from Virginia, Mason became the Confederate emissary to Great Britain. On September 23, 1861, Confederate Secretary of State Robert Hunter instructed Mason to sail to London. He was to gain England's recognition of the Confederacy, resulting in legitimacy and possibly an alliance against the United States.

But on November 8, Mason was captured by Union forces aboard the British vessel *Trent*. Britain deemed this a violation of its neutrality and nearly declared war on the United States. Great Britain never recognized the Confederacy.

National Archives, Records of the Office of the Chief Signal Officer
[111-B-4610]

JOHN SIDELL

Once a U.S. Senator from Louisiana, Sidell became the Confederate emissary to France. Union forces removed him, along with James Mason, from the British vessel *Trent*, provoking a diplomatic crisis that nearly led to war between Great Britain and United States.

This photograph, taken around 1861, reflects damage to the original glass plate negative that occurred before it was transferred to the National Archives.

National Archives, Records of the Office of the Chief Signal Officer
[111-B-4134]

CSS *Shenandoah*, 1864–65
U.S. Naval Historical Center

British Aggression?

A merchant vessel named the *Sea King* was built in Glasgow, Scotland, in 1863. Confederate agent James Bulloch bought the ship in October 1864. Once armed and at sea, it was renamed the CSS *Shenandoah*. This Confederate warship proceeded to capture or destroy 38 U.S. ships, including many from the Union's Pacific whaling fleet.

In March 1865, as it circumnavigated the globe, the *Shenandoah* destroyed 11 U.S. merchant vessels near Cape Town, South Africa. It then found safe harbor in Melbourne, Australia, a British possession. U.S. Secretary of State William Seward called the attacks and Britain's assistance to the *Shenandoah* a "new aggression of British subjects upon our national rights." Earl Russell, the British Foreign Minister, replied that Great Britain had merely fulfilled its obligations as a neutral power.

In April, Robert E. Lee surrendered at Appomattox. But the *Shenandoah's* captain, James Waddell, claimed that he had not learned of the "obliteration of the government under whose authority I had been acting" until August 2, 1865. Waddell sailed to Liverpool, England, where he surrendered to the British Government on November 6, 1865. It was the final surrender of a Confederate force. The British subsequently freed the *Shenandoah's* crew and officers but turned over the ship to U.S. Consul Thomas Dudley.

Despatch from Secretary of State Seward
to Charles F. Adams, U.S. Minister to
Great Britain, regarding the sinking of
Union ships by the CSS *Shenandoah* off
Cape Town, South Africa, March 25, 1865

*National Archives, General Records
of the Department of State*

Cornell's 1864 Atlas Map of Africa

Courtesy of the David Rumsey Historical Map Collection

DETAIL

"Cutting out of the *Florida* from
Bahia, Brazil, by
the USS *Wachusett*,"
October 7, 1864

U.S. Naval Historical Center

NAVAL ENCOUNTER NEAR BRAZIL

On October 7, 1864, the USS *Wachusett* captured
the CSS *Florida* in Brazilian waters. The Confederate
Senate issued this resolution condemning the
"flagrant outrage upon the territorial sovereignty
of Brazil." It also called upon the Brazilian
Government to seek restitution from the
United States for the capture of the *Florida*.

*National Archives, War Department Collection
of Confederate Records*

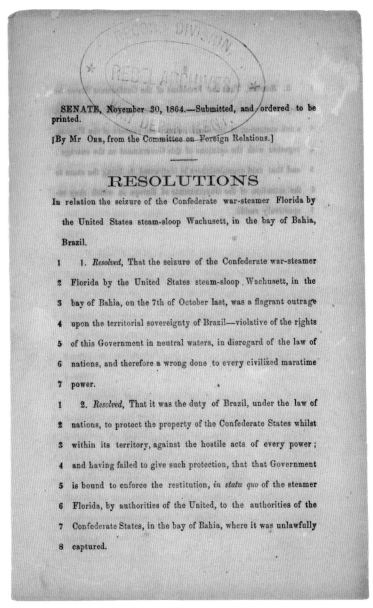

SENATE, November 30, 1864.—Submitted, and ordered to be
printed.

[By Mr ORR, from the Committee on Foreign Relations.]

RESOLUTIONS

In relation the seizure of the Confederate war-steamer Florida by
the United States steam-sloop Wachusett, in the bay of Bahia,
Brazil.

1 1. *Resolved,* That the seizure of the Confederate war-steamer
2 Florida by the United States steam-sloop Wachusett, in the
3 bay of Bahia, on the 7th of October last, was a flagrant outrage
4 upon the territorial sovereignty of Brazil—violative of the rights
5 of this Government in neutral waters, in disregard of the law of
6 nations, and therefore a wrong done to every civilized maratime
7 power.

1 2. *Resolved,* That it was the duty of Brazil, under the law of
2 nations, to protect the property of the Confederate States whilst
3 within its territory, against the hostile acts of every power;
4 and having failed to give such protection, that that Government
5 is bound to enforce the restitution, *in statu quo* of the steamer
6 Florida, by authorities of the United, to the authorities of the
7 Confederate States, in the bay of Bahia, where it was unlawfully
8 captured.

CONFEDERATE SHIPS: MADE IN ENGLAND
Michael Hussey

The Confederacy tried to expand its navy with ships built in Liverpool and other British shipyards. U.S. Consul Thomas Dudley tried to stop two such ships—the *Florida* and the *Alabama*—from ever leaving the shipyard where they were built.

On November 19, 1861, newly appointed U.S. Consul Thomas Dudley sailed to Liverpool, England. No sooner had he landed than he learned that two ships were "being fitted out for the so-called Confederate Government"—the vessels soon to be known as the *Florida* and *Alabama*. Although he was thousands of miles away from Union and Confederate troops, Dudley was right in the center of another Civil War front. The Confederacy was trying to build a navy in British shipyards—of which Liverpool was perhaps the most important. Blocking this Confederate effort became Dudley's main focus during the war years.

Legal Loophole?
Dudley quickly learned that the Liverpool populace tended to favor the Confederacy. "There seems to be strong feeling among the people and press in favor of recognizing the so called Southern Confederacy," he warned Secretary of State Seward in January 1862. Although Dudley did not want to raise undue alarm, he was convinced that the British Government itself also leaned towards recognizing the Confederacy and going to war with the United States. He alerted Seward that unless Union forces had some "decisive success within a short time, the Government here will recognize the so-called Southern Confederacy."

The threat of war with England would decrease over the course of the Civil War, but the threat of British-built Confederate warships to U.S. commerce did not.

In strict legal terms, the Confederacy should not have been able to contract with Liverpool shipyards to build warships. The British Foreign Enlistment Act strictly prohibited the Queen's subjects from constructing warships to be used against a nation with which the United Kingdom was not at war.

The Confederate naval agent James Bulloch found some maneuvering room, however. He claimed that if ships were not equipped as warships (i.e., with guns and munitions) while in English waters, then the Foreign Enlistment Act was not violated. The U.S. Government disagreed vociferously. But either from uncertainty or unspoken support of the Confederate cause, British officials were hesitant to enforce the law in favor of the United States.

And so the CSS *Florida* sailed out of Liverpool on March 22, 1862. Unable to prevent its departure, Dudley was even more determined to prevent the *Alabama* from leaving Liverpool. He wrote to William Seward: "When completed and armed she will be a most formidable and dangerous craft and if not prevented from going to sea will do much mischief to our commerce." Working with the U.S. Ambassador to Great Britain, Charles Francis Adams, Dudley set about marshalling sufficient evidence to convince British officials to prevent the *Alabama* from sailing.

Surveillance Begins
In the absence of British Government constraint, Bulloch signed a contract on August 1, 1861, with shipbuilders John Laird & Sons to build a warship initially known only as "the 290." This 290th ship built by Laird & Sons would later be renamed the *Alabama*. Dudley set out to learn everything he could about its construction, amassing an impressive collection of evidence to prove that the 290 was designed to be a warship. The evidence included the testimony of Laird & Sons' employees, detectives, and informants, which Dudley promptly forwarded to London and Washington, DC.

From a Laird & Sons foreman:
This ship was the "sister to the gun boat *Oreto* [later renamed the *C.S.S. Florida*] and has been built for the same parties and for the same purpose . . . that she was to be a privateer."

From Richard Brougan, Laird & Sons shipwright:
Bulloch "is at the yard and on the vessel every day and gives orders to the men and seems to have command . . . of the vessel . . . Bulloch represents himself as a commissioner for the Southern States and that this vessel is a privateer the same as the *Oreto*."

From Henry Redden, Laird & Sons employee:
"It is generally understood on board the said vessel that she belongs to the confederate government . . . [S]he is fitted in all respects as a man-of-war, to carry six broadside guns and four pivots, but has no guns or ammunition on board as yet."

SELECTED PAGE

Letter sent by Thomas Dudley
to Secretary of State Seward
on December 11, 1861

*National Archives,
General Records of the
Department of State*

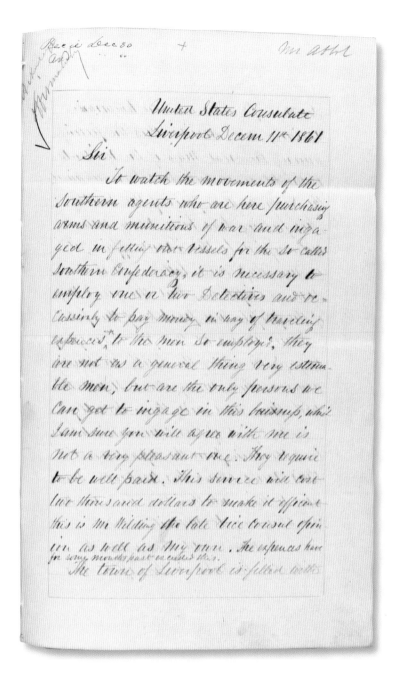

From Mathew Maguire, detective:
"I Matthew Maguire of Liverpool, agent, make oath and say as follows . . . On the second day of July . . . I saw . . . J. D. Bulloch on the [290 in] Laird & Co.'s yard. He appeared to be giving orders to the workmen who were employed about [the] . . . vessel."

From Robert John Taylor, 290 crewmember:
"One day while engaged in heaving up some of the machinery, we were singing a song, as seamen generally do, when the boatswain told us to stop that as the ship was not a merchant-ship, but a man-of-war."

With direct quotes from these and other sources, Dudley filled his State Department correspondence with specifics of the 290's design: "No pains or expense have been spared in her construction. Her engines are on the oscillating principle and are 350 horse power . . . Her screw . . . works in a solid brass frame casting weighing near two tons . . . The platform and gun carriages are now being constructed." Dudley also hired a photographer to obtain visual proof of the vessel's

design and intent. Unfortunately, high security around the shipyard prevented the photographer from securing this evidence.

The Outcome

Dudley was sure he had enough evidence to at least detain the 290. He hired British lawyers to put his case before Liverpool's Collector of the Port. "I have done about all that I can to stop this vessel. Much more I think than this Government ought to require any friendly Government to do. My counsel say I can do no more." He had acquired this mound of evidence despite the fact that "the strictest watch is kept over this vessel, no person except those immediately engaged up[on] her is admitted into the yard."

Dudley spent a lot of money obtaining information and presenting it before a British court. He hired detectives and provided financial support to witnesses in need of protection from British Confederate supporters. "One of the witnesses I have had to send to London to keep him from being tampered with and all those from the vessel will have to be

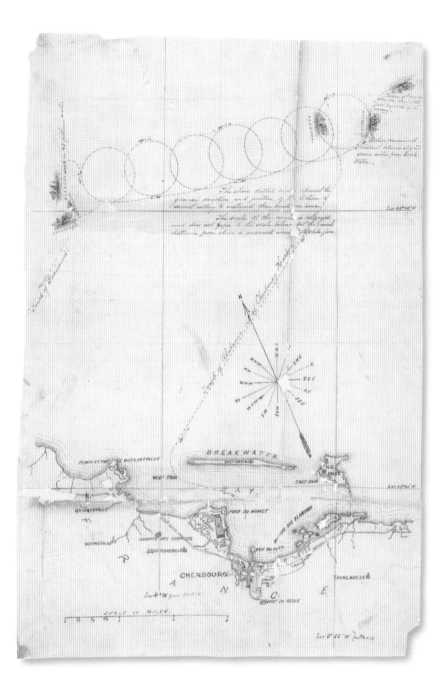

This map depicts the battle that took place on June 19, 1864, between the CSS *Alabama* and the USS *Kearsarge*.

National Archives, Naval Records Collection of the Office of Naval Records and Library

A still from the graphic novel entitled "The Voyage of the *Alabama*," this image brings the battle between the CSS *Alabama* and the USS *Kearsarge* to life for a modern audience.

Courtesy of Cortina Productions, Inc.

provided for," said Dudley. He informed Seward that Liverpool was a "hostile community . . . where the feeling and sentiment are against us." In spite of these obstacles, Dudley managed to obtain affidavits from these and other Laird & Sons employees.

Dudley was convinced that the Collector of the Port—"notwithstanding his sympathy for the Rebels and his indisposition to do anything against them"—could not deny the strength of the American case. Dudley also traveled to London with a copy of the witnesses' affidavits so that Ambassador Adams could present the U.S. case to the British Foreign Office.

Dudley and Adams were soon disappointed. On July 29, 1862, before the British could or would act, the 290 sailed out of Liverpool—ostensibly on a second test run. It never returned. Both the *Florida* and the *Alabama* would wreak havoc on Union merchant vessels.

NOTE ON SOURCES

State Department records provide a rich source of documentation on the U.S. effort to thwart the building of Confederate ships in Great Britain. The dispatches to the Department of State from the U.S. Legation in London and from the Consulate in Liverpool are contained within General Records of the Department of State, Record Group (RG) 59. Additional material is contained within the records that were retained in the legation and consulate. These are found in Foreign Service Post Records of the Department of State, RG 84, which are arranged by the posts' locations.

David H. Milton's *Lincoln's Spymaster: Thomas Haines Dudley and the Liverpool Network* (2003) and Coy F. Cross, II's *Lincoln's Man in Liverpool: Consul Dudley and the Legal Battle to Stop Confederate Warships* (2007) are both useful sources on this topic.

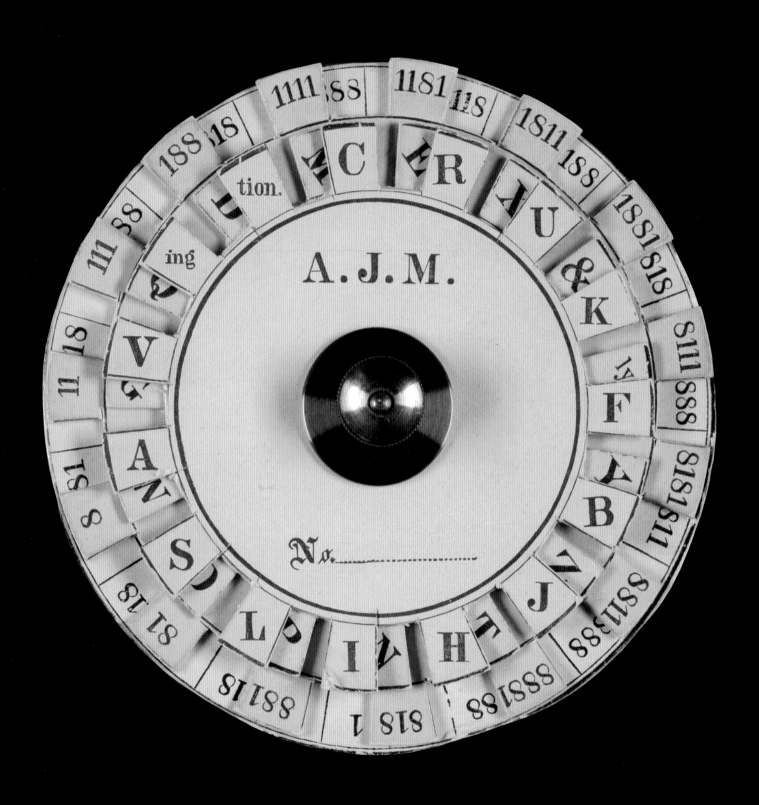

TURNING CIRCLES AROUND THE CONFEDERATES

Maj. Albert J. Myer, a U.S. Army Surgeon, created this cipher disk to protect Union Army communications. Letters on the upper two disks aligned with numbers on the lower two disks to encode a message. In this image, for example, the letter "A" would be sent as "81." The line marked "No." in the middle was completed with a number to help account for the device.

Before the Civil War began, Myer invented a signaling system that used a single flag, called wig wag signaling. In 1859, after it proved successful, he was promoted to major and appointed Chief Signal Officer of the Army. Lt. Col. Robert E. Lee chaired the review board that authorized the testing of Myer's system. Myer's assistants in his early work were future Confederate officers E. Porter Alexander and J.E.B. Stuart.

National Archives, Records of the Office of the Chief Signal Officer

CHAPTER 7

SPIES AND CONSPIRACIES

During the Civil War both sides used all of their resources to conduct intelligence operations that would give them an advantage. Even though these intelligence operations were often disjointed and uncoordinated, both sides experienced occasional successes.

- How did the North and South spy on each other?
- How did each side protect its communications?
- What conspiracies were formed during the war?

These and other records held by the National Archives allow us to better understand the covert Civil War.

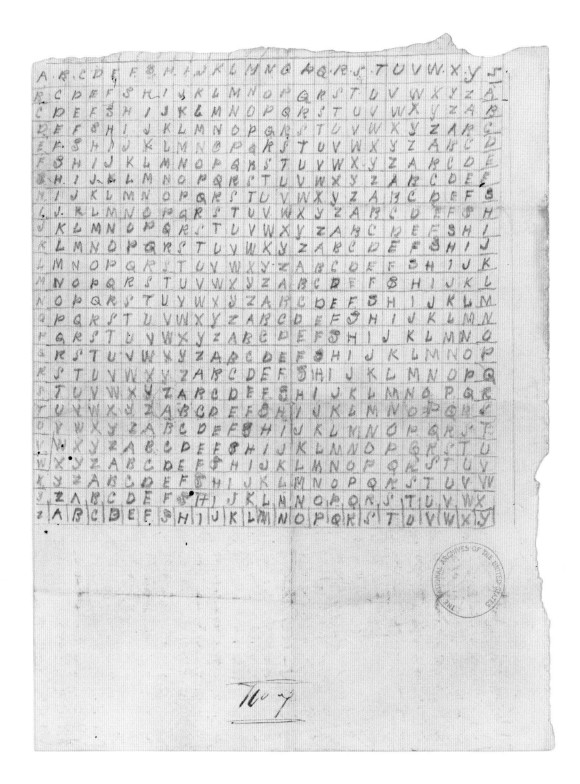

BOOTH'S SECRET CIPHER

This cipher was found among the possessions of Lincoln's assassin, John Wilkes Booth, in 1865. It is a form of the Vigenere Square, a tool used to produce messages in code. The Confederacy commonly used this type of cipher to protect its communications. How the cipher wound up in Booth's effects is unknown. But it is known that in October 1864, while making plans to kidnap President Lincoln, Booth traveled to Montreal, Quebec, and met with Confederate agents.

National Archives, Records of the Office of the Judge Advocate General (Army)

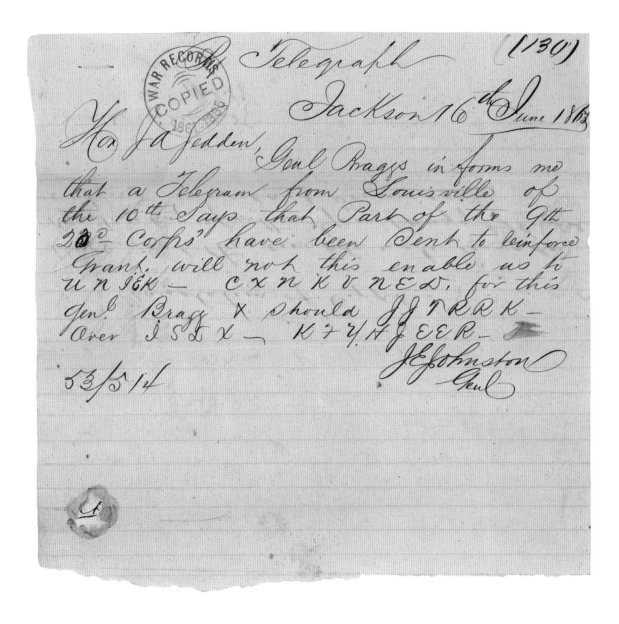

HIDING THE DETAILS

As this telegram shows, it was not always necessary to encrypt an entire message. Sometimes just a few key words or phrases were enough. Confederate Gen. Joseph E. Johnston sent this telegram to Secretary of War James A. Seddon on June 16, 1863. The decryption shows what Johnston was trying to hide: details advocating an invasion of Kentucky and his proposal to enlarge Gen. Braxton Bragg's area of responsibility.

The South used a very simple cipher with only three keywords—Manchester Bluff, Come Retribution, and Complete Victory—for the entire war. Phonetic spelling was often used in sending messages. Here, for example, "invade" was spelled "invad."

National Archives, *War Department Collection of Confederate Records*

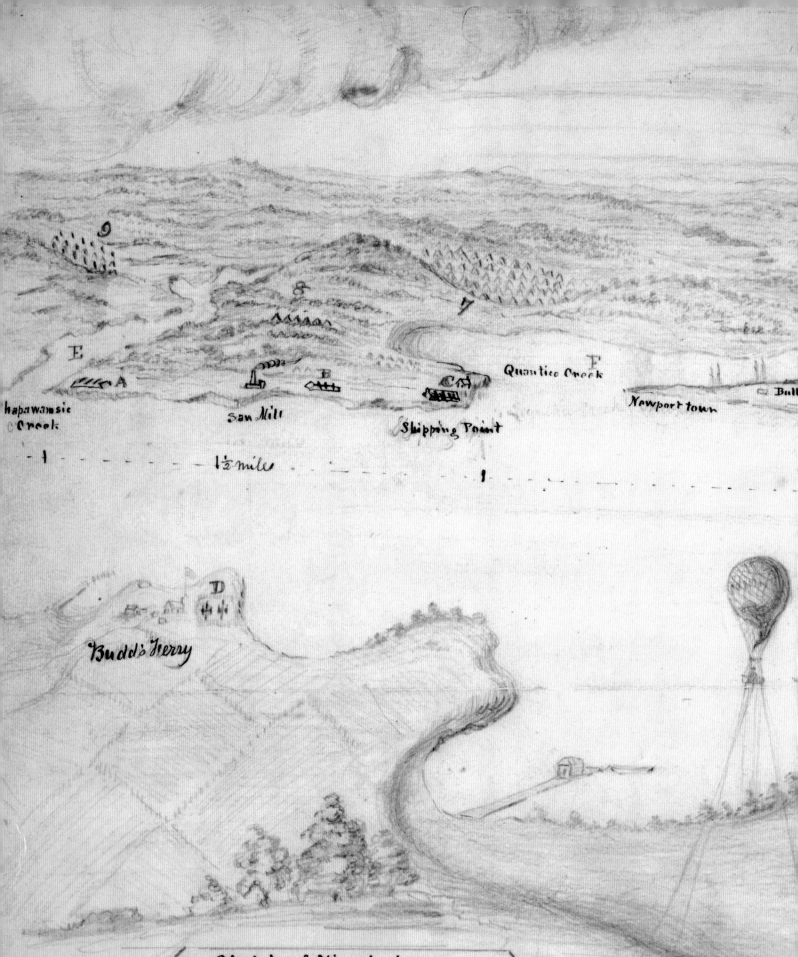

hapawamsic
Creek

Saw Mill

Shipping Point

Quantico Creek

Newport town

Bull

E
A
B
C
F

1½ mile

D

Budd's Ferry

Sketch of Virginia, and
the Rebel Camps and Batteries, in
front of Gen. Jos. Hooker's Division
in Charles County, Maryland.
Made from Prof. Lowe's Balloon, for the
Commander in Chief,   Dec. 8, 1861
By Col. Wm. F. Small, 26th Reg. Pa. Vols.

MAPPING ENEMY TERRITORY DETAIL

Col. William F. Small of the 26th Pennsylvania Infantry Regiment made this sketch while aloft in a balloon just south of Indian Head, Maryland, on December 8, 1861. The Potomac River flows through the middle of this drawing, with Virginia on the far shore. The balloon was the *Constitution,* designed by Prof. T.S.C. Lowe, Chief Aeronaut of the U.S. Army Balloon Corps.

National Archives, Records of the Adjutant General's Office, 1780's–1917

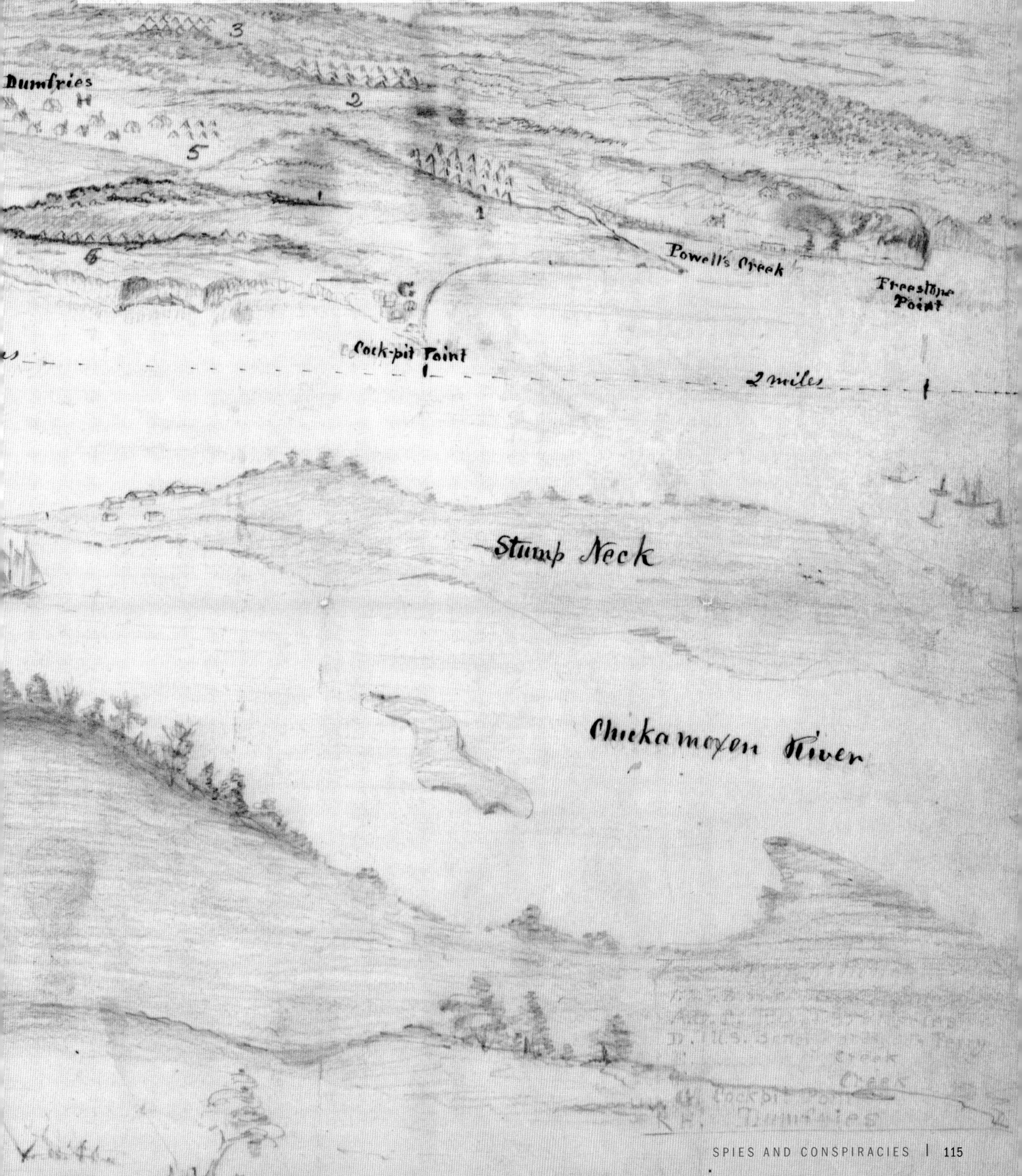
Dumfries
3
2
5
1
6
Powell's Creek
Freestone Point
G
Cock-pit Point
2 miles
Stump Neck
Chickamoxen River

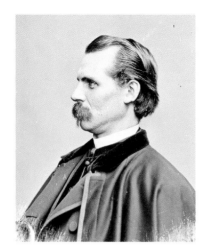

Chief Aeronaut of the U.S. Army Balloon Corps Prof. Thaddeus S. C. Lowe, ca. 1863

National Archives, Records of the Office of the Chief Signal Officer

[111-B-2514]

A Balloon Reconnoissance of the Enemy's Position at Manassas.

ALEXANDRIA, Va., Nov. 16, 1861.

To the Editor of The Boston Journal:

Every appliance that science can bring is secured to make the mighty volunteer army of the North irresistable; prominent among these appliances, and of incalculable value, are the balloon reconnoissances now so much depended upon by the young and active Gen. McClellan. At the commencement of the war our Generals in a measure comprehended the value of such aid, and in a very few weeks Profs. La Mountain at Fortress Monroe, and Lowe at Washington, were in their service. Since then, they have been constantly active, and the public probably are little aware of the value of their reconnoissances to our Government. Prof. Lowe is at present upon the Maryland side of the Potomac making topical ascensions for the purpose of numbering the forces connected with the batteries of the enemy.

NO STRINGS ATTACHED DETAIL

In this newspaper article, a Boston reporter describes an ascent made by Union balloonist John La Mountain on November 16, 1861, near Manassas, Virginia. Unlike Chief Aeronaut Lowe, who always remained tethered to the ground, La Mountain ascended without a tether. He overflew the enemy position in free flight, relying on air currents to carry him back safely.

National Archives, Records of the Adjutant General's Office, 1780's–1917

SPYING BY BALLOON

This photograph shows the *Intrepid,* one of Thaddeus S. C. Lowe's balloons, being inflated around 1862. During his ascents, Lowe stayed tethered to the ground.

National Archives, Records of the Office of the Chief Signal Officer

[111-B-681]

Calling card of George Bickley, founder of The Knights of the Golden Circle

National Archives, Records of the Office of the Judge Advocate General (Army)

Secret Efforts to Expand Slavery

In 1854, before the Civil War started, a self-styled general named George Bickley founded The Knights of the Golden Circle in Cincinnati. This large, well-organized, secret society had many branches, or "castles," around the country. It also had a constitution, by-laws, an official seal, and secret methods of recognizing fellow members.

The Knights of the Golden Circle wanted to bring into the Union as slave states a "Golden Circle" that included Mexico, Central America, and parts of the Caribbean. Toward that end, members twice tried to invade Mexico.

After the Civil War broke out, the Knights of the Golden Circle became the Order of American Knights, and later the Sons of Liberty. They often worked with Confederate agents based in Canada and with Copperheads—an extreme wing of Northern Democrats who opposed the war, sometimes violently.

Seal of The Knights of the Golden Circle

National Archives, Records of the Office of the Judge Advocate General (Army)

Union spymistress Elizabeth Van Lew
Virginia Historical Society

UNION SPIES
IN RICHMOND

As head of a very successful spy ring in Richmond, Virginia, Elizabeth Van Lew provided regular and timely information to Generals Benjamin Butler and Ulysses Grant, assisted escaped prisoners, and even placed a spy in Confederate President Jefferson Davis's home. After the war, her trusted lieutenant, William S. Rowley, sent this letter to Secretary of War Edwin M. Stanton claiming the government owed him money for his work as an agent.

Few official records of Van Lew's accomplishments exist. In December 1866, she asked the War Department for all records of her espionage activities. The records were never returned to the War Department. Van Lew probably destroyed them.

National Archives, Records of the Provost Marshal General's Bureau (Civil War)

Confederate spy Rose Greenhow

Courtesy of the Library of Congress

CONFEDERATE SPY IN THE DISTRICT OF COLUMBIA

Confederate spy Rose Greenhow lived in Washington, DC. Over four months in 1861 she passed information to Confederate General P.G.T. Beauregard. This message was found in pieces during a search of her house and reassembled after her arrest. Greenhow was imprisoned for several months. Although she is sometimes credited with providing information critical to the Confederate success at the First Battle of Bull Run, her messages did not influence Confederate decision making.

Greenhow was connected at the highest levels of government and society. Her friends included President James A. Buchanan, Senators John C. Calhoun and Jefferson Davis, Union General John Dix, and former first lady Dolley Madison.

Eventually Greenhow was banished to the South. The Confederate government used her as a fund raiser and emissary in Europe. In 1864 she was returning from Europe on a blockade-runner that was intercepted by a Union ship. Greenhow took to a rowboat to escape. It capsized in the rough surf, and she drowned—due in large part to the sizable amount of gold she had sewn into the hem of her dress.

National Archives, General Records of the Department of State

Head Quarters Assistant Provost Marshal General,

Indianapolis, Ind., Aug. 26th, 1864.

Brev. Maj. Genl. A. P. Hovey
Comdg. Dist. of Ind.

The following is a copy of a letter just now received from Huntington Ind. I know nothing of the writer

Respectfully your obt. servt.
Jas. G. Jones, Col. &
A. A. P. M. Genl. Ind.

Huntington August the 25th/64

Col. C. Baker - Sir

I have found out from reliable persons that the Copperheads of Ohio is in expectation of receiving their army in Columbus some time next Week They expect to receive them from Canada If However they should Meet with disappointment They Intend to fall back to the Lake Size the Landings and thow ground in Canada will Land them their army. They Intend to have all their army Distributed Before the Draft

But Should they be Disappointed In this they will wait until after the draft then rally in Mass to the Lake Shore Size the Landings, get their army and

Commence their hellish work of killing union men where Ever found They Meet and Drill 3 times a week In Ohio They Drill with Wooden guns made of Butternut This I know to be true and if you think It of any Benefit all Right I will Be able to give you more Information In a few Days

Yours J M Bratton

A "HELLISH" PLOT UNCOVERED

J. M. Bratton sent this August 25, 1864, letter to Col. C. Baker, informing him of a Copperhead plot to disrupt the upcoming draft. The plan called for "Copperheads of Ohio" to receive an army from Canada. This army, once assembled, was to "commence their hellish work of killing union men where ever found." Bratton also reported that the Copperheads met and drilled three times a week in preparation for their role in the scheme.

Copperheads were an extreme wing of Northern Democrats who opposed the war and wanted a peace settlement with the South. Their opponents called them "copperheads" after the poisonous snake that strikes without warning. Eventually they took the name as their own and pinned copper pennies to their lapels.

National Archives, Records of the Office of the Judge Advocate General (Army)

DETAIL

City Point, Virginia, after the August 9, 1864, explosion.
By Mathew Brady Studios, ca. 1864

*National Archives, Records of the Office of
the Chief Signal Officer*
[111-B-558]

WHAT REALLY HAPPENED AT CITY POINT
William J. Sandoval

The explosion of a Union supply barge at City Point, Virginia, was assumed to be an accident—until the Union Army captured Richmond, Virginia, and a report written by the saboteur.

City Point, Virginia—now incorporated into the nearby city of Hopewell—sat at the confluence of the Appomattox and James Rivers, about 10 miles northeast of Petersburg. It was a small village of a few houses sitting on even fewer streets. That all changed when Union Lt. Gen. Ulysses Grant wrapped up his Overland Campaign and began the Siege of Petersburg.

City Point was the ideal location for a major Union military base supporting the siege. A brigade of Colored Troops from the Union's Army of the James secured City Point on May 5, 1864. As they pushed at the weakly defended Confederate lines around Petersburg, Maj. Gen. George G. Meade's Army of the Potomac applied pressure to Confederate General Robert E. Lee's Army of Northern Virginia north and east of

Richmond. Five weeks later, Grant arrived and claimed the yard of Dr. Richard Eppes's home, "Appomattox," as the headquarters of the U.S. Army.

A City Transformed

Over the course of those five weeks, City Point changed dramatically. It was now well on its way to becoming one of the busiest ports in the world, with hundreds of ships and barges calling daily. They disgorged thousands of tons of munitions, food, medical supplies, and other material necessary to sustain more than 100,000 men and 65,000 horses and mules in the field. The warehouses in City Point held more than 30 days' rations and 20 days' forage at all times. Every day hundreds of wagons and 18 trains loaded with supplies left City Point for the front.

Telegram from General Ulysses S. Grant to Maj. Gen. Henry Halleck reporting on the explosion at City Point, Virginia

National Archives, Records of the Office of the Secretary of War

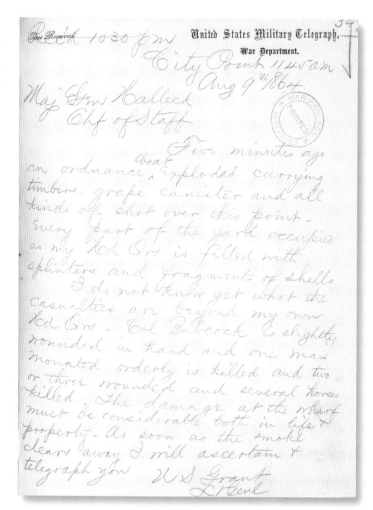

In addition to being a major supply point, City Point was home to the Headquarters of the entire United States Army. It housed an array of other units and activities required to support the Army of the Potomac and the Army of the James, including:

- Army staff bureaus
- Provost units
- 7 hospitals, including Depot Field Hospital, which could accommodate more than 10,000 patients
- A bakery that could produce up to 123,000 loaves of bread daily
- Stables, repair shops, and a prison for Union troops.

The pace of operations quickly assumed a sense of normalcy.

Explosion!

That routine was shattered shortly before noon on August 9, 1864. The supply barge *J. E. Kendrick*, fully loaded with tons of ammunition, blew up. The explosion obliterated the *Kendrick*, the vessel next to it, and a newly constructed 600-square-foot warehouse. Smoke billowed a mile high. The sound of the blast carried more than 10 miles. Debris rained down all over the crowded point. Hundreds were wounded and missing; dozens more were killed. Warehouses, 180 feet of wharf, and tons of supplies were damaged or destroyed.

Five minutes after the explosion, Lt. Gen. Ulysses S. Grant wired Maj. Gen. Henry Halleck providing minimal details of the explosion. Grant reported that his headquarters was strewn with debris. A mounted orderly was killed, one of Grant's aides and at least two mounted orderlies were slightly wounded, and several horses were killed. Grant promised to send further details once the smoke cleared.

Lt. Morris Schaff, the ordnance officer in charge of transshipping the munitions coming into City Point, tabulated the staggering losses:

- 700 boxes of artillery ammunition
- 2,000 boxes of small arms munitions
- between 600 and 700 blank cartridges
- 43 people known to be killed
- an additional unknown number (estimated to be hundreds) of black laborers who worked the docks killed
- 126 people wounded

The total cost of the blast exceeded $2 million. Clean-up took several days.

A court of inquiry determined that the cause of the explosion was an accident. While not charged with anything, Lieutenant Schaff was transferred to Reading, Pennsylvania, where he spent the remainder of the war inspecting cannons and projectiles. The story might have ended there—except that the court of inquiry was wrong. The explosion was not an accident.

Confederate Senate Bill 194

This story actually begins in mid-January 1864, when the Confederate Congress considered Senate Bill 194, "A bill to organize bodies for the capture and destruction of the enemy's property by land or sea, and to authorize compensation for the same." We do not know the exact wording of S. 194 because it is not included in the Engrossed Bills of the Confederacy at the National Archives or in any of the printed laws of the Confederacy. But we can trace its passage through the closing days of the Fourth Session of the First Confederate Congress.

Introduced by Louisiana Senator Edward Sparrow on January 20, 1864, it spent its entire legislative life in secret session. It was referred to the Military Affairs Committee in both the Senate and House. The only amendment offered was by Louisiana Representative Charles M. Conrad. He proposed that the last section include the only language we know was in the bill: that something was "payable in 4% bonds." Two days later the Senate agreed to the House Amendment. The Speaker of the House signed S. 194 on

> C. S. A. War Department
> Richmond. Va February 29th. 1864.
>
> Z. McDaniel is hereby authorized to enlist a company of men, not to exceed fifty in number, for secret service against the enemy, under the regulations prescribed by this Department for such organizations.
>
> When he shall have enlisted and mustered his company into the service for the War, he will receive a Commission as Captain in the Provisional Army of the Confederate States, without pay—
>
> Transportation will be furnished to him for his recruits to the place of rendezvous, and to such points as he may select for his operations.
>
> J. A. Seddon
> Secretary of War.

DETAIL

Confederate Secretary of War James A. Seddon, authorized Z. McDaniel to raise "a company of men . . . for secret service against the enemy."

National Archives, War Department Collection of Confederate Records

February 16, 1864, and sent it back to the Senate for signature. The President Pro Tempore signed the bill on the 17th and sent it to President Jefferson Davis for his signature, which was affixed to the bill.

We can surmise that S. 194 authorized the formation of an organization that specialized in the capture or destruction of enemy property. It also authorized the payment of men based upon a percentage of the value of the captured or destroyed property. This is the payment authorized by Conrad's amendment, to be made in 4 percent Confederate bonds.

Twelve days after Davis signed S. 194 into law, the Confederate War Department authorized Z. McDaniel to raise a company of no more than 50 men and muster them into the Confederate service. McDaniel was probably Zedekiah or Zere McDaniel from Kentucky, who operated along the Mississippi River early in the war. McDaniel mustered his company, which became Company A, Confederate Secret Service, and received a captain's commission. He served without pay and reported to Confederate Brig. Gen. Gabriel J. Rains, commander of the Confederate Torpedo Bureau.

Mission Accomplished

City Point is the best known and perhaps most successful operation carried out by the men of McDaniel's company. John Maxwell, a Confederate secret service agent, sent a report to Capt. Z. McDaniel on December 16, 1864. The report detailed how Maxwell, with the assistance of R. K. Dillard, infiltrated the Union lines around City Point, Virginia, on August 9, 1864, and successfully planted a "horological torpedo" or time bomb aboard the Union supply barge *J. E. Kendrick*.

Maxwell and Dillard watched from a short distance away as the timer counted down. The results were everything Maxwell had hoped. His 12-pound explosive device led to widespread devastation. In his report, Maxwell estimated the amount of damage. He was pretty close with the number of men killed: 58. He was right in estimating the number of wounded: 126. However, he was far off in his estimate of the value of the destroyed goods and facilities. He put the number at twice the amount tabulated by Schaff: $4 million.

Why did he get everything else right but not the amount of damage? Was it an attempt to receive greater compensation for his efforts? Four percent of $4 million is a lot more than four percent of $2 million.

Maxwell's report was captured at the end of the war, and Union authorities finally learned of the deliberate nature of the explosion. Although the explosion was very successful from a Confederate point of view, it ultimately had little impact on the Siege of Petersburg. Union troops did not go hungry. They did not suffer from a lack of ammunition. Security around City Point was tightened. The damage was repaired. And the siege continued.

The overall impact of S. 194 was similarly weak. Maxwell did not return to Confederate lines until December 1864, and he achieved very little. No other members of Company A experienced a success as notable as that of City Point.

NOTE ON SOURCES

The legislative history of Senate Bill 19 is found in Entry 3 of War Department Collection of Confederate Records, Record Group (RG) 109, Chapter VII, Legislative and Executive, volumes 4, 7, 11, 13, 15, and 20, hold the records of the Journals of the House and Senate, in both Open and Secret Sessions, in which references to S. 194 can be found. McDaniel's claim for payment for sinking the USS *Cairo* may be found at C. 225, in Entry 159 (Vessel Papers 1861-1865) of RG 109. Grant's telegram to Halleck is found in Entry 34, Telegrams Received from LTG Grant, March 10, 1864–Sept. 20, 1864, Vol. 1, p. 349, Records of the Office of the Secretary of War, RG 107. Noah Andre Trudeau's Chapter 7 of *The Last Citadel* (Baton Rouge, 1993) has an excellent account of the City Point Explosion that draws from several eyewitness sources.

T. Wilkins' Imp Ambulance Carriage.

Patented Nov. 22. 1864.

45,200.
Gree
I claim,
axles, A B,
E, resting
or wood,
board bein,
wheels, an
Second, 7
tached, suc

Fig. 3.

ax
ax
L
k
ax
H
ax

Fig. 1.

i   j   i
J
d   d   d
G
H
I
D   a'   F   F'
C   b'   a
A
c

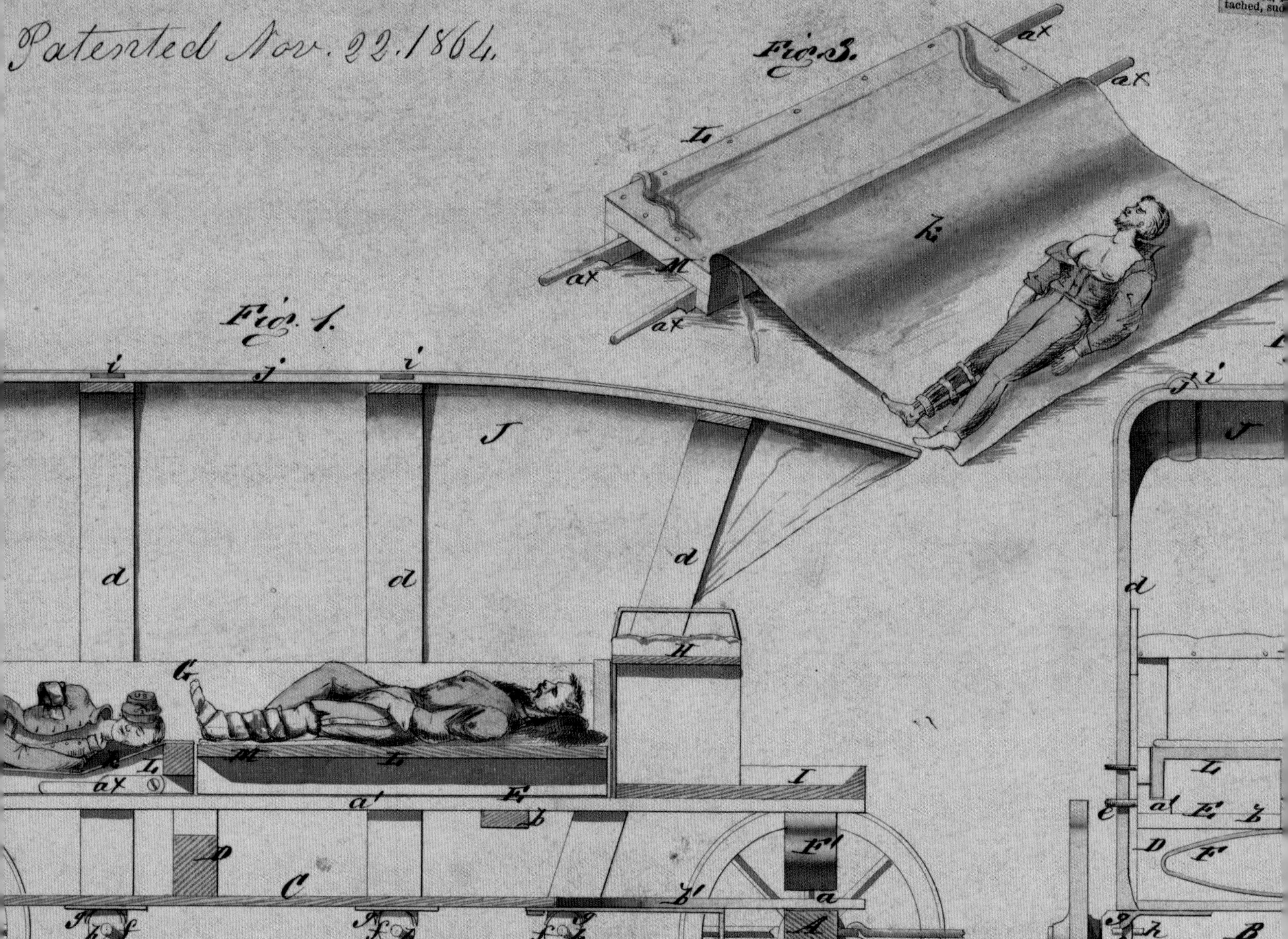

Witnesses
C L Topliff
Theo Busch

Carriage Oct 25. 1864

WAR RECORDS PRINTED 1861-1865

CHAPTER 8

INVENTION AND ENTERPRISE

Both Union and Confederate governments increased spending during the Civil War. Millions of dollars were spent on new or improved cannons, guns, shells, tents, ambulances, and artificial limbs.

Also, the role of the telegraph and the railroad expanded. Railroads rapidly transported troops and supplies. The telegraph provided near-instantaneous communication over great distances.

But these advances raised new and troubling questions:
- Would fraud accompany increased government spending?
- Would the government attempt to control the telegraphic flow of information?

The documents in this chapter will help you explore these issues.

"Improvement in Ambulance Carriages," patent 45,200 issued to Thomas Wilkins, November 22, 1864

National Archives, Records of the Patent and Trademark Office

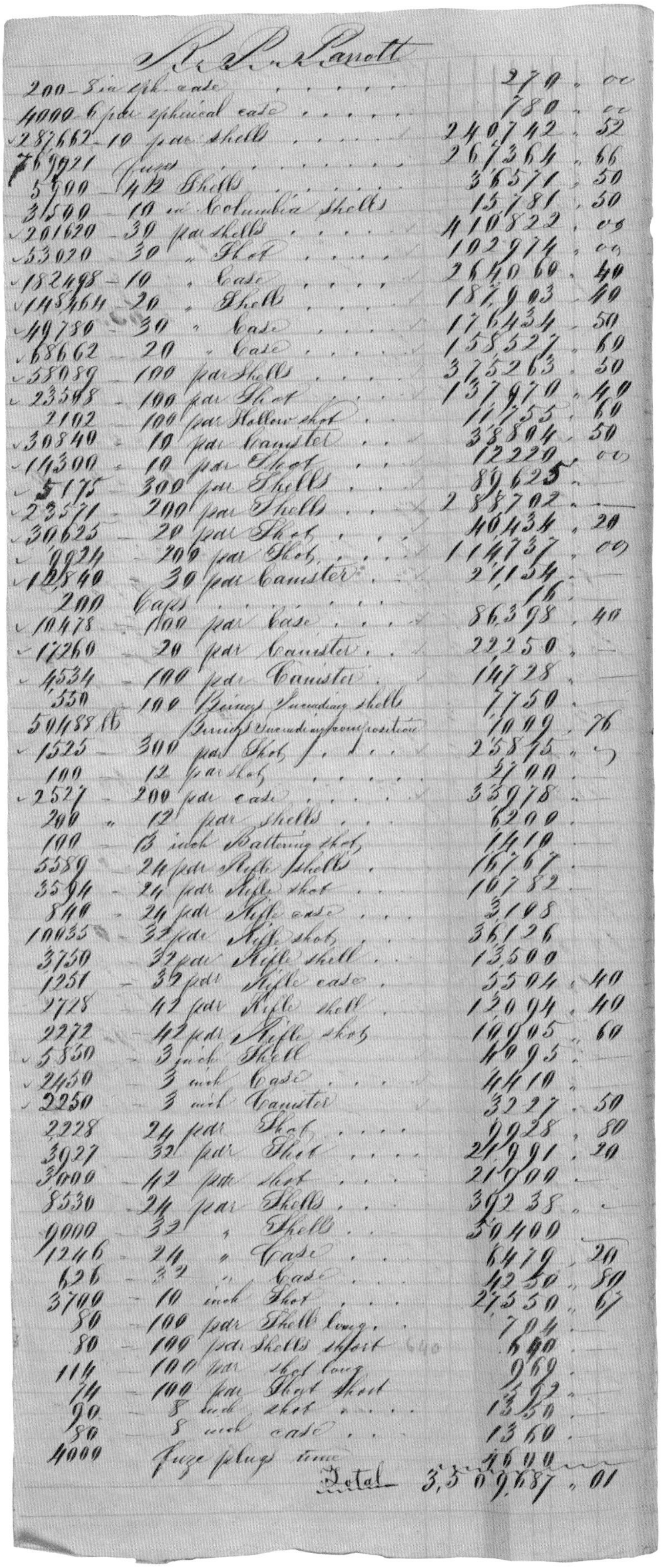

R. P. Parrott

200	8 in sph case	270	00
4000	6 pdr spherical case	780	00
287662	10 pdr shell	240742	52
769921	Fuzes	267364	66
5500	4½ Shells	36571	50
31500	10 in Columbia shells	15781	50
201620	30 pdr shells	410822	00
53020	30 " Shot	102974	00
182498	10 " Case	264060	40
145464	20 " Shell	187903	40
49780	30 " Case	176434	50
68662	20 " Case	155527	60
58089	100 pdr Shells	375263	50
23598	100 pdr Shot	137970	40
2102	100 pdr Hollow shot	11755	60
30840	10 pdr Canister	33804	50
14300	10 pdr Shot	12220	00
5175	300 pdr Shells	89625	
23571	200 pdr Shells	288702	
30625	20 pdr Shot	40434	20
9924	200 pdr Shot	114737	00
12840	30 pdr Canister	27154	
200	Cases	16	
10478	100 pdr Case	86398	40
17260	20 pdr Canister	22250	
4534	100 pdr Canister	14728	
550	100 Berney's Incendiary shell	7750	
504888 lb	Berney's Incendiary composition	1009	76
1525	300 pdr Shot	25875	
100	12 pdr shot	5700	
2527	200 pdr case	33978	
200	12 pdr shells	6200	
100	13 inch Battering shot	1410	
5589	24 pdr Rifle Shells	16767	
3594	24 pdr Rifle shot	16782	
840	24 pdr Rifle case	3108	
10035	32 pdr Rifle shot	36126	
3750	32 pdr Rifle shell	13500	
1251	32 pdr Rifle case	5504	40
2728	42 pdr Rifle shell	12094	40
2272	42 pdr Rifle shot	10905	60
5850	3 inch Shell	4095	
2450	3 inch Case	4410	
2250	3 inch Canister	3237	50
2228	24 pdr Shot	9928	80
3927	32 pdr Shot	24991	20
3000	42 pdr shot	21900	
8530	24 pdr Shells	39238	
9000	32 " Shell	50400	
1246	24 " Case	6479	20
626	32 " Case	4250	80
3700	10 inch Shot	27550	67
80	100 pdr Shell long	704	
80	100 pdr Shells short	640	
114	100 pdr shot long	969	
74	100 pdr Shot short	629	
90	8 inch shot	1350	
80	8 inch case	1360	
4000	Fuze plugs time	4600	
	Total	3,509,687	01

THE ECONOMIC COST OF WAR

During the Civil War, the U.S. Government spent nearly $18 million for artillery and associated ordnance. One of the largest of the firms to produce such weaponry was Parrott and Company of Cold Springs, New York. This ledger itemizes the number of guns and shells purchased from Parrott and the amount paid. Parrott and Company sold the Government approximately $5 million of artillery and ordnance. In current dollars, this amounts to nearly $80 million.

National Archives, Records of the Office of the Chief of Ordnance

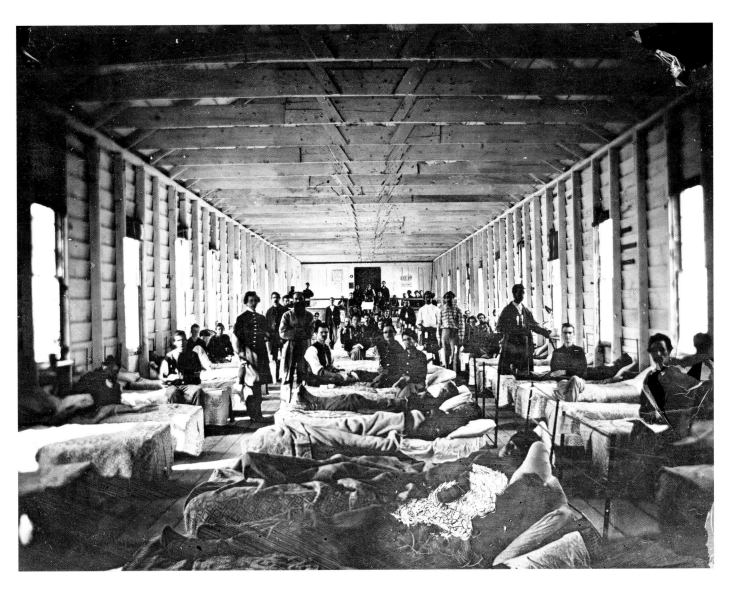

THE PERSONAL COST OF WAR

New and improved guns, shells, and other weapons took their toll on the bodies of soldiers on both sides of the war. This photograph shows wounded Union soldiers in a hospital around 1863.

National Archives, Records of the Office of the Chief Signal Officer [111-B-286]

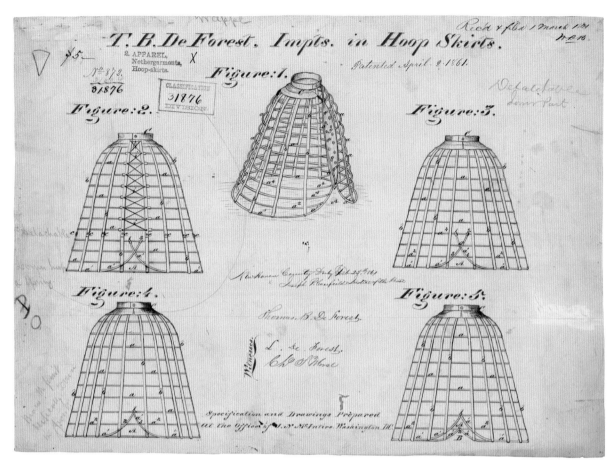

Drawing from T. B. DeForest's patent for improvements in hoop skirts, April 2, 1861

National Archives, Records of the Patent and Trademark Office

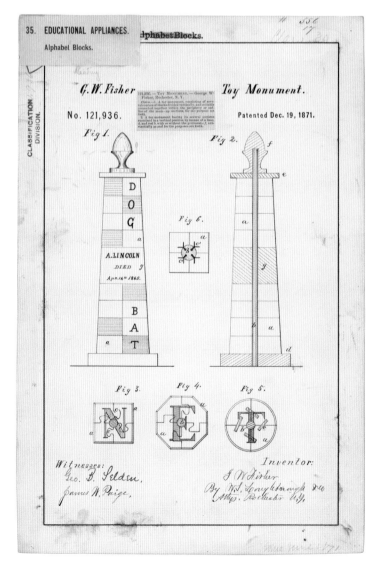

Drawing from George W. Fisher's patent for an "Improvement in Toy Monuments," December 19, 1871. An inscription reads, "A. Lincoln died Apr. 14th 1865."

National Archives, Records of the Patent and Trademark Office

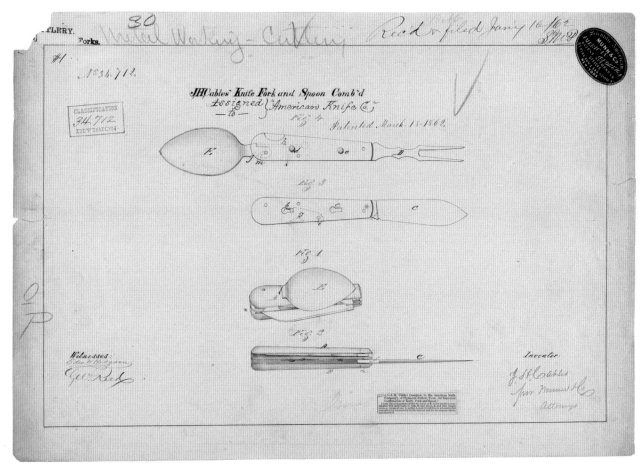

"Combination of Knife, Fork, and Spoon," patent 34,712 issued to J. H. Cable, March 18, 1862

National Archives, Records of the Patent and Trademark Office

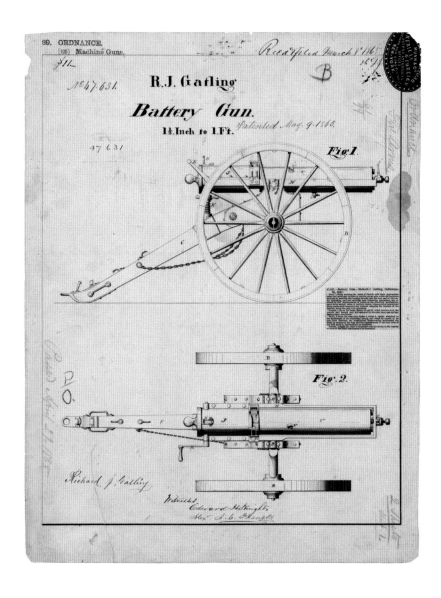

Drawing from Richard J. Gatling's patent for a "Battery Gun," May 9, 1865

National Archives, Records of the Patent and Trademark Office

S.S.BALTIC.OFF SANDY HOOK APR.EIGHTEENTH.TEN THIRTY A.M. .VIA

NEW YORK. . HON.S.CAMERON. SECY.WAR. WASHN. HAVING DEFENDED

FORT SUMTER FOR THIRTY FOUR HOURS UNTIL THE QUARTERS WERE EN

TIRELY BURNED THE MAIN GATES DESTROYED BY FIRE.THE GORGE WALLS

SERIOUSLY INJURED.THE MAGAZINE SURROUNDED BY FLAMES AND ITS

DOOR CLOSED FROM THE EFFECTS OF HEAT .FOUR BARRELLS AND THREE

CARTRIDGES OF POWDER ONLY BEING AVAILABLE AND NO PROVISIONS

REMAINING BUT PORK.I ACCEPTED TERMS OF EVACUATION OFFERED BY

GENERAL BEAURECARD BEING ON SAME OFFERED BY HIM ON THE ELEV

ENTH INST.PRIOR TO THE COMMENCEMENT OF HOSTILITIES AND MARCHED

OUT OF THE FORT SUNDAY AFTERNOON THE FOURTEENTH INST.WITH

COLORS FLYING AND DRUMS BEATING.BRINGING AWAY COMPANY AND

PRIVATE PROPERTY AND SALUTING MY FLAG WITH FIFTY GUNS. ROBERT

ANDERSON.MAJOR FIRST ARTILLERY.COMMANDING.

Telegram from Major Robert Anderson to the Secretary of War regarding the surrender of Fort Sumter to the Confederates, April 18, 1861

National Archives, Records of the Adjutant General's Office, 1780's–1917

Telegraph and Telegrams

The telegraph dramatically increased the speed with which military officers communicated with each other and with civilian authorities. Newspapers also used the telegraph and rapidly delivered war-related information to readers.

Early in war, however, the Lincoln administration censored telegraphic communication, arguing that while news of the war could be delivered with great speed, military secrets could also be quickly divulged. There was a fine line between military necessity and censoring the merely embarrassing or politically disadvantageous.

Telegram from Gen. Robert E. Lee to James A. Seddon, Confederate Secretary of War, announcing the death of Gen. Thomas "Stonewall" Jackson, May 10, 1863

National Archives, War Department Collection of Confederate Records

DIAL OR DASH? (-.. .. .- .-.. / --- .-. / -.. .- ... .-..)

Union forces used two types of telegraphy, the dial (or Beardslee) and the Morse. This illustration shows operators using the dial telegraph on the battlefield. It could be set up quickly, giving it great flexibility. Operators needed to be literate but not as highly trained as Morse operators. Chief Signal Officer Albert Myer advocated the dial system; the Military Telegraph Service used the Morse system.

By the end of 1863, however, the Signal Corps moved towards the Morse system with its relatively stronger signal strength. When Secretary of War Stanton removed Myer as chief signal officer in November 1863, the military primacy of the Morse telegraph was complete.

National Archives, Records of the Office of the Chief Signal Officer

Samuel Morse, inventor of the Morse telegraph, around 1860–65

National Archives, Records of the Office of the Chief Signal Officer

[111-B-2591]

SHODDY GOODS

In February 1861, Isaac Comstock wrote to the Select Committee on Government Contracts of the U.S. House of Representatives. Comstock informed the Committee of possible fraud. While some manufacturers placed a small amount of filler material known as "shoddy" in their blankets, a particular government contractor's goods, he wrote, were mainly filler: "These blankets contain fifteen percent wool the balance entirely made from shoddy."

In short, they were "shoddy goods." A previously neutral manufacturing term became a pejorative during the Civil War.

National Archives, Records of the U.S. House of Representatives.

Report of Board on Artificial Limbs, May 5, 1865   SELECTED PAGE

National Archives, Records of the Adjutant General's Office, 1780's–1917

Recommendations on Artificial Limbs

Beginning in 1862, Congress appropriated money to provide Civil War veterans who had lost arms or legs with prosthetic limbs. Former Confederate states such as Virginia, North Carolina, and South Carolina instituted similar programs after the war.

In March 1865, a board of medical officers gathered in New York City to examine models of prosthetic limbs. After testing each, the board commented on its "relative superiority." From March through early May, the officers tested 26 artificial legs, 16 artificial arms, and other devices.

In its report of May 5, the Board recommended Dr. Douglas Bly's "universal ankle joint motion" leg first among such prosthetics. The next two recommendations, in order of quality, were for the legs of Sephlo & Co. and B. F. Palmer.

For above-the-elbow arm prosthetics, the Board recommended the device patented by John Condell as best, followed by those of the National Arm & Leg Company and of Marion Lincoln.

In May 1866, J. K. Barnes, Surgeon General of the United States, reported to Congress that 6,075 prosthetics had been issued to veterans. By 1868, Congress had amended the law so that officers could also receive artificial limbs.

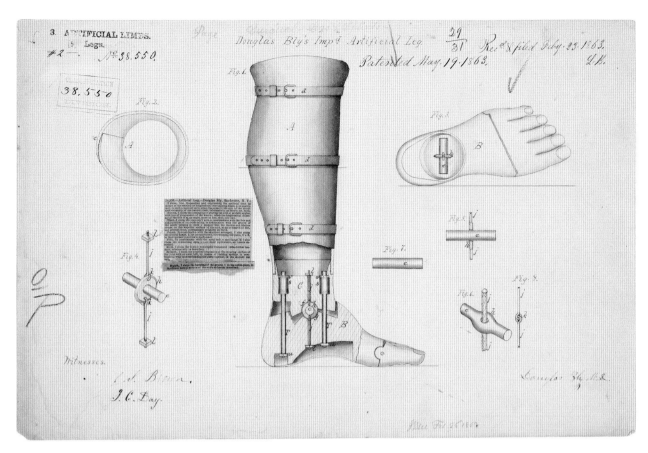

D. Bly's Artificial Leg (Utility Patent Number 38,550), recommended first among such prosthetics

National Archives, Records of the Patent and Trademark Office

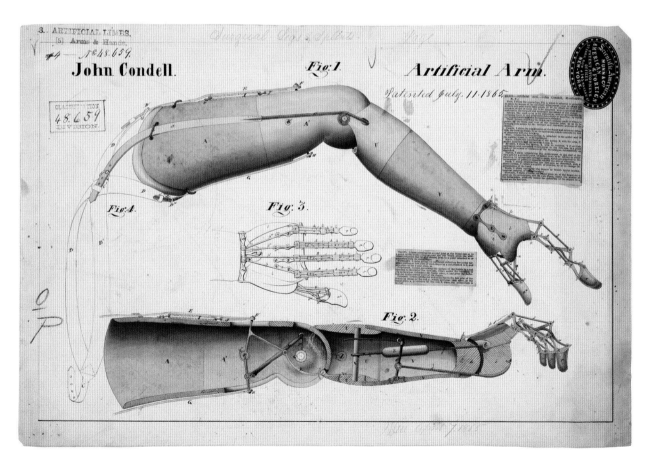

Patent drawing of Artificial Arm by John Condell, titled "Improvement in Artificial Arms," issued as patent 48,659, dated July 11, 1865

National Archives, Records of the Patent and Trademark Office

THE GREAT CENSORSHIP DEBATE
Michael Hussey

Was there censorship of the telegraph during the Civil War? The House of Representatives decided to investigate.

Documents reveal fascinating details of the debate that ensued between Government officials and the press.

In April 1861, secessionist mobs cut telegraph lines between Washington, DC, and the north. With the nation's capital effectively cut off from its most efficient means of communication, the Lincoln administration responded by taking control of the privately owned telegraph industry. As a congressional report described:

> During the "dark days" of April, 1861, the government assumed exclusive control of the telegraph lines leading from this city. This was an act of necessity, arising from the extraordinary perils then surrounding the government.

Agreement to Cooperate

For all of its advantages, the telegraph posed potential dangers to the Government and society as a whole. While military information could be delivered with great speed, military secrets could also be quickly divulged. Maj. Gen. George McClellan and a group of prominent journalists discussed this reality at a meeting on August 2, 1861. Present were correspondents from the *New York Herald*, the *Philadelphia Inquirer*, the Washington *Evening Star*, the *New York Tribune*, the *Cincinnati Gazette*, the *Boston Journal*, the Associated Press, and others.

The group agreed to the following set of rules governing war-related information.

- All editors would "refrain from publishing, either as editorial, or as correspondence . . . any matter that may furnish aid and comfort to the enemy."

- The editors would "signify to their correspondents here and elsewhere their approval of the foregoing suggestion, and to comply with it in spirit and letter."

- The Government was "respectfully requested to afford to the representatives of the press facilities for obtaining and immediately transmitting all information suitable for publication, particularly touching engagements with the enemy."

This voluntary agreement acknowledged the need for some measure of secrecy regarding ongoing military operations. At the same time, it urged a cooperative spirit on the part of the Government so that newspapers could provide war-related information to their readers.

Government's Grip Tightens

When responsibility for telegraph censorship was transferred to the State Department, the scope of banned topics expanded. On October 22, 1861, Assistant Secretary of State Frederick Seward issued this order:

> For the present it is deemed advisable to prohibit all telegraphic dispatches from Washington, intended for publication, which relate to the civil or military operations of the government.

Clearly, some information needed to be barred from the telegraph. There was a fine line, however, between military necessity and censoring the merely embarrassing or politically disadvantageous. Seward's instructions seemed to blur this line to the point that some correspondents were unsure exactly what they could or could not telegraph regarding Government matters.

Congress Resolves to Investigate

On December 5, 1861, the House of Representatives passed a resolution calling on its Judiciary Committee to:

> . . . inquire if a telegraphic censorship of the press has been established in this city . . . to report if such censorship has not been used to restrain wholesome political criticism and discussion, while its professed and laudable object has been to withhold from the enemy information in reference to the movements of the army.

The Committee agreed that the protection of military information such as troop movements was a "laudable object." It was the possible suppression of civilian and political aspects of Government operations that concerned them.

The Committee questioned Telegraph Superintendent H. Emmons Thayer about his role as censor. Did he object to matters relating to the President's Cabinet being sent telegraphically by newspaper correspondents? Thayer replied:

> Where correspondents have written on matters which took place or were said to have taken place at meetings of the Cabinet, or between

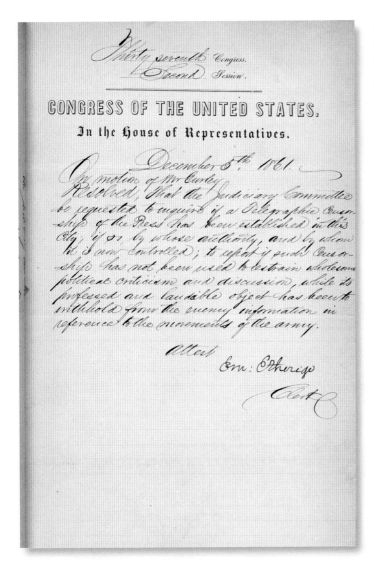

The House of Representatives passed this resolution on December 5, 1861, to investigate whether there had been Government censorship of the telegraph.

National Archives, Records of the U.S. House of Representatives

So far as civil matters are concerned, I have been informed that nothing would be allowed to pass in regard to rumored changes in the Cabinet. The resignation of General Cameron was not allowed to be sent, even though that fact had been official [sic] communicated to the Senate. The censor had told Adams that he had written instructions to 'allow no changes to be sent over the wires in regard to the Cabinet' as it would injure the credit of the Government.

Adams believed that the censorship had spread far beyond the agreement reached between the press and General McClellan. He found himself not reporting matters on which he "would have staked [his] veracity." He wanted to have a cordial relationship with the censors, because he knew:

> . . . they possessed control over my dispatches. I have always endeavored to write such dispatches as would go through thinking it a better policy than to make a fuss about the matter.

When pressed for examples of subjects that he had avoided, Adams noted that without the censors "I should have on a great many occasions made statements of extravagance in purchase by officers of the War Department."

W. Bartlett of the *New York Evening Post* testified that he believed if he were to write a "despatch couched in severe language upon Mr. Lincoln or Mr. Seward, it would be suppressed, unless the censor has been alarmed by this investigation."

Bull Run Defeat Suppressed

It was not only civil matters upon which correspondents and censors disagreed. This was particularly the case with the Battle of Bull Run. Adams testified that on the day of the battle, July 21, 1861, he sent the following telegram to Richard Smith of the *Cincinnati Gazette:*

> Letter is received. The Gov't. would not permit me to telegraph you of the defeat of our forces at both Bull Run battles, but on the contrary insisted on it being represented as a victory. I explain by mail. The fault was not mine.

members of the Cabinet, or between [the] President and members of the Cabinet, I have considered that private business, and that correspondents had not right to use it—that was calculated to have a bad effect and to embarrass the Government.

But suppose, asked the Committee chairman, that "after a Cabinet meeting a member of the Cabinet had come out and stated what had taken place would that have changed your determination?" Thayer replied: "It would have if that member had endorsed it."

The Press Testifies

Rumors regarding one Cabinet member, Secretary of War Simon Cameron, were widespread in Washington but almost uniformly suppressed when correspondents attempted to telegraph the rumors to their newspapers. Abram S. Mitchell, correspondent for the *New York Times*, stated:

> Every man was talking about the difficulty between the President and General Cameron. It was not a secret, and nobody considered it as such.

George W. Adams—correspondent for the *New York World*, the *Philadelphia Bulletin*, and the *Chicago Times*—testified along similar lines:

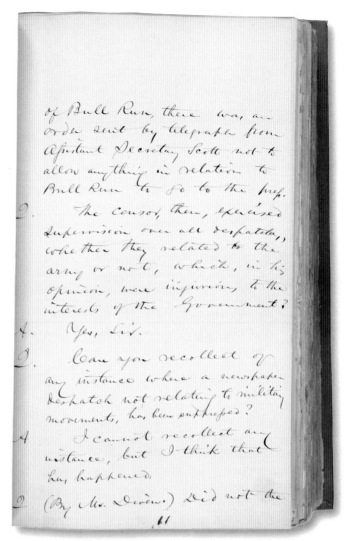

This is part of the testimony delivered on January 25, 1862, by censor Alfred B. Talcott to the House of Representatives regarding the prohibition on releasing information related to the Union defeat at Bull Run. SELECTED PAGES

National Archives, Records of the U.S. House of Representatives

Adams informed the Committee that his telegram was edited by the censor to read:

> Letter is received. The Gov't would not permit the telegraphing of the defeat of our forces at that time. I explain by mail, etc.

Censor Alfred Talcott testified to the Committee that Assistant Secretary of War Thomas Scott had ordered him not to allow any information regarding the Union defeat at Manassas to reach the press via telegraph. On the same day Adams's telegram was censored, Jefferson Davis sent a telegram announcing the Confederate victory.

Mitchell informed the Committee of perhaps the most ironic moment in Civil War censorship. Overall he did "not find so much fault with their suppression." However, on one occasion he tried to send a dispatch in which he complained of the "manner in which the censorship was exercised by the agent of the Government. That dispatch was suppressed, and to that I did take exception."

The Committee's Verdict
Ultimately, the House Judiciary Committee concluded that:

> . . . [d]espatches, almost numberless, of a political, personal, and general character have been suppressed by the censor, and correspondents have been deterred from preparing others because they knew they could not send them to their papers by telegraph.

The Committee recognized that the Government could censor telegraphic messages that contained military information that would "aid the public enemy." Still, the telegraph had become "a most important auxiliary to the press of the country." As such, it should be "left as free from government interference as may be consistent with the necessities of the government in time of war."

The Committee left the difficult task of determining when "interference" was necessary, and when it was not, in the hands of the censors.

NOTE ON SOURCES

The extensive transcripts of the hearings held by the House Judiciary Committee into telegraphic censorship form the basis for this essay. They are held in Records of the U.S. House of Representatives, Record Group 233. The investigation was authorized by the 37th Congress on December 5, 1861. Jeffery Alan Smith's *War & Press Freedom: The Problem of Prerogative Power* (New York, 1999) is a helpful secondary source.

A BULLDOG GRIP ON NEW TECHNOLOGY
Tom Wheeler

Telegrams sent by Lincoln reveal how the embattled President embraced this new technology and used it effectively to lead, manage, and eventually win the Civil War.

The late summer of 1864 was a dark hour for Abraham Lincoln and the cause of the Union. The Civil War had been raging for more than three years. The Union Army's advance on the Confederate capital of Richmond had stalled. General-in-Chief Ulysses Grant was the target of mounting criticism for sustaining high casualties without the desired result. Confederate troops were advancing down the Shenandoah Valley, a well-worn path toward Washington and the Northern states. The fall Presidential election was only a few months away. Unable to deliver either victory or peace, and facing widespread draft resistance, Lincoln anticipated electoral defeat.

Lincoln Telegrams Grant
It was in this environment that President Lincoln read an August 15 telegram from General Grant to the Army Chief of Staff. In the telegram Grant fretted that the draft riots could pull troops away from the front:

> If we are to draw troops from the field to keep the loyal states in harness it will prove difficult to suppress the rebellion in the disloyal states.

With this glimpse into his general's thoughts, the Commander-in-Chief used the same electronic messenger to relay his resolve and allay Grant's concerns. On August 17, Lincoln telegraphed:

> I have seen your despatch [sic] expressing your unwillingness to break your hold where you are. Neither am I willing. Hold on with a bull-dog grip, and chew and choke, as much as possible.

It was almost as good as walking into Grant's headquarters, sizing up the general's state of mind, and responding face-to-face. Even the choice of words such as "bull-dog grip" and "chew and choke" connoted the firmness of the President's mindset. When Grant read the President's message, he laughed out loud and exclaimed to those around him:

> The President has more nerve than any of his advisors.

The General's observation was correct, of course. More importantly, however, Grant held in his hands a tool that Lincoln used to reinforce his resolve and ensure that neither

In August 1864, Gen. Ulysses Grant protested a proposal that some of his troops be removed from around Petersburg. President Lincoln agreed with Grant and sent him this message of encouragement.

National Archives, Records of the Office of the Secretary of War

Timothy O'Sullivan took this photograph of Gen. Ulysses S. Grant at City Point, Virginia, his headquarters during the siege of Petersburg.

National Archives, Records of the Office of the Chief Signal Officer [111-B-36]

distance nor intermediaries could diffuse his leadership—the telegram.

Recognizing the Power of Technology

I first saw the handwritten copy of Lincoln's bulldog telegram at the National Archives. Standing with the document in front of me and reading the tight, forward-leaning cursive was like having just one degree of separation between me and Abraham Lincoln. The document pulsed like a living object and opened up a new world of discovery about our 16th President.

When Lincoln arrived as President-elect in 1861, the nation's leaders did not fully appreciate the relatively new technology of the telegraph. The famous words "What hath God wrought!" had been telegraphed from the Capitol building almost 17 years earlier. But to most people of the 1860s, the very idea of electricity—much less the notion of sending messages long distances by sparks of electricity—was only a vague scientific concept. Leaders remained flummoxed as to how the Federal Government could use the new technology. There was no telegraph station at the White House, or at the Navy Yard, or at the War Department. When the U.S. Army wanted to send a telegram, it handed the text to a clerk, who then stood in line at the central telegraph office.

To Abraham Lincoln, however, this new technology offered a capability unavailable to any other leader in history. Traditionally, leaders had traveled with their armies, like Henry V at Agincourt and Bonaparte in Russia. Lincoln now had the ability to communicate in real time with armies in the field from the political capital. But he had to figure out how to use the new technology to his greatest advantage—without the guidance of precedent, without a text to study, without a tutor's guidance, and in the midst of the Civil War.

Fortunately, Lincoln was instinctively comfortable with new technology. He was the only President to hold a patent and had been involved with the spread of innovations such as the railroad in his native Illinois. He embraced the telegraph to interject his leadership from afar—and this was essential to winning the Civil War.

Lincoln's Eyes and Ears

Reading the approximately 1,000 telegrams Lincoln sent during his Presidency reveals a journey of discovery regarding how to apply the new technology. For the first 14 months, he used the telegraph rarely. In 1862, however, he began issuing direct orders to generals in the field—a turning point in the nature of national leadership. For the last 35 months of his life, Lincoln expanded and refined his use of the telegraph, making it an essential element of his leadership.

Lincoln's greatest discovery was that the telegraph could become an extension of his eyes and ears. Lincoln spent more time in the War Department telegraph office next to the White House than he did in any other location except the Executive Mansion and his retreat cottage at the Soldiers' Home. The telegraph office became the first Situation Room

The gigantic mortar known as "The Dictator," was one weapon used by Union forces to lay siege to Petersburg in 1864.

National Archives, Records of the War Department General and Special Staffs [165-SB-75]

as the President gained insight into operations in the field by patiently reading every telegram that arrived, even those not addressed to him.

Whenever he arrived at the telegraph office, Lincoln made a beeline for the file drawer that held the flimsy copies of all the telegrams received. He took that stack to a desk that belonged to the head of the telegraph office and that overlooked Pennsylvania Avenue. There the President reviewed each message, setting aside those that required more information or that he wanted to deal with later. It was during just such an exercise that Lincoln discovered General Grant's telegram to the Army Chief-of-Staff. Lincoln responded immediately, even though the message had not been directed to him.

Lincoln's telegrams provide valuable insight into his real-time thinking. He did not keep a diary. All that we know from Lincoln himself about his thought process comes from just three sources: his speeches, his letters, and his telegrams. The speeches and letters are set pieces designed to stand on their own to convey the desired message. Only his handwritten telegrams reveal the real-time inner workings of his thought process. They are off-the-top-of-the-head, spur-of-the-moment jottings. Many have scratch-outs and insertions that allow us to witness the President's mind at work as he struggles to find the right word and concept. Lincoln's handwritten telegrams are as close to the transcript of a conversation with the man himself as we will ever get.

A Model for the Future

At the desk next to a window overlooking Pennsylvania Avenue, Abraham Lincoln singularly conceived and implemented the model for modern electronic leadership. His pioneering use of electronic communications changed the leadership of war, influenced the movement and management of armies, and in this way impacted the ultimate outcome of the Civil War.

The President's embrace of new technology encourages us to behave with similar initiative and creativity as we face ever-changing and sometimes confusing technological development. Most importantly, Lincoln's handwritten telegrams allow us to experience firsthand the story of how a great man at a hinge moment in history used a new technology to assure that the hinge swung forward, not backward.

A NOTE ON SOURCES

Gen. Ulysses Grant's initial August 15, 1864, telegram to the Army Chief of Staff and President Lincoln's August 17, 1864, "bull-dog grip" response to General Grant are both among the Telegrams Sent and Received by the War Department Central Telegraph Office, 1861–82, Records of the Office of the Secretary of War, Record Group 107. Grant's telegram is in Telegrams Sent by Lt. Gen. Ulysses S. Grant to Washington, DC, March 10, 1864–February 2, 1865, vol. 60. Lincoln's response is in Telegrams Sent by the President, Vol. 1A. Horace Porter's *Campaigning with Grant* (1991) provides the details of Grant's reaction to Lincoln's response. Tom Wheeler, *Mr. Lincoln's T-Mails: The Untold Story of How Abraham Lincoln Used the Telegraph to Win the Civil War* (2006) discusses Lincoln's use of this new technology.

ICE for the Soldiers.

Saratoga, Aug. 13, 1863.

I have just received from the Colonel and Quartermaster at Hilton Head an urgent request for ICE for the sick and wounded at that place, ending, "FOR GOD'S SAKE SEND SOME ICE TO THESE SUFFERING MEN."

It is proposed that the visitors at Saratoga furnish money to purchase a *Cargo* or two, to be shipped at *once* from Boston to comfort these men, many of whom were wounded at Charleston.

GEO. H. STUART,

Chairman U. S. Christian Commission.

Contributions received at the office of this Hotel.

CHAPTER 9

PRISONERS AND CASUALTIES

The life of a Civil War soldier or sailor involved week after week of routine drills, inspections, and housekeeping. Combat relieved the tedium, but often with bitter consequences such as death, injury, or captivity that changed lives forever. A variety of diseases ran through the ranks, causing even more misery than battle.

- What risks did soldiers face?
- What kinds of care did the wounded, sick, and dead receive?
- How were prisoners treated by their captors?

The records here and others in the National Archives document the terrible costs of battle through the stories of those who survived as well as those who fell.

WANTED: ICE

When faced with disease accompanied by a fever, Civil War doctors could do little but make patients as comfortable as possible. Ice helped hold down the fever and quench parched mouths. The United States Christian Commission—a nationwide voluntary organization that raised money, supplies, and food for the relief of Union soldiers—circulated this appeal for money to "comfort these men."

National Archives, Records of the Adjutant General's Office, 1780's–1917

BURYING THE DEAD

This 1864 photo taken by Timothy O'Sullivan in Fredericksburg, Virginia, shows Confederate soldiers lying alongside the coffins in which they will be buried. Sickness, not combat, killed most Civil War soldiers. Three of five U.S. soldiers and two of three Confederate soldiers who perished died from disease.

National Archives, Records of the Office of the Chief Signal Officer [111-B-4953]

Circular:

Surgeon Generals Office
January 29, 1863.

Sir:

Grave complaints have been made to this office that Surgeons in charge of General Hospital are derelict in taken proper measures to secure the identification of soldiers dying in hospital under their charge. — They will be instructed in future to cause to be affixed upon the breast of every sol- dier thus dying, a strong card, on which will be legibly written the full name of the man, and the com- pany and Regiment to which he belongs.

Very respectfully
Your Obt. Servant,
By order of the Surg. Genl.
J. R. Smith, —
Surgeon. u.s.a.

Medical Directors to whom sent
See Book No. 2. Mily. — Page 527

NAMING THE DEAD

Neither the United States nor the Confederacy issued identification badges for soldiers. Many men purchased their own badges from private firms. They also wrote their names in Bibles or on letters and scraps of paper so that if they died, they could be identified. This circular issued by the Union Surgeon General's Office ordered name tags to be attached to the bodies of those who died in hospitals—one small step toward identifying war casualties.

National Archives, Records of the Office of the Surgeon General (Army)

WHO WERE THEY?

We know little about the three Confederate soldiers listed on this 1862 coffin receipt. Pvt. John Y. Pitts was mustered into Captain Barnes's Company of the "Ouachita Greys" at Little Rock, Arkansas, on May 31, 1861. He was 18. Pvt. E. Underwood joined Captain Wilson's Company of the 8th Arkansas Infantry for 12 months at Camp Price, Arkansas, on July 6, 1861. He was 22. The service record for Pvt. Joseph Avering was not located.

National Archives, War Department Collection of Confederate Records

WOUNDED IN ACTION DETAIL

After the Battle of Spotsylvania in May 1864, wounded soldiers wait for help at Marye's Heights, Fredericksburg. Ideally, wounded soldiers would be quickly evacuated and sent to a nearby makeshift hospital. Slightly wounded soldiers would be treated and returned to their units. The more seriously injured would be sent farther behind the lines to a divisional hospital.

National Archives, Records of the Office of the Chief Signal Officer [111-B-349]

WOUNDED . . . AND RE-WOUNDED

Union Maj. Henry Barnum received a bullet wound to his groin at the Battle of Malvern Hill on July 1, 1862. Left for dead, he was captured and exchanged for a Confederate prisoner of war. While still recovering, Barnum returned to the Union Army, fought at the Battle of Gettysburg, and was wounded again at Lookout Mountain. This "Surgeon's Certificate" from his pension application describes his condition 12 years after receiving the initial wound.

National Archives, Records of the Department of Veterans Affairs

4

DUPLICATE.

4

SURGEON'S CERTIFICATE

OF

BIENNIAL OR ANNUAL EXAMINATION ON WHICH THE PENSIONER DRAWS HIS PENSION.

Office of the Board of Pension Examining Surgeons,

Chicago, Ill., Sept. 16 , 1875.

We hereby certify, *That we have carefully examined* Henry A. Barnum *who was a* Maj. 12 ° N. Y. Vol *in the war* 1861+5 , *and was granted an Invalid Pension under Certificate No.* 78753 , *to be paid now at the Agency in* Canandaigua , *by reason of alleged disability resulting from* G S Wd left Ilium (or Thigh) , *which he states to have been received in the line of duty while he was in the military service of the United States.*

In our opinion the said Pensioner's disability, from the cause aforesaid, continues at

A more particular description of the Pensioner's condition is subjoined: Height, 5 - 9¾ *weight,* 175 ; *complexion* Light ; *age,* 43 *respiration,* 18 ; *pulse,* 80

Ball struck near left groin and emerged thro' ilium near sacro. iliac junction. wound still open entirely through the body. requiring the use of a drainage tube. Constantly. Requiring constant attention and physical strength impaired. See Surg. Genl Report Circular No 6. Washington DC
Rated Total 25 00

A LIFETIME OF SUFFERING

Henry Barnum of the 12th New York Infantry included this photograph in his pension application. Taken decades after the war, it shows the former soldier in uniform with a still unhealed wound and drainage tube.

National Archives, Records of the Department of Veterans Affairs

Cert. No. 78.753 -

H. A. Barnum
New York
his photo was taken some ... prior to 1880.
H A Barnum

PARENTS' GRIEF

In this letter, the parents of Leander Hamlin ask about their son's death: "Was he Killed instantly or was he wounded and afterward died if so how did he die what did he say in regard to dieing." It is similar to many Civil War letters inquiring about a soldier's fate. Hamlin's parents may have wanted details of Leander's death because they—like many 19th-century Americans—believed that his state of mind at death could predict how he would spend his afterlife.

Fortunately, Hamlin's parents had been misinformed about his death. Leander had been captured by Confederates and survived the war.

National Archives, Records of the Adjutant General's Office, 1780's–1917

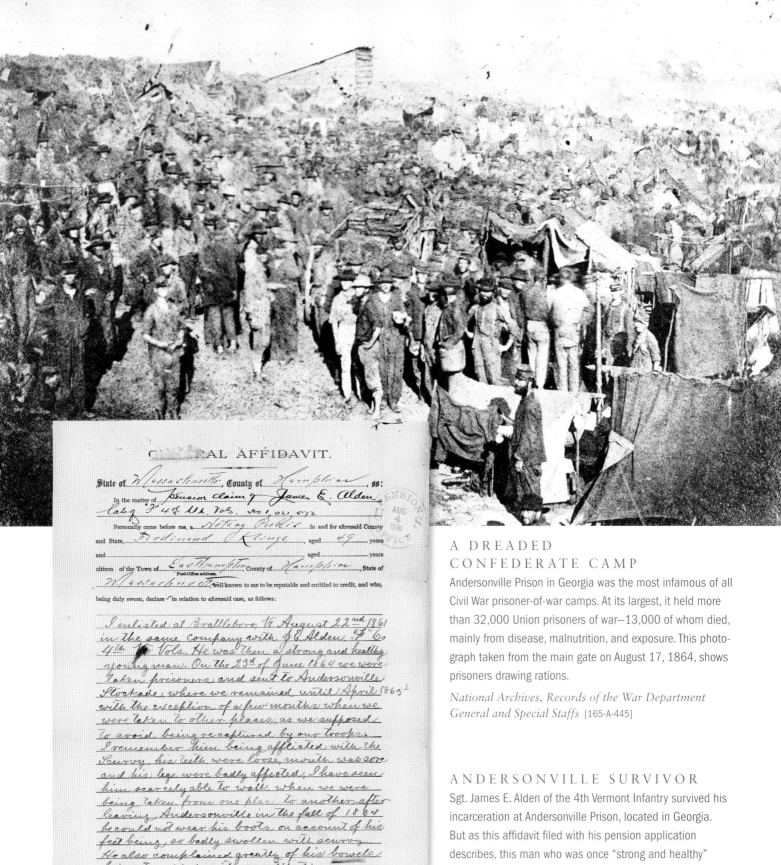

GENERAL AFFIDAVIT.

State of *Massachusetts*, County of *Hampshire*, ss:

In the matter of *pension claim of James E. Alden Co. "F" 4th Vt. Vols. No 1,021,572*

Personally came before me, a *Notary Public* in and for aforesaid County and State, *Ferdinand Kluge*, aged *49* years and aged years citizen of the Town of *East Hampton* County of *Hampshire*, State of *Massachusetts*, well known to me to be reputable and entitled to credit, and who, being duly sworn, declare in relation to aforesaid case, as follows:

I enlisted at Brattleboro, Vt. August 22nd 1861 in the same company with J.E. Alden "F" Co. 4th Vt. Vols. He was then a strong and healthy young man. On the 23d of June 1864 we were taken prisoners, and sent to Andersonville Stockade, where we remained until April 1865 with the exception of a few months when we were taken to other places, as we supposed to avoid being recaptured by our troops. I remember him being afflicted with the Scurvy, his teeth were loose, mouth was sore and his legs were badly affected, I have seen him scarcely able to walk when we were being taken from one place to another after leaving Andersonville in the fall of 1864 he could not wear his boots on account of his feet being so badly swollen with scurvy. He also complained greatly of his bowels being troubled with constipation. He was a carriage trimmer by occupation but was obliged to give it up after we returned to Brattleboro May 1865. I have seen him several times since, and he has told me that his trouble with bowels still made him a great deal of trouble, and that he could not labor

He further declare that *he has* no interest in said case, and *is* not concerned in its prosecution.

Ferdinand Kluge
Signature of Affiant.

NOTE.—In the execution of papers and evidence, whenever a person or witness signs by mark, (†,) two persons who *can write* must attest the signature by signing their names opposite. The official before whom papers are executed is *not a competent witness to a mark*.

A DREADED CONFEDERATE CAMP

Andersonville Prison in Georgia was the most infamous of all Civil War prisoner-of-war camps. At its largest, it held more than 32,000 Union prisoners of war—13,000 of whom died, mainly from disease, malnutrition, and exposure. This photograph taken from the main gate on August 17, 1864, shows prisoners drawing rations.

National Archives, Records of the War Department General and Special Staffs [165-A-445]

ANDERSONVILLE SURVIVOR

Sgt. James E. Alden of the 4th Vermont Infantry survived his incarceration at Andersonville Prison, located in Georgia. But as this affidavit filed with his pension application describes, this man who was once "strong and healthy" was terribly ill for the rest of his life. Ferdinand Kliuge, who was in the same company with Alden, writes:

> I remember him being afflicted with the scurvy his teeth were loose, mouth was sore and his legs were badly affected. I have seen him scarcely able to walk. When were being taken from one place to another after leaving Andersonville in the fall of 1864 he could not wear his boots on account of his feet being so badly swollen with scurvy.

National Archives, Records of the Department of Veterans Affairs

SEVERE OVERCROWDING AT CAMP DOUGLAS

Camp Douglas, the Union prison camp in Chicago, Illinois, grew quickly and was poorly administered by a series of commandants. Prisoners accused several guards of cruelty. The camp had a maximum capacity of 6,000. But by 1864 it housed more than 12,000 Confederate soldiers as well as a few civilians suspected of sympathizing with the Confederacy or planning escapes. The official death count at Camp Douglas was 4,454. Some 1,500 men, however, were "unaccounted for." This photograph shows Confederate prisoners outside their barracks.

Courtesy of the Chicago History Museum [ICHi22084]

Head Quarters Trinity La
July 30th 1864

Lieut Col H. A. McCaleb
Comdg U.S. Forces
Vidalia La

Sir

In the skirmish of the 22nd July 1864 a negro man named Wilson was captured by the Confederate forces. He is wounded in the calf of the leg (Flesh wound) and is receiving such medical attention as we have, When he is well if his owner lives in the Confederate lines he will be delivered to him, if not he will be held to slavery by the Government, I have to inform you that negroes are not considered prisoners of war, but all who surrendered to us are treated as property and either delivered to their original owner or put at labor by the Government.

I am very respectfully
Your Obedient Servant
(Signed) Wm P Hardeman
Col Comdg Post

A True Copy
J. M. Guest
Lieut and AAAG

In this letter, Confederate Col. William P. Hardeman outlined Confederate policy on black prisoners of war.

National Archives, Records of the Adjutant General's Office, 1780's–1917

P.O.W. or Slave?

In 1862 the Union and Confederate armies agreed to exchange prisoners. The agreement broke down after the Emancipation Proclamation—in part over the issue of how captured black troops should be treated. Confederate leaders wanted black U.S. soldiers treated as rebellious slaves, subject to execution or sale into bondage. Union leaders wanted them treated as prisoners of war, just like white soldiers.

On July 22, 1864, Pvt. Wilson Wood of the 6th U.S. Colored Heavy Artillery was wounded and captured by Confederate forces. Confederate Col. William P. Hardeman informed the Union commanders of Wood's capture and outlined his position on Private Wood's status. He wrote that blacks "who surrender will be treated as property and either delivered to their original owner or put at labor by the government." Union Brig. Gen. J. M. Brayman replied: "When the United States made negroes soldiers it assured towards them the same obligations as were due to any others who might wear its uniform and bear its flag." Brayman went on to warn that "for every black soldier reduced to slavery," he will "put a rebel in like condition."

Wood was held by Confederate forces until he was released by U.S. forces on June 1, 1865, in Natchitoches, Louisiana. It is unclear from his service record how he was treated by his captors.

CIRCULAR,)   WASHINGTON, D. C.

No. 8.   )   *July* 14, 1862.

No candidate for service in the Women's Department for nursing in the military hospitals of the United States, will be received below the age of thirty-five years, (35) nor above fifty.

Only women of strong health, not subjects of chronic disease, nor liable to sudden illnesses, need apply. The duties of the station make large and continued demands on strength.

Matronly persons of experience, good conduct, or superior education and serious disposition, will always have preference; habits of neatness, order, sobriety, and industry, are prerequisites.

All applicants must present certificates of qualification and good character from at least two persons of trust, testifying to morality, integrity, seriousness, and capacity for the care of the sick.

Obedience to rules of the service, and conformity to special regulations, will be required and enforced.

Compensation, as regulated by act of Congress, forty cents a day and subsistence. Transportation furnished to and from the place of service.

Amount of luggage limited within a small compass. Dress plain— colors, brown, grey, or black, and, while connected with the service, without ornaments of any sort.

No applicants accepted for less than ~~three~~ months' service; those for longer periods always have preference.

                           D. L. DIX,

APPROVED :

          WILLIAM A. HAMMOND,

              Surgeon General.

DETAIL

"MATRONLY PERSONS . . . WILL ALWAYS HAVE PREFERENCE"

In 1861, shortly after the Battle of Bull Run, U.S. Surgeon General William Hammond appointed Dorothea Dix as Superintendent of U.S. Army Nurses. This circular lays out Dix's requirements for women who wanted to serve. Strict age and marriage requirements stemmed from fears that mixing young unmarried women with soldiers would lead to scandal. Dix appointed approximately 3,000 women to nursing positions. Approximately 30,000 women served in nursing and relief operations on both sides of the conflict.

Dorothea Dix (1802–1887) was a social reformer who devoted her life to causes such as assisting the mentally ill and prison reform. She became interested in wartime nursing after visiting military hospitals in Europe following the Crimean War.

National Archives, Records of the Judge Advocate General (Army)

DETAIL

WANTED: POPPIES

This circular appeals to Confederate women to provide an "essential service" by growing garden poppies that could then be processed into opiates such as morphine. Civil War physicians had few effective medicines for curing diseases and treating wounds. Sometimes all they could offer was morphine as a painkiller.

Using natural medicines was especially widespread in the Confederacy because the Union naval blockade prevented the import of medicines from abroad. The Confederate Surgeon General created several laboratories that manufactured drugs from plants and herbs.

National Archives, War Department Collection of Confederate Records

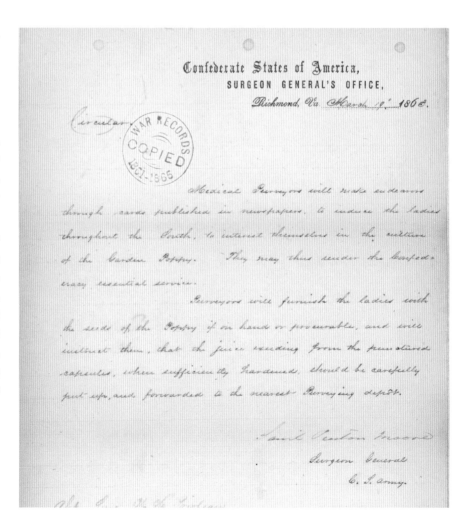

A CONFEDERATE PRISONER WHO TOOK THE UNION OATH

Jennifer N. Johnson

In 1864, as prison camp conditions deteriorated, the Union offered Confederate prisoners of war an opportunity to take the Union oath and become "Galvanized Yankees." Among those who took the oath was Pvt. Henry Scott, a prisoner at Point Lookout in Maryland.

Prison camp conditions during the Civil War were harsh. Death rates were so high that a soldier had less chance of surviving in a prison camp than he did on a battlefield. Dozens of camps were set up during the war, but nearly all were inadequate for the number of soldiers imprisoned in them. Neither the Union nor the Confederacy provided sufficient facilities, food, or clothing for their prisoners. The notoriously poor conditions were due partly to poor management and partly to inexperience: the Army had never dealt with such a high number of prisoners.

Point Lookout, Maryland

One of the largest Union prison camps was at Point Lookout in Maryland. Officially named Camp Hoffman, Point Lookout was situated on land that was formerly a resort area. By 1863 it was a military complex that included a hospital, storehouses, quarters for troops and doctors, and the prison camp. The complex sat facing Virginia on a peninsula formed by a junction of the Potomac River and Chesapeake Bay. Point Lookout Military Prison took up roughly 40 acres of the complex and consisted of tents surrounded by fences.

About 130 prisoners arrived at Point Lookout from Gettysburg in July 1863. Around the same time, the regular prisoner exchange system between the Union and Confederacy broke down. Prison camps on both sides became very crowded, very quickly. Before then prison camps had been used primarily as temporary holding camps while exchanges were negotiated. Now conditions at Point Lookout, stark to begin with, quickly deteriorated as more and more prisoners arrived. By Christmas the prison population at Point Lookout numbered approximately 9,000.

Although winter on the Chesapeake could be harsh, prisoners continued to be quartered in tents. During the colder months, campfires were their main source of warmth. The tents were overcrowded, and blankets and wood were scarce as the peninsula had few trees or shrubs. Most of the men grew up in the South and were not used to the cold winter. What's more, flooding was not infrequent, leaving the men—with their lack of solid structures—especially exposed.

Conditions Worsen

By 1864 disease was epidemic in the camp. Chronic diarrhea, dysentery, and typhoid fever were rampant as a result of the lack of fresh water. Food rations were severely lacking. One prisoner described them as "just sufficient to maintain life, yet leaving one in a continual state of hunger." Some prisoners resorted to

The Union service card for 21-year-old Pvt. Henry Scott records his brief stay with the 1st U.S. Volunteers.

National Archives, Records of the Adjutant General's Office, 1780's–1917

Henry Scott's Confederate service card shows that although he was absent because of illness, he had rejoined the 10th Louisiana by the summer of 1864.

National Archives, War Department Collection of Confederate Records

SELECTED PAGE

The loyalty oath taken by Henry Scott and other Confederate prisoners at Point Lookout included a pledge to support the Constitution and "support all proclamations of the President . . . having reference to slaves." Scott's name can be found eight names from the last on this register.

National Archives, War Department Collection of Confederate Records

capturing and eating whatever they could find, be it rodents or seafood. Unfortunately, the conditions at Point Lookout were not unique. Overcrowded facilities, disease, starvation, and lack of supplies and clothing were typical of all prison camps—Union and Confederate.

Gen. Benjamin Butler, Commander of the Department of Virginia and North Carolina, was responsible for the operation of Point Lookout. In late 1863, he expressed to Secretary of War Edwin M. Stanton his desire to enlist prisoners in the Army. By January, General Butler had President Lincoln's permission—with certain conditions. Each prisoner was to be asked a series of questions, composed by President Lincoln himself, and their answers recorded. The men were asked if they wanted to be exchanged, to take the oath and serve, to engage in labor, or to go home (if that home was within U.S. Army lines). One question inquired: "Do you desire to take the oath of allegiance and parole, and enlist in the Army or Navy of the U.S., and if so which?" Men who answered "yes" to that question were recruited.

Battles in 1864 exacerbated the conditions at Point Lookout. Droves of prisoners swarmed into camp. One of those who arrived in mid-May was Pvt. Henry Scott of Company A,

10th Louisiana Volunteers. Like most men of the 10th Louisiana, Scott was an immigrant and wore a Zouave uniform, an exotic dress inspired by French colonial troops from North Africa. He had joined the Confederate Army on July 22, 1861, and mustered in at Camp Moore, Louisiana. Scott's service card noted that he was born in Tankirk, France, and identified him as a sailor. Private Scott and the 10th fought in several bloody engagements, including the battles of Chancellorsville and Gettysburg. However, it wasn't until the Battle of Spotsylvania in May 1864 that Scott's luck ran out. He was one of hundreds captured by the Union Army.

A Possible Way Out

Eager to make prison life more bearable, prisoners volunteered to help out as clerks, cooks, other kitchen staff, hospital workers, or gravediggers. Now, in 1864, another option became available—to take the oath and pledge allegiance to the United States. It was not a decision taken lightly. Men who took the oath had a variety of motivations—including a genuine change of loyalty, despair at their situation as prisoners, and perhaps a chance to desert at the first opportunity.

By spring 1864, General Butler had enough men at Point

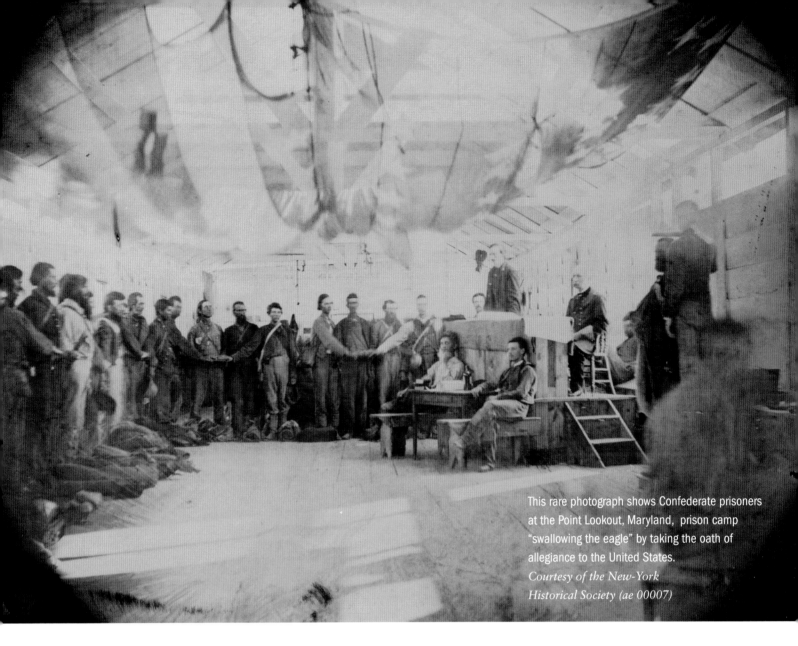

This rare photograph shows Confederate prisoners at the Point Lookout, Maryland, prison camp "swallowing the eagle" by taking the oath of allegiance to the United States.
Courtesy of the New-York Historical Society (ae 00007)

Lookout to create a regiment, which was officially named the 1st U.S. Volunteer Infantry. A volume from Point Lookout lists about 1,500 prisoners who took the oath. It includes details about each soldier, such as where he was born and what Confederate regiment he served in. Private Scott is included in that volume. Within a few weeks of arriving at Point Lookout, he had enlisted with the 1st U.S. Volunteers.

The 1st U.S. Volunteers was one of six regiments composed of "Galvanized Yankees"—former Confederates who had "swallowed the eagle" and sworn allegiance to the United States. Most took the oath under the condition that they would not fight former comrades. Originally the 1st were sent to North Carolina, where they had a small skirmish with guerillas. But General Grant was vehemently opposed to using former Confederates against Confederates, and the 1st U.S. Volunteers was quickly transferred to Milwaukee, Wisconsin, and then on to Indian territory.

But not Private Scott. He deserted on July 30, 1864, in Pasquotank County, North Carolina. It appears that he returned to his regiment, because his Confederate service card reads: "Took the oath of allegiance to escape Yankee prison." As of September 1864, "absent captured" was replaced by "absent on detail or duty by order."

Desertion was clearly one motivation for the Confederate men who became Galvanized Yankees. But thousands of others served the nation in the West after the end of the Civil War, at a time when a military presence was much needed and the military was much in need of men. During their time in service to the Army, these Galvanized Yankees protected settlers against the Sioux in Minnesota, manned forts along the Mississippi River, and marched through Kansas to open a new stage route.

NOTE ON SOURCES

Essential for providing the "face" to this article were The Register of Prisoners Enlisting in the United States Army and Navy, Point Lookout, MD, and Henry Scott's service records for the Union and Confederacy: 1st U.S. Volunteer Infantry, *Compiled Service Records of Former Confederate Soldiers Who Served in the 1st Through 6th U.S. Volunteer Infantry Regiments, 1864–1866* (National Archives Microfilm Publication M1017, roll 12). War Department Collection of Confederate Records, Record Group (RG) 109; and 10th Louisiana, *Compiled Service Records of Confederate Soldiers Who Served in Organizations from the State of Louisiana* (M320, roll 223), RG 109.

Other sources used were *"Trading Gray for Blue, Ex-Confederates Hold the Upper Missouri for the Union,"* by Michele T. Butts, *Prologue* 37, No. 4 (Winter 2005), 14-21; D. Alexander Browns's *The Galvanized Yankees* (Illinois, 1973); Lonnie R. Speer's *Portals to Hell* (Pennsylvania, 1997); and Charles W. Sanders, Jr.'s, *While in the Hands of the Enemy: Military Prisons of the Civil War* (Baton Rouge, 2005).

Congress of the United States,

At the Second Session

BEGUN AND HELD AT THE CITY OF WASHINGTON

in the District of Columbia

on Monday the _third_ day of December one thousand eight hundred and _sixty_.

Joint Resolution to amend the Constitution of the United States.

Resolved by the Senate and House of Representatives of the United States of America in Congress assembled, That the following article be proposed to the legislatures of the several States as an amendment to the Constitution of the United States, which, when ratified by three fourths of said legislatures, shall be valid to all intents and purposes, as part of the said Constitution, viz:

Article XIII. No amendment shall be made to the Constitution which will authorize or give to Congress the power to abolish or interfere, within any State, with the domestic institutions thereof, including that of persons held to labor or service by the laws of said State.

Approved March 2. 1861.

Wm. Pennington

James Buchanan   Speaker of the House of Representatives.

John C. Breckinridge
Vice President of the United States,
& President of the Senate.

CHAPTER 10

EMANCIPATIONS

In March 1861, Congress proposed a 13th amendment to the U.S. Constitution. It would have stopped the Federal Government from interfering with slavery, but it was never ratified by the states. Four years later, another U.S. Congress passed a very different 13th Amendment that abolished slavery forever and freed four million people. It *was* ratified.

- What changed between the passage of these two amendments?
- How did a war over secession become one for human freedom?
- What role did Lincoln's Emancipation Proclamation play?

From documents in the National Archives, we know that the path to emancipation was a gradual and uneven one. It was shaped by military events, by Government policies, and by the actions of enslaved people who pursued and fought for their freedom.

1861: A PROPOSED 13TH AMENDMENT

As Southern states began seceding during the winter of 1860–61, several compromises were proposed to hold the nation together. One was a constitutional amendment that would have prevented Congress from passing legislation that would interfere with a state's "domestic institutions . . . including that of persons held to labor or service." Amendment sponsors hoped its approval would keep border states in the Union and reassure Southerners that Republicans opposed only the extension, not the existence, of slavery.

The compromise failed. Congress approved the amendment, but only two state legislatures ratified it.

National Archives, General Records of the U.S. Government

> Head Quarters 2'd Reg. C.V.
> Camp Welles. Washington D.C. June 12/61
> To Captain Theodore Talbot. Asst' Adj'. Genl:
> Sir:
> In accordance with a verbal order from General Mansfield I have the honor to report to you that on the 10th inst, six men of color representing themselves to be fugitive slaves from Howard County in the State of Maryland appeared in the Camp of my Regiment and still remain upon my grounds. They also represent that their Masters are secessionists in sentiment and opinion and members of secret military organizations hostile to the Government.
> Alfred H. Terry
> Col. 2 Reg. C.V.

AN OFFICER'S DILEMMA DETAIL

The escape of six men from slavery to a Union camp during the early months of the war presented its commanding officer with a dilemma. The fugitives were from Maryland, a state that had not seceded. Slavery was legal there, but the men were the property of an owner who supported secession. The officer was told to consider the men "contraband"—property seized from rebels. He could refuse to return them.

National Archives, Records of U.S. Army Continental Commands, 1821–1920

A group of "Contrabands" in a Union Army camp, Bermuda Hundred, Virginia, ca. 1863. Another caption for this photograph describes these men as "teamsters."

Donated Material in the National Archives [200-(s)-2594]

FREE IN SOUTH CAROLINA

This photograph shows formerly enslaved men and women planting sweet potatoes on Edisto Island, South Carolina, in 1862. They were among the first persons freed when U.S. Navy and Army forces captured the Sea Islands in late 1861. Confederate landowners abandoned their plantations, but many of their former slaves refused to leave. They ransacked their former owners' homes and started to work the land for their own benefit.

Courtesy of the New-York Historical Society

To Mr. A. Smith Esq

Clerk of the Circuit Court of the District of Columbia

In pursuance of the act of Congress, entitled "An act for the
release of certain persons held to service or labor in the District of Columbia,"
passed on the 16th April 1862, and in accordance with the 9th section thereof
you are hereby authorised and required to file and record in your office
the following Statement and schedule, under said act, of persons from whom
I claimed service as slaves at the time of the passage of said act: viz:

	Age	Name	Sex	Color	Height	Particular description.
1.	65	Peter Jenkins	Male	Black	5.8½	For life - Good farm hand
2.	58	Mary Jenkins	Female	"	5.2	" - Good Cook
3.	60	Ellen Jenkins	"	"	5.7	" "
4.	36	Susan Carroll	"	Dark mulatto	4.11⅞	For a term - till 44 years old : 8 years to serve. House servant
5.	7	Dennis Carroll	Male	Light Mulatto	3.10	For life
6.	3	Ann Maria Carroll	Female	"	Child	"
7.	2	Wm Carroll	Male	"	"	"
8.	25	Richd Williams	"	Dark Mulatto	5.10½	" Shoemaker, Carpenter, good farm hand.
9.	45	Chapman Toyer	"	Black	6.	" Good farm hand
10.	51	Sarah Toyer	Female	"	5.1	" Good Laundress
11.	59	Mary Young	"	"	5.	" Good Cook.
12.	37	Kitty Silass	"	Light Mulatto	5.2½	" Laundress & Cook
13.	8	Gilbert Silass	Male	"	4.2½	
14.	5	Wm Silass	"	"	3.10	
15.	8 months	Philip Silass			Child	
16.	24 yrs	Saml Yates	"	Dark Mulatto	5.2½	" Good house Servant
17.	31	Judah Yates	"	"	5.3½	" House servant. Coachman farm hand
18.	41	John Thomas	"	Black	5.8¾	" Coachman, & farm hand.
19.	25	Henry Toyer	"	Dark Mulatto	5.10½	" Farm hand
20.	24	Josh Toyer	"	Black	5.8½	" "
21.	23	Louisa Toyer	Female	"	5.7	" Good Cook
22.	4 months	Danl Toyer	Male		Child	"
23.	18 years	Eliza Toyer	Female	Dark Mulatto	5.1	" Good house servant
24.	36	Jane Yates	"	"	5.1¼	" Good Cook
25.	20	Mary Brown	"	Light Mulatto	5.7⅞	" House Servant
26.	16	Betty Briscoe	"	Dark Mulatto	5.2	" "

EMANCIPATION IN DC

On April 16, 1862, 8½ months before the Emancipation Proclamation, President Lincoln signed a bill ending
slavery in the District of Columbia. It provided for immediate emancipation and compensation to owners loyal to
the Union of up to $300 for each person freed. Margaret Barber filed this list with the U.S. District Court seeking
compensation for her freed slaves. Over nine months, the Board of Commissioners appointed to administer the
act approved 930 petitions, completely or in part, seeking compensation for the freedom of 2,989 people.

National Archives, Records of District Courts of the United States

CELEBRATION OF THE ABOLITION OF SLAVERY IN THE DISTRICT OF COLUMBIA BY THE COLORED PEOPLE, IN WASHINGTON, April 19, 1866.—[Sketched by F. Dielman.]

For years after the Civil War ended, black Washingtonians celebrated emancipation in the District of Columbia with parades and festivals as in this 1866 image.

Courtesy of the Library of Congress

By the President of the United States of America:

A Proclamation.

Whereas, on the twenty-second day of September, in the year of our Lord one thousand eight hundred and sixty-two, a proclamation was issued by the President of the United States, containing, among other things, the following, to wit:

"That on the first day of January, in the "year of our Lord one thousand eight hundred "and sixty-three, all persons held as slaves within "any State or designated part of a State, the people "whereof shall then be in rebellion against the "United States, shall be then, thenceforward, and "forever free; and the Executive Government of the "United States, including the military and naval "authority thereof, will recognize and maintain "the freedom of such persons, and will do no act "or acts to repress such persons, or any of them, "in any efforts they may make for their actual "freedom.

"That the Executive will, on the first day

President Abraham Lincoln issued the Emancipation Proclamation on January 1, 1863, as the nation approached its third year of bloody civil war. The proclamation declared "that all persons held as slaves" within the rebellious states "are, and henceforward shall be free."

Despite this expansive wording, the Emancipation Proclamation was limited in many ways. It applied only to states that had seceded from the Union, leaving slavery untouched in the loyal border states. It also expressly exempted parts of the Confederacy that had already come under Northern control. Most important, the freedom it promised depended upon Union military victory.

Although the Emancipation Proclamation did not end slavery in the nation, it captured the hearts and imagination of millions of Americans and fundamentally transformed the character of the war. After January 1, 1863, every advance of Federal troops expanded the domain of freedom. Moreover, the Proclamation announced the acceptance of black men into the Union Army and Navy, enabling the liberated to become liberators. By the end of the war, almost 200,000 black soldiers and sailors had fought for the Union and freedom.

From the first days of the Civil War, slaves had acted to secure their own liberty. The Emancipation Proclamation confirmed their insistence that the war for the Union must become a war for freedom. It added moral force to the Union cause and strengthened the Union both militarily and politically. As a milestone along the road to slavery's final destruction, the Emancipation Proclamation has assumed a place among the great documents of human freedom.

National Archives, General Records of the U.S. Government

Resolution

adopted at a

Great Public Meeting

of the

Inhabitants of Bolton in the County of Lancaster

February 24th 1863

James Barlow Esqre in the Chair.

Resolved

That this meeting being convinced that Slavery is the cause of the tremendous struggle now going on in the American States, and that the object of the Leaders of the Rebellion is the perpetuation of the unchristian and inhuman system of chattel slavery, earnestly prays that the rebellion may be crushed and its wicked object defeated, and that the Federal Government may be strengthened to pursue its emancipation policy till not a slave be left on the American Soil. That a Copy of this resolution be sent to his Excellency the President of the United States.

Signed on behalf of and by order of the meeting

James Barlow Chairman

SUPPORT FROM OVERSEAS

News of the Emancipation Proclamation spread around the world. In Europe it solidified support for the Union cause, especially among working people. In February 1863, citizens of Bolton, England, passed this resolution praising Lincoln's action and sent him their own elaborate proclamation.

National Archives, General Records of the Department of State

TO COLORED MEN!

FREEDOM,
Protection, Pay, and a Call to Military Duty!

On the 1st day of January, 1863, the President of the United States proclaimed FREE-
DOM to over THREE MILLIONS OF SLAVES. This decree is to be enforced by all the power of
the Nation. On the 21st of July last he issued the following order:

PROTECTION OF COLORED TROOPS.

"WAR DEPARTMENT, ADJUTANT GENERAL'S OFFICE,
WASHINGTON, July 21.

"*General Order*, No. 233.

"The following order of the President is published for the information and government of all concerned:—

EXECUTIVE MANSION, WASHINGTON, July 30.

"'It is the duty of every Government to give protection to its citizens, of whatever class, color, or condition, and especially to
those wh are duly organized as soldiers in the public service. The law of nations, and the usages and customs of war, as carried on
by civilized powers, permit no distinction as to color in the treatment of prisoners of war as public enemies. To sell or enslave any
captured person on account of his color, is a relapse into barbarism, and a crime against the civilization of the age.
'"The Government of the United States will give the same protection to all its soldiers, and if the enemy shall sell or enslave any
one because of his color, the offense shall be punished by retaliation upon the enemy's prisoners in our possession. It is, therefore,
ordered, for every soldier of the United States, killed in violation of the laws of war, a rebel soldier shall be executed; and for every
one enslaved by the enemy, or sold into slavery, a rebel soldier shall be placed at hard labor on the public works, and continued at such
labor until the other shall be released and receive the treatment due to prisoners of war.
'"ABRAHAM LINCOLN."'

"'By order of the Secretary of War.
'"E. D. TOWNSEND, Assistant Adjutant General."'

That the President is in earnest the rebels soon began to find out, as witness the following order from his Secretary of War:

"WAR DEPARTMENT, WASHINGTON CITY, August 8, 1863.

"SIR: Your letter of the 3d inst., calling the attention of this Department to the cases of Orin H. Brown, William H. Johnston,
and Wm. Wilson, three colored men captured on the gunboat Isaac Smith, has received consideration. This Department has directed
that three rebel prisoners of South Carolina, if there be any such in our possession, and if not, three others, be confined in close custody
and held as hostages for Brown, Johnston and Wilson, and that the fact be communicated to the rebel authorities at Richmond.
"Very respectfully your obedient servant,
"EDWIN M. STANTON, Secretary of War.

"The Hon. GIDEON WELLES, Secretary of the Navy."

And retaliation will be our practice now—man for man—to the bitter end.

LETTER OF CHARLES SUMNER,
Written with reference to the Convention held at Poughkeepsie, July 15th and 16th, 1863, to promote Colored Enlistments.

BOSTON, July 13th, 1863.

"I doubt if, in times past, our country could have expected from colored men any patriotic service. Such service is the return for
protection. But now that protection has begun, the service should begin also. Nor should relative rights and duties be weighed with
nicety. It is enough that our country, aroused at last to a sense of justice, seeks to enrol colored men among its defenders.
"If my counsels should reach such persons, I would say: enlist at once. Now is the day and now is the hour. Help to overcome
your cruel enemies now battling against your country, and in this way you will surely overcome those other enemies hardly less cruel,
here at home, who will still seek to degrade you. This is not the time to hesitate or to higgle. Do your duty to our country, and you
will set an example of generous self-sacrifice which will conquer prejudice and open all hearts.
"Very faithfully yours,
"CHARLES SUMNER."

NEW RECRUITS

President Lincoln's Emancipation Proclamation allowed black men to "be received into the armed service of
the United States." With the President's signature, formerly enslaved men living in Confederate states became
potential recruits—and potential weapons against the rebellion.

By the end of the war, 200,000 African Americans would serve in the U.S. Army and Navy, the vast majority
of whom had been born in slavery.

National Archives, Records of the Adjutant General's Office, 1780's–1917

FIGHTING IN LOUISIANA

On May 27, 1863, at Port Hudson, Louisiana, more than 1,000 black troops from the Louisiana Native Guards attacked a heavily fortified position. They suffered heavy casualties. Afterwards, one Union officer wrote to his wife: "There can be no question about the good fighting qualities of negroes."

National Archives, Records of the National Archives and Records Administration

WAR RECORDS
COPIED
1861–1865

Freedom to Slaves !

Whereas the President of the United States did on the first day of the present month, issue his Proclamation declaring "that all persons held as slaves in certain designated States, and parts of States, are henceforward and shall be free," and that the Executive Government of the United States, including the Military and Naval authorities thereof, would recognize and maintain the freedom of said persons.

And whereas the county of Frederick is included in the territory designated by the Proclamation of the President, in which the slaves should become free, I therefore hereby notify the citizens of the city of Winchester, and of said county, of said Proclamation, and of my intention to maintain and enforce the same.

I expect all citizens to yield a ready compliance with the Proclamation of the Chief Executive, and I admonish all persons disposed to resist its peaceful enforcement, that upon manifesting such disposition by acts, they will be regarded as rebels in arms against the lawful authority of the Federal Government and dealt with accordingly.

All persons liberated by said Proclamation are admonished to abstain from all violence, and immediately betake themselves to useful occupations.

The officers of this command are admonished and ordered to act in accordance with said Proclamation and to yield their ready cooperation in its enforcement.

R. H. Milroy
Brig Genl Commanding.

Jany 5th 1863

STERN WARNING

Four days after President Lincoln issued his Emancipation Proclamation, U.S. Brig. Gen. R. H. Milroy put the citizens of Frederick County and Winchester, Virginia, on notice with this order. It warned that all those who opposed the Proclamation would be treated as "rebels in arms." Confederate forces found this copy of Milroy's order and passed it on to Gen. Robert E. Lee as evidence of the effect of the Emancipation Proclamation in Northern Virginia.

National Archives, War Department Collection of Confederate Records

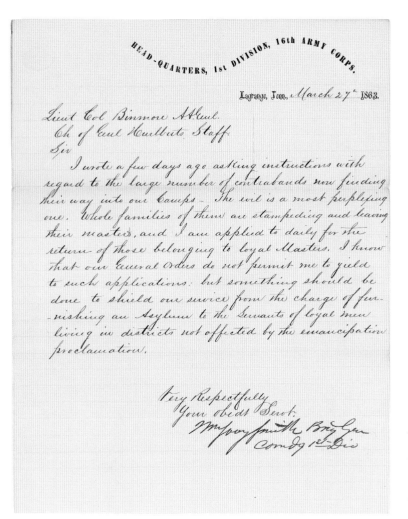

> "Whole families of them are stampeding and leaving their masters, and I am applied to daily for the return of those belonging to loyal citizens."

A PERPLEXING SITUATION

After the Emancipation Proclamation, the stream of slaves running to freedom swelled to a flood. Gen. W. Sooy Smith, who commanded Union troops in Tennessee, faced a dilemma. Men loyal to the Union wanted their property returned, but Smith's orders were to refuse such requests.

This letter asks how to avoid "the charge of furnishing Asylum to the Servants of loyal men." The War Department usually advised that runaways be employed by the Army.

National Archives, Records of U.S. Army Continental Commands, 1821–1920

> "you will please let me know if we are free."

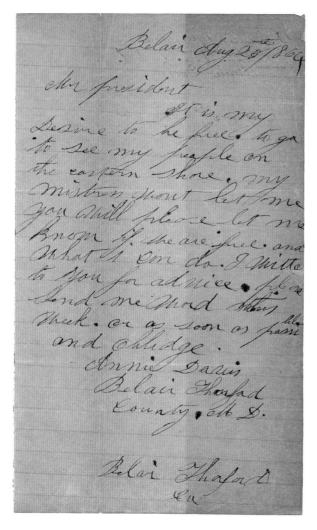

LETTER TO LINCOLN

On April 25, 1864, Annie Davis, a slave living in Maryland, wrote this brief but touching letter to President Abraham Lincoln. In it, she asked if she was free. No reply from the President has been located. The answer to Davis's question, however, would have been "no." Slavery existed in Maryland until November 1, 1864.

National Archives, Records of the Adjutant General's Office, 1780's–1917

Thirty-Eighth Congress of the United States of America;

At the _Second_ Session,

Begun and held at the City of Washington, on Monday, the _fifth_ day of December, one thousand eight hundred and sixty-_four._

A RESOLUTION

Submitting to the legislatures of the several States a proposition to amend the Constitution of the United States.

Resolved by the Senate and House of Representatives of the United States of America in Congress assembled, (two-thirds of both houses concurring), that the following article be proposed to the legislatures of the several States as an amendment to the Constitution of the United States, which, when ratified by three-fourths of said Legislatures shall be valid, to all intents and purposes, as a part of the said Constitution, namely: Article XIII. Section 1. Neither slavery nor involuntary servitude, except as a punishment for crime whereof the party shall have been duly convicted, shall exist within the United States, or any place subject to their jurisdiction. Section 2. Congress shall have power to enforce this article by appropriate legislation.

Schuyler Colfax
Speaker of the House of Representatives.

H. Hamlin
Vice President of the United States
and President of the Senate

Abraham Lincoln

Approved, February 1. 1865.

1865: FINAL 13TH AMENDMENT

Four years into the war, and four years after Congress approved a constitutional amendment protecting slavery, Congress proposed another constitutional amendment. This one abolished slavery in the United States. After being signed by President Lincoln, the proposal was ratified by the necessary three-quarters of the states.

On December 18, 1865, it became the 13th Amendment to the Constitution.

National Archives, General Records of the U.S. Government

VOLUNTEERS DISCOVER A TREASURE
Budge Weidman

As members of the National Archives' dedicated volunteer corps combed through the files performing a routine administrative task, the project manager came upon a poignant letter from a former slave that has been one of the corps' most valued finds.

In 1995, volunteers from the National Archives' Civil War Conservation Corps were preparing the compiled military service records of the 55th Massachusetts Infantry (Colored) for microfilming. As I sifted through the boxes of military forms and applications, I came across something very special. Glued to an application from Robert Cabble, a slave-owner in Brunswick, Missouri, was a moving letter from one of his former slaves, Samuel Cabble. The letter informed Cabble's wife, who was still in slavery, of his whereabouts. "Dear wife," it began, "I have enlisted in the army." Samuel Cabble, it appears, had escaped from slavery at the age of 21 and made it to Iowa, where he enlisted in the Union Army. He was then sent to Massachusetts, where he joined the state's 55th Infantry.

The letter goes on to express not only Cabble's longing to see his wife again but his hopes and optimism for the future:

> . . . though great is the national difficulties yet I look forward to a brighter day When I shall have the opportunity of seeing you in the full enjoyment of freedom . . . great is the outpouring of the colored people that is now rallying with the hearts of lions against that very curse that has separated you an me yet we shall meet again and oh what a happy time that will be.

Cabble's former owner confiscated the letter before it reached Cabble's wife and used it to apply for compensation. At that time the Union Government provided up to $300 to loyal border state slave holders for each slave released to the U.S. Army.

Letter that escaped slave Samuel Cabble wrote to his wife—but that never reached her
National Archives, Records of the Adjutant General's Office, 1780's–1917

"*I shall use my utmost endeavor to strike at the rebellion and the heart of this system that so long has kept us in chains.*"

ESCAPED SLAVE SAMUEL CABBLE

rebellion shall be put down and the Curses of our land is trampled under our feet i am a soldier now and i shall use my utmost endeavers to strike at the rebellion and the heart of this system that so long has kept us in chains. write to me just as soon as you git this letter tell me if you are still living in the cabin where you use to live. tell eliza i send her my best respects and love ike an sucy likewise i would send you some money but i now it is impossible for you to git it i would like to see little jenkins now but i no it is impossibl at present so no more but remain your own afectionate husband until death

Samuel. Cabble

There is no evidence that Robert Cabble ever received compensation, probably because he failed to prove his loyalty to the Union and meet other requirements.

The letter became one of the volunteer corps' most treasured finds. Condoleeza Rice, Secretary of State under President George W. Bush, is among those who own a framed copy. I was moved to tears the first time I saw it—as was almost everyone else we shared it with. It was extremely dangerous to attempt to escape from slavery. This letter shows, with such passion, why Cabble and so many others took that risk. You just knew this determined man was going to succeed.

But did he? Curious to know more about Samuel Cabble and what happened to him, I researched other National Archives records, including the Civil War pension files. I learned that Cabble's regiment was sent to South Carolina, where he suffered a leg injury from a cannon discharge. He remained with the regiment, despite his injury, and served for three years until the 55th was mustered out in August 1865.

After being discharged, Cabble returned to Brunswick, where he was at last reunited with his wife, Leah. They were now both free and could be legally married. They had a son—Samuel Cabble, Jr.—and headed west to Denver, Colorado. Cabble applied for and received a military pension in 1891. In late 1905, alone and unable to care for himself, he moved to the National Military Home in Leavenworth, Kansas. He died on May 31, 1906. But more than a century later, his letter remains preserved in the collections of the National Archives—helping us better understand not only the personal struggles of those who fought for emancipation, but the dreams that sustained them.

A UNION ARMY OFFICER CONFRONTS EMANCIPATION IN LOUISIANA
Bruce I. Bustard

A U.S. Army captain in Louisiana bemoaned "the perplexities of my position" as he discovered that confusing Federal policies raised more questions about emancipation than they answered.

CONTRABANDS COMING INTO CAMP

Union-controlled areas were havens for slaves seeking freedom. Called "contrabands" because they were considered "property" seized by the United States, the legal status of these individuals depended on where and when they had escaped, and whether they had been the property of a loyal or secessionist owner. *From* Harper's Weekly, *January 31, 1863   Courtesy of the Library of Congress*

Presidents proclaim, legislatures act, and generals order. But junior military officers—lieutenants and captains—often end up carrying out the grand designs set in motion by the powerful. This was certainly the case when a 27-year-old U.S. Army captain from Massachusetts tried to implement Federal policy toward the emancipation of slaves in the small town of New Iberia, Louisiana, in April 1863. His efforts to understand his commanders' intentions and to put confusing Federal policies into practice in occupied territory provide a brief but fascinating Civil War era illustration of how difficult it can be for military officers "on the ground" to carry out orders set in faraway locales by their superiors.

Early Northern justifications for the armed suppression of the rebellion focused on preserving the Union rather than on granting freedom for the millions of black men and women held in bondage in the Confederacy. Early Federal wartime policies toward slavery in occupied territory reassured slaveholders that their property would be safe even as their communities fell under Union control. From President Lincoln on down, most Federal officials hoped to encourage southern Unionists, to keep Border States from seceding, and to avoid inflaming racist Northern public opinion. When a few Union commanders such as David Hunter in South Carolina or John Freemont in Missouri tried to do more by

Capt. Alanson B. Long issued this circular in an attempt to clarify U.S. policies about slavery and emancipation.

National Archives, Records of U.S. Army Continental Commands, 1821–1920

CIRCULAR.

New Iberia, La., April 24, 1863.

The generally received impression, that the slaves of this Parish, are free, by force of the presence of the Union army, *is erroneous.*

This Parish, (St. Martin) is excepted by name, in the Emancipation Proclamation, of President Lincoln, issued at Washington, D. C., January 1, 1863.

No farther interference, with the institution of slavery will be allowed by the Army Authorities, than may necessarily result from the police regulations.

United States Army Officers, are forbidden, by law of Congress, to use force in the restoration of slaves to masters.

If slaves flee from their masters, they must work on Government works, receiving therefor, full rations, for full day's work.

If slaves voluntarily return to their masters, they will not be molested.

If masters use force, in abducting run-away slaves, the masters will be arrested.

If masters inhumanly punish or whip their slaves, they must be arrested.

No punishment of slaves, will be permitted, except such as are practiced in the Army.

A. B. LONG,
Capt., & Provost Marshal,
Commanding Post.

freeing slaves in their jurisdictions, President Lincoln reversed their orders.

Confusion in Louisiana

An early test of this conciliatory approach came in Louisiana. On April 28, 1862, New Orleans surrendered to U.S. naval forces. The city's new military commander, Gen. Benjamin F. Butler, informed citizens that "all forms of property of whatever kind, will be held inviolate." He put slaves seized from disloyal owners to work on Federal projects, but he also left unemployable runaways subject to the "ordinary laws of the community." Nevertheless, over the next few weeks hundreds of slaves ran for the protection of Federal lines. Over the next year the slave system continued to teeter as Confederate plantation owners abandoned their lands and slaves and as Union soldiers sympathetic to abolition protected runaways, and Federal raiders seized more slaves than could be employed—including women, old people, and children. Lincoln's Emancipation Proclamation of January 1, 1863, only confused the situation in Louisiana, because it specifically exempted some parishes from its scope.

The Federal occupation of Louisiana and the Emancipation Proclamation raised several questions for Northern officers:

- Who was free, and who remained a slave?
- How should black people be employed?
- What were the rights of slaves and the rights of owners?
- Who would care for the sick and the infirm?
- Who would punish lawbreaking or unruly ex-slaves?

Enter Capt. Alanson B. Long

One man who grappled with these questions was Capt. Alanson B. Long of the 52nd Massachusetts Infantry. Long was an unlikely soldier. Born in 1835, he grew up on a farm in northern Massachusetts, graduated from Dartmouth College, and enrolled in Harvard Law School. But at 24, Alanson was "smitten with paralysis" and left school. Over many months, he recovered enough to make sea voyages that improved his health. He took a job as high school principal, then enlisted for nine months with the newly formed 52nd. He was chosen captain of Company A.

The 52nd Massachusetts traveled to New York City, then by ship to New Orleans, and finally up the Mississippi River to Baton Rouge, where it landed on December 17, 1862. Initially, the 52nd spent most of its time bivouacked, foraging for food and enduring epidemics of typhoid fever and measles that would sicken 80–90 men and kill dozens. But it also carried out a number of "expeditions" into Confederate-held territory, burning plantations owned by rebels and looking to "gobble up" caches of weapons, cotton, sugar, molasses, and livestock to ship to New Orleans.

It was during one of the largest of these expeditions that Captain Long found himself in the middle of emancipation policy. On April 15, 1863, after days of skirmishing with retreating rebels, the 52nd occupied the small town of New Iberia in St. Martin Parish. Four companies, including Company A, were ordered to stay in town while the rest of

TO THE PEOPLE
OF THE
TRANS-MISS. DEPARTMENT.

Office Chief Quartermaster, Trans-Miss. Department.
Shreveport, La., September 15th, 1863.

In this struggle for all that makes life desirable; as a band of brothers we must stand shoulder to shoulder, be true to ourselves, sacrifice freely, and never give up.

Do this, and we are, and will remain freemen; decline to do it, and we will be subjugated, our property wrested from us, and our country lost. Nothing can be gained by submission. By Lincoln's law you are told your property is confiscated, yourselves are rebels, and that "rebels have no rights."

Your country needs labor, as well as men to fight. The negro men our enemies would arm against us, can be well employed as teamsters, cooks, mechanics and laborers; better then, far better to let the Government have them than the enemy. They will be well cared for, and a fair compensation paid for their services. You cheerfully yield your children to your country, how can you refuse to hire your servants?

We appeal to the slave holders of the Trans-Mississippi Department generally, and particularly to that portion of the Department likely to be visited by the enemy in any raid he may make, to let the Government have their able-bodied men, thereby saving them from falling into the hands of our enemies, and enabling the Lieut. Gen'l Commanding, to place in the ranks thousands of men now employed as teamsters, laborers, etc., for want of other labor for that service.

The Government requires from two to three thousand laborers. and the Chief Quartermasters of the Districts of Arkansas, Louisiana and Texas will receive them; any one person or neighborhood furnishing twenty able-bodied men, can designate a person to take charge of them, who will be employed by the Government for that purpose.

The Government will pay for any servants that may be killed by the enemy, but will not be responsible for those that die from disease, or run away. Any person wishing to furnish hands under this call, will please address the Chief Quartermasters of the Districts of Arkansas, Louisiana or Texas, or the undersigned, setting forth the number he will furnish, and steps will be taken at once to receive them. None but able-bodied men received.

J. F. MINTER,
Major and Chief Quartermaster, Trans-Miss. Dept.

Caddo Gazette Print.)

For the Confederate Quartermaster of the "Trans-Mississippi Department," slaves were source of labor to be exploited. They needed to be protected from Union raids such as the one that Capt. Alanson Long accompanied. This broadside promises slave owners compensation for contributing their slaves to the cause, asking: "You cheerfully yield your children to your country, how can you refuse to hire your servants?"

National Archives, War Department Collection of Confederate Records

the regiment continued its march up the Bayou Teche. Long was appointed provost marshal and commander. As provost marshal, he was in charge of relations between civilians and the U.S. Army in New Iberia as well as the surrounding area—including touchy questions about the status and treatment of black people and the rights of their owners.

Captain Long took his new duties very seriously and plunged into the murky waters of U.S. Government policy on slavery and emancipation. On April 24, 1863, Long issued a one-page "Circular" to the community outlining what he understood to be the Government positions on a variety of issues.

Interpreting the Policies
Long's circular is a seemingly contradictory series of statements concerning U.S. policies. It began by pointing out that despite "the generally received impression," slaves in St. Martin Parish were not free either by "the presence of the Union army" or by the Emancipation Proclamation. In fact, St. Martin had been specifically exempted "by name" from the Proclamation. The Army would carry out "no further interference, with the institution of slavery" except for "police regulations." Long then backed away from the implications inherent in carrying out such a strict policy. Slaves, for instance, might voluntarily return to their masters, but the Army could not "use force in the restoration of slaves to masters." Nor could masters "use force" to kidnap slaves or "inhumanely punish or whip" them. In fact, "no punishment of slaves, will be permitted, except such as are practiced in the Army." Masters who tried these tactics faced arrest.

Although Captain Long was trying to clear up public confusion with his circular, he—like many Northern soldiers—was uncertain about what he was supposed to do. On April 23 and April 30, he wrote two letters to the Provost Marshal General's office inquiring about policies "with regard to citizens, property, and slaves," and outlining "the perplexities of my position." He admitted he "perhaps" failed to understand Federal policy. He had always "encouraged the idea of freedom among slaves," but he had not realized that the Emancipation Proclamation had exempted St. Martin Parish from its provisions.

For Long, freedom-seeking slaves had become "a continual source of anxiety and trouble." For example, the Confederate government had brought in many slaves from outside the area to work "on gunboats and arsenals etc." Now free, they wanted to go home. Long was letting them leave. But he knew that the Union needed their labor to "prosecute govt works that can not be completed with out their aid." He asked, "are they to be advised to return to their masters or compelled"? Furthermore, those who stayed to work for the government needed food, clothing, and shelter. To make matters worse, "armed bands of negroes" were roaming the countryside, inciting "insurrections," committing "depredations," and bringing whites to "a state of fear and anxiety."

Implementing the Policies
In his first request for instructions, Long asked, "What policy shall be pursued now towards the hundred who come flocking here?" It was a question with no simple answer. That may explain why the captain never received a response. He did, however, try to put into practice his understanding of Federal policy.

- He attempted, when he could, "to return [slaves] to their masters (if they wish to)," but he also tried to feed and clothe former slaves who were "willing laborers for the Gov't."
- He arrested and imprisoned a white man who shot "a Negro boy." But he also endorsed an expedition by the 22nd Maine to punish some of the black "rioters" who had terrorized the white inhabitants of the parish.
- Long may have also sent men from the 52nd to a nearby town where whites had fought and disarmed a group of blacks. Local citizens hanged the 10 black leaders of the group.

Long's "perplexities," at least for him, were soon resolved. The companies under his command left the town on May 13, stopping along the way at plantations where they would "get all we wanted to eat" because residents feared "they would do worse" than just confiscate food. They were accompanied by 1,200 blacks. Their status as freedpeople may not have been legal, but it was established de facto because of the Federal Government's desire to deprive the rebels of manpower and its own need for labor and troops. Many of these former slaves were gathered into large "labor depots" and probably ended up working on large Government-run plantations.

And what of Capt. Alanson Long? The 52nd's only major engagement was in June 1863 at Fort Donalson, where Alanson won praise for leaving his sickbed and walking six miles to lead his men. By August he was back in Greenfield and would stay in New England for a few years, studying law. Then he returned to New Orleans, passed the bar, and was eventually appointed U.S. District Attorney for Louisiana. On October 30, 1876, his still fragile health betrayed him, and he died.

NOTE ON SOURCES
Capt. Alanson B. Long's Compiled Military Service Record in Records of the Adjutant General's Office, 1780's-1917, Record Group (RG) 94, is very brief, containing only the barest facts about his career with the 52nd. Long's Circular and his two letters to the Provost Marshal can be found in Part 1, Provost Marshal Records of the Department of the Gulf, Records of U.S. Army Commands, 1821-1920, RG 393. The circular is reproduced in Ira Berlin, et al., Freedom: A Documentary History of Emancipation, 1861-1867, Series 1, Vol. 1, The Destruction of Slavery (Cambridge, 1985), p. 244. J. F. Moors's History of the Fifty-second Regiment Massachusetts Volunteers (Boston, 1893) describes the regiment's time in Louisiana and includes letters from soldiers who stayed in New Iberia with Captain Long. While somewhat dated, C. Peter Ripley's Slaves and Freedmen in Civil War Louisiana (Baton Rouge, 1976) remains a good starting point for the history of the Union occupation of Louisiana.

Sir

    Understanding that your army is advancing on this Capitol I have to request under proper safe conduct, a personal interview at such time as may be agreeable to you, for the purpose of con upon the subject of a Suspension of hostilities, with a view to further communications with the authorities of the United States touching the final termination of the existing war.

    If you concur in the propriety of such a proceeding, I shall be obliged by an early reply

        with high respect

        Your obedient Servant

Genl. Wm. T. Sherman
   Commanding United States Forces   Z. B. Vance

CHAPTER 11

ENDINGS AND BEGINNINGS

At the end of the Civil War, the South lay devastated. Many of its people were refugees. About 250,000 Confederate soldiers had died. And 4 million newly freed people were living alongside their former owners.

Many Americans—North and South—desired reconciliation. But there were no guidelines on how to create a new social, political, and economic order.

- How did the South begin to rebuild itself?
- How did former slaves begin to shape their lives as free people?
- What role did the Federal Government play?

Here is some of the evidence that tells us about this complicated and controversial era.

END OF HOSTILITIES

When Robert E. Lee surrendered at Appomattox on April 9, 1865, there were still Confederate armies in the Trans-Mississippi, Alabama, and North Carolina. Days later, North Carolina Governor Zebulon Vance wrote to Union Gen. William T. Sherman requesting a "personal interview" to end hostilities. In the confusion of the ensuing days, Vance never received a reply. On April 17, however, General Sherman and Confederate Gen. Joseph E. Johnston met and negotiated both the surrender of Johnston's army and peace terms.

National Archives, Records of the Adjutant General's Office, 1780's–1917

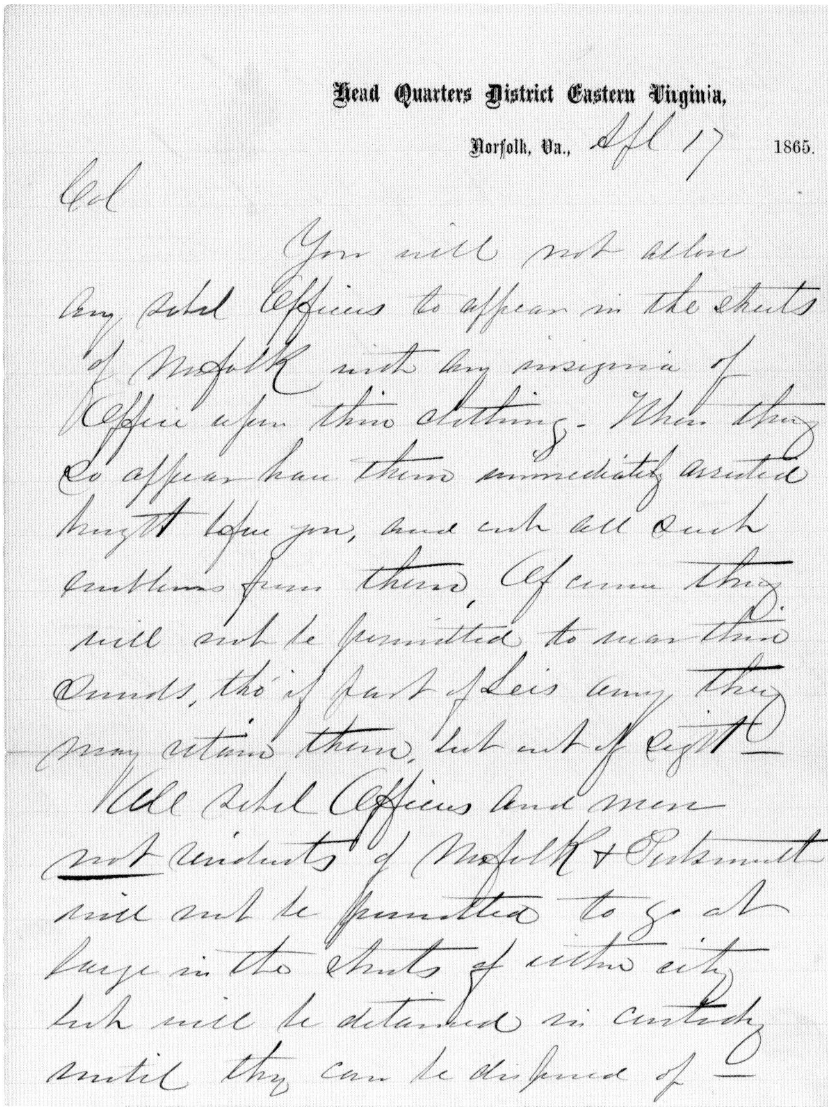

Head Quarters District Eastern Virginia,

Norfolk, Va., *Apl 17* 1865.

Col

You will not allow any rebel Officers to appear in the streets of Norfolk with any insignia of Office upon their clothing. When they do appear have them immediately arrested & brought before you, and cut all such emblems from them. Of course they will not be permitted to wear them Arms, tho' if part of Lee's army they may retain them, but out of sight—

All rebel Officers and men not residents of Norfolk & Portsmouth will not be permitted to go at large in the streets of either city but will be detained in custody until they can be disposed of—

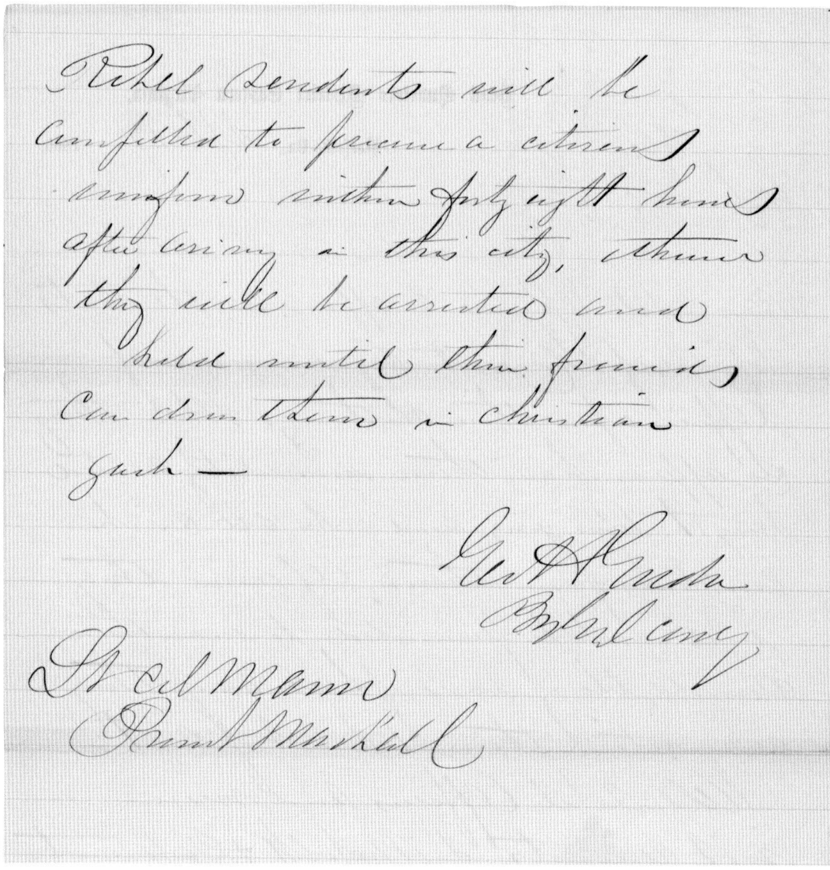

Rebel residents will be compelled to procure a citizens uniform within forty eight hours after arriving in this city, otherwise they will be arrested and held until their friends can dress them in christian garb—

Geo H Gordon
Bvt Maj Genl

Lt Col Mann
Provost Marshall

CONFEDERATE
INSIGNIA BANNED

After the surrender at Appomattox, and particularly after Lincoln's assassination, the U.S. Army's Department of Eastern Virginia moved to establish its authority over the former Confederate-held areas. This April 17, 1865, letter from the Department's commanding general instructs former Confederate officers in Norfolk, Virginia, not to wear "any insignia of office."

National Archives, Records of U.S. Army Continental Commands, 1821–1920

Robert E. Lee without his insignia, April 20, 1865

National Archives, Records of the Office of the Chief Signal Officer [111-B-1564]

Soon after taking office, President Andrew Johnson issued proclamations appointing provisional governors in each state and requiring that each state hold constitutional conventions to rewrite their prewar constitutions. This Proclamation for Florida, dated July 13, 1865, appointed William Marvin as Provisional Governor and ordered Floridians to take the actions necessary to obtain "the enjoyment of a Republican form of Government."

National Archives, General Records of the U.S. Government

BY THE PRESIDENT OF THE UNITED STATES OF AMERICA:
A PROCLAMATION.

WHEREAS, the 4th Section of the 4th Article of the Constitution of the United States declares that the United States shall guarantee to every State in the Union, a Republican form of Government, and shall protect each of them against invasion and domestic violence, and, *Whereas*, the President of the United States is, by the Constitution, made Commander-in-Chief of the Army and Navy, as well as Chief Civil Executive Officer of the United States, and is bound by solemn oath faithfully to execute the office of President of the United States, and to take care that the laws be faithfully executed; and, *Whereas*, The rebellion, which has been waged by a portion of the people of the United States against the properly constituted authorities of the Government thereof, in the most violent and revolting form, but whose organized and armed forces have now been almost entirely overcome, has, in its revolutionary progress, deprived the people of the State of *Florida*, of all Civil Government; and, *Whereas*, it becomes necessary and proper to carry out and enforce the obligations of the United States to the people of *Florida* in securing them in the enjoyment of a Republican form of Government:—

Now, THEREFORE, in obedience to the high and solemn duties imposed upon me by the Constitution of the United States, and for the purpose of enabling the loyal people of said State to organize a State Government, whereby justice may be established, domestic tranquility ensured, and loyal citizens protected in all their rights of life, liberty and property, I, ANDREW JOHNSON, President of the United States, and Commander-in-Chief of the Army and Navy of the United States, do hereby appoint *William Marvin* Provisional Governor of the State of *Florida*, whose duty it shall be, at the earliest practicable period, to prescribe such rules and regulations as may be necessary and proper for convening a Convention, composed of delegates to be chosen by that portion of the people of said State, who are loyal to the United States, and no others, for the purpose of altering or amending the Constitution thereof; and with authority to exercise, within the limits of said State, all the powers necessary and proper to enable such loyal people of the State of *Florida* to restore said State to its constitutional relations to the Federal Government, and to present such a Republican form of State Government as will entitle the State to the guarantee of the United States therefor, and its people to protection by the United States against invasion, insurrection, and domestic violence: *Provided that*, in any election that may be hereafter held for choosing delegates to any State Convention as aforesaid, no person shall be qualified as an elector, or shall be eligible as a member of such Convention, unless he shall have previously taken and subscribed the oath of amnesty, as set forth in the President's Proclamation of May 29th, A. D., 1865, and is a voter qualified as prescribed by the Constitution and laws of the State of *Florida*, in force immediately before the *tenth day of January* A. D., 1861, the date of the so-called ordinance of Secession; and the said Convention when convened, or the Legislature that may be thereafter assembled, will prescribe the qualification of electors, and the eligibility of persons to hold office under the constitution and laws of the State, a power the people of the several States composing the Federal Union have rightfully exercised from the origin of the Government to the present time.

FREEDMEN'S BUREAU

The Bureau of Refugees, Freedmen, and Abandoned Lands—also known as the Freedmen's Bureau—was established in March 1865. Bureau agents, who were often the only Federal presence in Southern communities, focused on overseeing the establishment of a paid labor system. They also provided food, medicine, clothing, shelter, and education to former slaves.

This illustration of the Office of the Freedmen's Bureau in Memphis, Tennessee, was published in *Harper's Weekly* on June 2, 1866.

Courtesy of the Chicago History Museum
(ICHi-61620)

OFFICE OF THE FREEDMEN'S BUREAU, MEMPHIS, TENNESSEE.

SEPARATED FOREVER?

As one consequence of slavery and war, many former slaves, including children, were separated from their families. Freedpeople traveled far and wide searching for their relatives. Although reunions did happen, many quests ended in failure. This roster of orphans, all under the age of 12, notes that five of the children's parents were "lost" during the war.

National Archives, Records of the Bureau of Refugees, Freedmen, and Abandoned Lands

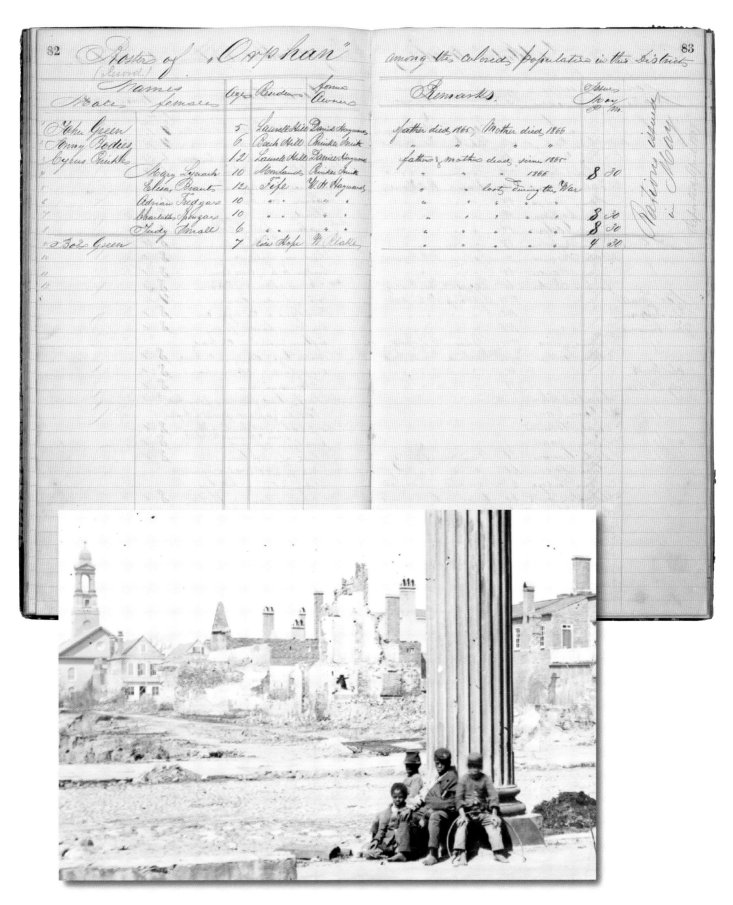

"View of ruined buildings through porch of circular church, Charleston, South Carolina, April 14, 1865"   DETAIL

Courtesy of the Library of Congress (cwpb 03049)

Office of Bureau of Refugees Freedmen &c
for Robeson Co
Lumberton Aug 28th 1865

This instrument witnesseth that Robert Mc Kenzie of Robeson Co agrees to pay Truss B. Hall $4.00 per month until 25th day of December next for and in consideration of the said Truss B. Hall rendering the Robert McKenzie true and faithful service and obey all lawful commands as he use to when a slave.

Robert McKenzie

Witnessed and approved
James Sinclair agent of Bureau.

Truss B. Hall his mark

FREE LABOR
SYSTEM?

Thousands of acres of land lay fallow after the war, and many former slaves lived and worked on former plantations. The Freedmen's Bureau helped freedmen arrange labor contracts and negotiate fair wages for steady work. This contract, for example, dated August 28, 1865, obligated Robert McKenzie to pay former slave Truss B. Hall for a set period of time and for a set monthly wage.

National Archives, Records of the Bureau of Refugees, Freedmen, and Abandoned Lands

ENSURING
FREEDMEN'S
RIGHTS

During the first two years after the Confederate surrender, Southern states tried to limit the rights of freedmen through laws known as "Black Codes." In response, Congress passed several Reconstruction Acts starting in March 1867. The Freedmen's Bureau distributed this May 1 circular in the Richmond area. It instructed officers and agents to inform freedmen of their rights, especially their right to vote.

National Archives, Records of the Bureau of Refugees, Freedmen, and Abandoned Lands

Bureau of Refugees, Freedmen and Abandoned Lands,

Head Quarters Assistant Commissioner, State of Virginia.

RICHMOND, VA., May 1st, 1867.

CIRCULAR NO. 9.

Officers and Agents of this Bureau will take care that the Freedmen, within their respective jurisdictions, are made acquainted with their rights under the Act of Congress " to provide for the more efficient government of the Rebel States," and the Act supplementary thereto, passed respectively, March 2nd, and March 23rd, 1867.

2. Such measures will be taken as will inform all Freedmen entitled to be registered, of the necessity for, and the time and place of registration, and of the time and place of voting. They will also be instructed that, as they will not be allowed to suffer from the honest exercise of the right of suffrage, they should disregard all threats or undue influence tending to prevent or restrain the same.

Prompt report will be made to the President of the local Board of Registration of any case in which the rights of a Freedman, under the above-mentioned Acts, are withheld or interfered with.

By order of Brevet Brigadier General O. BROWN,

Assistant Commissioner.

GARRICK MALLERY.

Captain 43rd Infantry, A. A. A. G.

OFFICIAL

Acting Assistant Adjutant General.

[ED. FORM. No. 5.]

MONTHLY REPORT of Schools, Teachers, Societies, Pupils, and Buildings, called for by Circular Letter of October 6, 1868, from Commissioner Bureau R., F., and A.L.   State of *Virginia*, Month of *March*, 1869.

Location of School.	Name of Teacher.	Under what patronage.	No. Pupils.	No. Buildings.	Owner of Building.
Accomac Co.					
Pungateague	Lucinda H. Spivey	American M. Assoc	55	1	Freedmen.
Onancock	Phoebe A. Henson	—do— do—	06	1	—do—
Drummondtown	D. P. Allen	—do— do—	45	1	Bureau R. F. + A L.
Bridgton	H. A. Orcutt	—do— do—	56	1	Freedmen.
Albemarle Co					
Charlottesville	Anna Gardner	N. England B.F.M. Com.	27		
—do—	Philena Carkin	—do— do—	54	1	Bureau R. F. + A. L.
—do—	Isabella Gibbons	—do— do—	49		
—do—	Paul Lewis	—do— do—	58		
Augusta Co					
Staunton	John Scott / Miss S. H. Davison	American M. Assoc.	60		
—do—	Margaret Burk	—do— do—	41	1	Freedmen

Asst.-Com., and Supt. Education.

FOCUS ON EDUCATION

Before the war, most Southern states had laws against educating slaves. The Freedmen's Bureau and Northern benevolent societies invested heavily in education. They established and supported day, evening, Sunday, and industrial schools. Education was a high priority within black communities. Even poor communities often provided land and pay for schools and teachers.

This monthly education report, dated March 1869, is from Virginia.

National Archives, Records of the Bureau of Refugees, Freedmen, and Abandoned Lands

Interior of a freedmen's school with an African American teacher, ca. 1870

Courtesy of the Library of Congress

Senator Hiram Rhodes Revels. ca. 1870

National Archives, Records of the U.S. Information Agency
(306-PSE-77-875)

FIRST AFRICAN AMERICAN SENATOR

An educator and minister, Hiram Rhodes Revels was born free in
North Carolina. In 1870 he became the first African American elected
to the United States Senate. He occupied the same seat vacated by
Jefferson Davis almost 10 years earlier. After serving in the Senate,
he was named president of Alcorn College, Mississippi's first college
for African American students.

National Archives, Records of the U.S. Senate

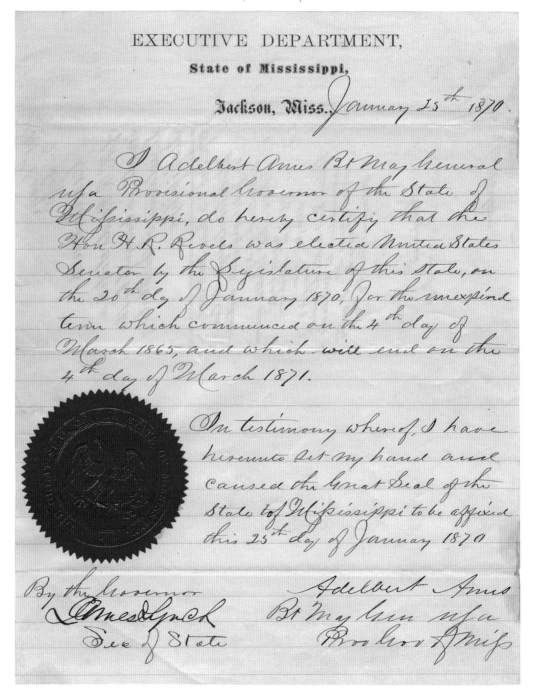

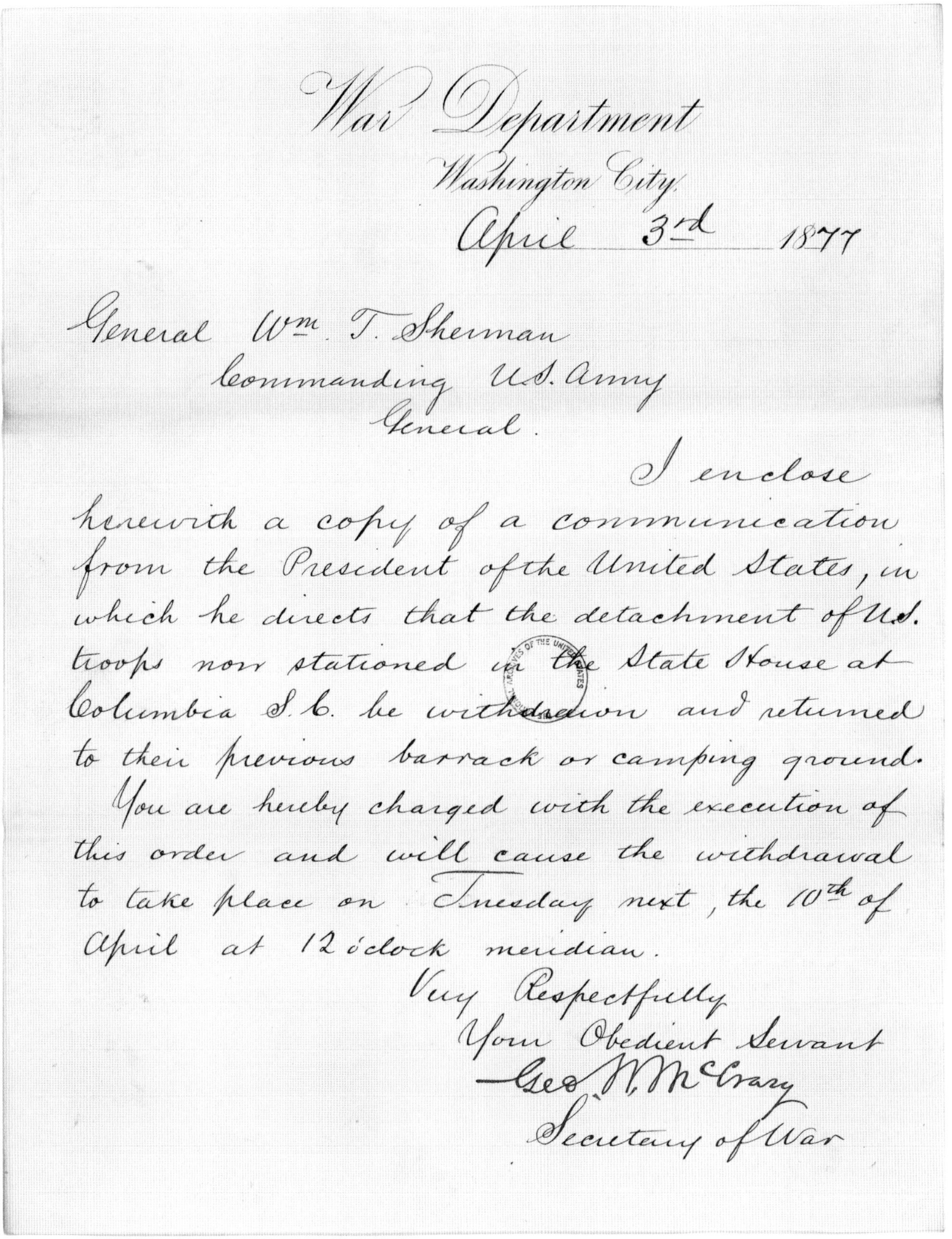

War Department
Washington City,
April 3rd 1877

General W^m. T. Sherman
Commanding U.S. Army
General.

I enclose herewith a copy of a communication from the President of the United States, in which he directs that the detachment of U.S. troops now stationed in the State House at Columbia S.C. be withdrawn and returned to their previous barrack or camping ground.

You are hereby charged with the execution of this order and will cause the withdrawal to take place on Tuesday next, the 10th of April at 12 o'clock meridian.

Very Respectfully
Your Obedient Servant
Geo. W. McCrary
Secretary of War

OCCUPATION ENDS

In this letter, Secretary of War George W. McCrary ordered Gen. William T. Sherman, Commander of the U.S. Army, to pull the remaining troops out of South Carolina. The letter is dated April 3, 1877—12 years after the war ended. It signaled the end of Federal occupation in the South. South Carolina, the first state to secede from the Union, was one of the last states from which troops withdrew.

National Archives, Records of the Adjutant General's Office, 1780's–1917

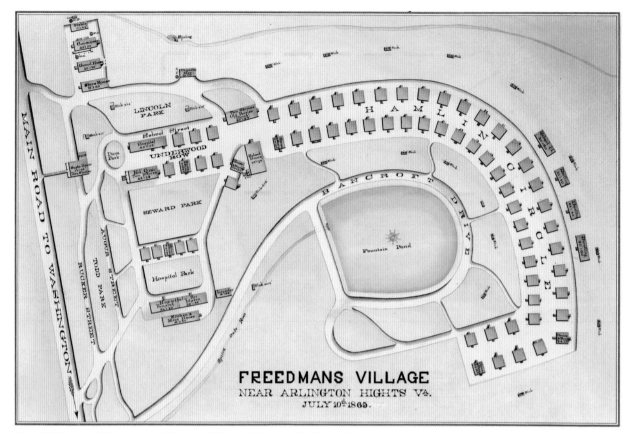

This 1865 plan of "Freedmans Village [sic]", near Arlington, Virginia, reflects an idealized vision of what the community would look like.   *National Archives, Records of the Office of the Quartermaster General*

Freedmen's Village

One result of the 1862 abolition of slavery in the District of Columbia was an influx of enslaved people into the District, especially from Maryland and Virginia. These freedom seekers needed food, shelter, and work. As the black population in Washington, DC, grew, the U.S. Army set up a camp for freedpeople on the abandoned estate of Robert E. Lee just across the Potomac River in Arlington, Virginia. Named Freedmen's Village, its male residents were expected to work for pay on the defenses of the city, while its women sewed uniforms and worked the village gardens and fields.

With the end of war, control of Freedmen's Village passed from the Army to the Freedmen's Bureau. By 1866, almost 1,000 people called it home. What had been intended as a temporary camp became a thriving community with 50 dwellings, churches, a school, a hospital, and a home for the needy. This showcase for the results of emancipation continued to grow, but relations between the Government and residents were often strained.

In 1883 the property became a military reservation. For the next decade its residents were pressured to leave by the Government and by developers. By 1900 those residents remaining had to vacate their homes.

This drawing of Freedmen's Village, with a black Union soldier in the foreground, appeared in an 1864 issue of *Harper's Weekly*. Freedmen's Village was the best known of all the camps for newly freed people around the country because of its location on the Lee family plantation.   *Courtesy of the Library of Congress*

VIOLENCE IN TEXAS
Jennifer N. Johnson

As the South worked to rebuild itself, the Freedmen's Bureau struggled to help newly freed men and women achieve their rights despite an outpouring of violent crimes.

For the South, the end of the Civil War in April 1865 was also a beginning. A whole new social, economic, and political order had to be established. There was no guidebook, no consensus on how to rebuild. As former slaves tried to define their new status, defeated Southerners were negotiating their new situation with the Federal Government—all in an environment of uncertainty, resentment, and devastation. As Frederick Douglass said:

> Verily, the work does not end with the abolition of slavery, but only begins.

The Freedmen's Bureau

To help former slaves make the transition to freedom, a temporary Federal agency was established in March 1865. The Bureau of Refugees, Freedmen, and Abandoned Lands (also known as The Freedmen's Bureau) was the main Federal presence in the South, along with the troops still stationed there. Organized under the War Department, the Freedmen's Bureau was meant to serve as a coordinated national program of relief. Its goal was to help freedpeople achieve independence and realize their rights, so they did not remain in "some sort of limbo between slavery and freedom." Bureau agents were responsible for putting into practice directives from headquarters, in faraway Washington, DC, about fair wages and equal rights. This was very difficult work. Most agents were not welcome in the areas they were assigned. To some whites the Freedmen's Bureau represented tyranny and corruption. To former slaves, however, the local Freedmen's Bureau office was one of the few places they could turn for help or a sympathetic ear.

There were often sharp differences of opinion between white Southerners, the Freedmen's Bureau, and newly freedpeople about who should control the South's future. Some whites used intimidation and violence to control and terrorize former slaves. Freedmen's Bureau agents had little power to punish—or to make local authorities punish—the perpetrators. The best they could do was to record the instances of violence in their reports and send them to headquarters. Those responsible for the violence against freedpeople, or against sympathetic whites, were rarely held accountable.

Volumes of Violence

Freedmen's Bureau records in the National Archives contain reports of murders and "outrages" from nearly every state in which the Bureau operated. Some of the most shocking and graphic examples are contained in three volumes from Texas titled "Criminal Offenses Committed in the State of Texas." The three volumes record more than 2,000 acts of violence between 1865 and 1868.

The volumes are filled with details about each particular crime, the names and race of the perpetrator and victim, where the crime was committed, and any action taken by the Bureau or local authorities. Agents described crimes ranging from aggravated assault to murder. There were occasional acts of violence against whites, but most of the violence recorded was committed by white males on freedmen. Among the offenses in the volume are more than 1,500 violent acts committed by white men on freedmen, and just a few dozen committed by freedmen on whites.

Because of its size and Confederate leanings, Texas posed especially difficult challenges for the Army and the Freedmen's Bureau in their efforts to establish order and enforce the law. Bureau agents, who often acted alone, faced resistance and even open hostility from whites. They had difficulty getting local authorities to back them up—a fact often noted in reports to Washington.

- In one entry, an agent recorded that civil authorities had "tried and fined one cent!!!" a white man who "assaulted and maltreated" a freedman.

- In another entry, a 14-year-old boy was murdered. The action taken by civil authorities was recorded as "no bill found by grand jury."

Other crimes were "dismissed" or had "no action taken." In some localities, hostility toward agents included physical attacks, gunfights, and even assassinations.

It had been a painful and costly war. Some whites used violence to discipline former slaves who sought political, economic, or social equality. Other incidents seemed to be completely random. One agent recorded:

> A deliberate and cold-blooded murder. No provocation whatever except that the freedman objected to have his wife whipped. The father and son almost quarreled as to who should shoot him for the insult!!!

No.	DATE OF REGISTRY Period Given	County offence Committed in	NAMES Name of Criminal	Race	Nature of Offence	Name of party injured	Law PREC
236	Houston	Harris	Jno McCoy	White	Kicking a woman	Mackey	Black twin
237	Houston	Montgomery	Caughey Campbell	White	Beating one, bad welts—arms &c. seldom with heavy stick	—	Black
238	Houston	Montgomery	Jno Rodgers	White	Beating on his back, badly bruising	Jno Bonegil	Black
239	Houston	Montgomery	Saml Kaydue	White	Beating one on neck & shoulders with heavy stick	Charlotte Lee	Black
240	Houston	Harris	James Catton	White	Beating woman over the head with club	Mrs ham	Black
241	Houston	Brazoria	Jno Huston	White	Beating woman with pine on her face & shoulders	L Grey	Black & two
242	Houston	Harris	Christy & Hullock	White	Assault & Batty	Washington	Black
243	Houston	Harris	Jno Janaway	White	Cutting with a hatchet	William	Black
244	Houston	Polk	J Smith	White	Shooting	G.B	Black
245	Houston	Polk	J Smith	White	Fracturing Skull	J Hopkins	Black
246	Houston	Harris	Buck Hanson & Tethas	White	Assault & Batty	Duncan	Black
247	Houston	Jefferson	Citizens	White	Homicide	Chas Hemming	White

Labor, Politics, and Society

O. O. Howard, commissioner of the Freedmen's Bureau, believed there were plenty of opportunities for work for newly freed people. He therefore charged his agents to help arrange paid labor contracts. But these contracts could not reorganize the labor system or change attitudes about what fair wages meant. Whites used violence to discipline blacks for not working fast enough, for sickness, or for perceived laziness or carelessness. In Upsher County, Ann Ship, a freedwoman, was "whipped twice about 100 lashes in all—because [her employer] thought she didn't hoe fast enough." Some whites did not approve of freed people seeking work elsewhere. In Davis County, "a gang of men (white) went round and whipped all Freedmen who would not make contracts."

Political participation for black men, like many of the Bureau's goals, was seen by most whites as temporary until the Federal Government moved out. Shortly after the war, "Black Codes" were passed throughout the South restricting African Americans' economic and political rights. Blacks who tried to vote, organize, or hold meetings were vulnerable to violence or intimidation. Bureau agents had limited success policing such crimes and usually depended on the availability of nearby U.S. Army troops to arrest and prosecute those who carried out such acts.

Southern whites also fiercely protected traditional social mores, retaliating swiftly when they were broken. The way a freedman addressed a former master, the speed with which he or she obeyed, or the attendance of a freedman at a church or celebration could all incite brutality. In Marion County, an agent described the homicide of a freedman like this: "a cold blooded murder—no provocation—was shot because he didn't stand to attention while the desperado was passing." The agent also recorded that no action was taken by the civil authorities after he himself had tried, but failed, to arrest him.

Surrounded by poverty, devastation, and widespread destitution, postwar Southerners were often overwhelmed by the task of rebuilding society and creating a new order. The atmosphere throughout the South was volatile. Some white

Freedmen's Bureau agents compiled this volume over the course of three years, recording descriptions of violence committed in Texas from September 1865 though December 1868.

National Archives, Records of the Bureau of Refugees, Freedmen, and Abandoned Lands

Southerners were protective of their antebellum status. Freedpeople were hungry to build new lives. Bureau agents, under pressure and acting alone, could not themselves manage the mountain of resentment felt by some white Southerners. As the three Texas volumes document, this conflict of expectations often created an atmosphere that was turbulent and violent.

NOTE ON SOURCES

The reports of violence in this article are from the National Archives Freedmen's Bureau records, Criminal Offences Committed in the State of Texas, Vol. 1 of 3, Assistant Commissioner, Austin, Texas, Records of the Bureau of Refugees, Freedmen, and Abandoned Lands, Record Group 105. An article that was invaluable to me and provided the statistical information was "A Spirit of Lawlessness: White Violence; Texas Blacks, 1865–1868," by Barry A. Crouch, *Journal of Social History* 18, No. 2 (Winter 1984) 217–32. Other sources include Eric Foner's *Reconstruction, 1863–1877* (New York, 1988); Paul A. Cimbala's *The Freedmen's Bureau: Reconstructing the American South after the Civil War* (Florida, 2005); Paul A. Cimbala and Randall M. Miller's *The Freedmen's Bureau and Reconstruction* (New York, 1999), and "Rights and the Constitution in Black Life during the Civil War and Reconstruction," by Eric Foner, *Journal of American History* 74, No. 3 (Dec. 1978), 863–88.

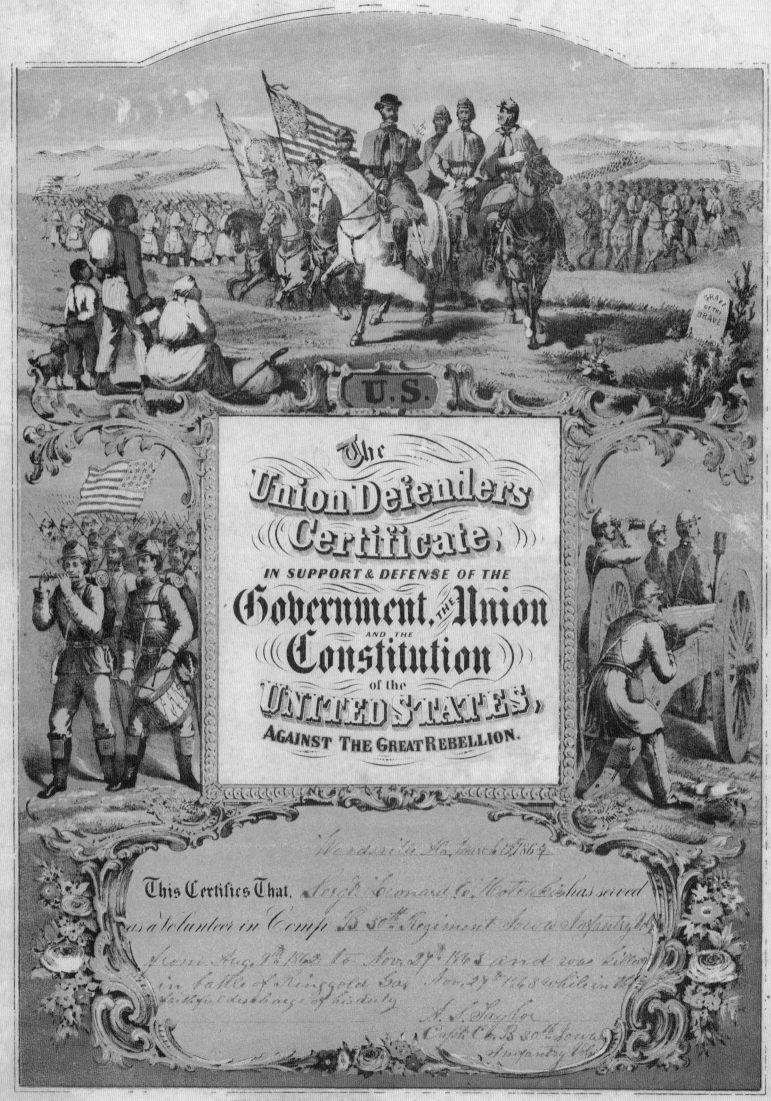

CHAPTER 12

REMEMBERING

Even before the Civil War ended, Americans sought ways to give it meaning and purpose. This remembering took many forms, including books, monuments, cemeteries, and commemorative events. Later generations continued to look back—sometimes selectively, and especially during moments of crisis.

- How have Americans remembered the war's military campaigns and battlefield sacrifices?
- How have we recalled the war's causes and political furies?

Witness some of the many different ways the Civil War has been remembered by exploring these documents from the vaults of the National Archives.

PROOF OF UNION SERVICE

In 1862 the U.S. Congress passed legislation granting monthly pensions to dependent mothers whose sons died while serving in the Armed Forces. Hannah Hotchkiss's son, Leonard, died while serving with Company B of the 30th Iowa Infantry. When Hotchkiss applied for a pension, she included this colorful "Union Defenders Certificate" signed by Leonard's commanding officer as proof of his Federal service.

National Archives, Records of the Department of Veterans Affairs

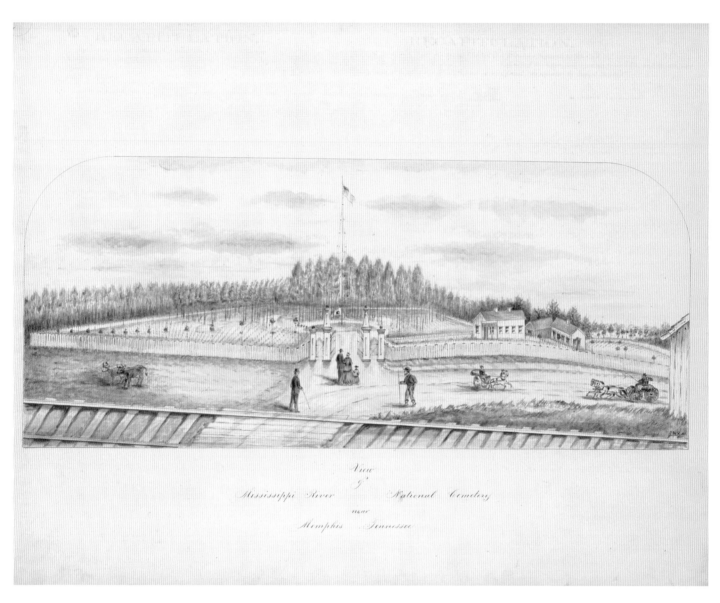

View 9

Mississippi River National Cemetery near Memphis Tennessee

NATIONAL CEMETERIES

In March 1865, Edmund B. Whitman of the U.S. Army's Quartermaster Corps began a survey "to locate the scattered graves of Union soldiers." Over the next four years Whitman and those under his command traveled through Kentucky, Tennessee, Georgia, Mississippi, and Alabama. They located, disinterred, and reburied almost 115,000 bodies.

In his *Final Report,* Whitman included drawings of several of the 20 new national cemeteries constructed for the Union dead. This one is of Mississippi River National Cemetery in Tennessee, which is now renamed Memphis National Cemetery.

National Archives, Records of the Office of Quartermaster General

N. B. Forrest Camp, No. 4
United Confederate Veterans

L. T. DICKINSON
ADJUTANT

Chattanooga, Tenn._____ April 3rd, 1906

Resolved by N. B. Forrest Camp No. 4 U. C. V. at Chattanooga, Tennessee, that the thanks of this Camp be and they are hereby tendered to Senator J. B. Foraker, the Congress of the United States and to the President for their generous course in passing and approving the act known as the Foraker Act providing for the location and marking of the graves of Confederate prisoners of war who died in prison and were buried near the places where they died.

Resolved, Second, that a copy of this resolution be sent by the adjutant of this camp to Senator J. B. Foraker and one to Representative John A. Moon for presentation to the respective Houses of Congress, and that a copy also be sent by the Adjutant to the President of the United States.

I take pleasure in transmitting to you the above resolutions passed unanimously by N. B. Forrest Camp.

Respectfully,

L. T. Dickinson

Adjutant.

S.

CONFEDERATE GRAVES IN THE NORTH

By the time a Confederate veterans association passed this resolution in 1906, wartime passions had cooled. The resolution thanks Congress and President Theodore Roosevelt for approving legislation that permits marking graves of Confederate prisoners who died in Northern captivity.

The U.S. Government made no provision for the burial of Confederate soldiers or marking of Confederate graves at the war's end. In the South, private efforts, many led by women, saw to the creation of Confederate cemeteries and commemorations.

National Archives, Records of the U.S. House of Representatives

UNVEILING CEREMONIES

MEMORIAL TO
DR.
BENJAMIN
FRANKLIN
STEPHENSON

FOUNDER OF
THE
GRAND ARMY
OF THE
REPUBLIC

FRATERNITY

CHARITY

LOYALTY

WASHINGTON

JULY 3, 1909

EARLY VETERANS ORGANIZATION

The memorial to Dr. Benjamin Franklin Stephenson described in this program is located right across the street from the National Archives Building in Washington, DC.

Stephenson was an Illinois physician who organized the largest Union fraternal organization—the Grand Army of the Republic (G.A.R.). Formed to keep alive the memory of veterans' service, the G.A.R. had 400,000 members at its peak. Members enjoyed "encampments" where they swapped stories and relived their wartime exploits. They also lobbied for increased pensions for veterans and provided charity to veterans, widows, and orphans.

National Archives, Records of the Office of Public Buildings and Public Parks of the National Capital

MULTITUDE OF MONUMENTS

In the decades following the end of the Civil War, erecting monuments to the Confederate and Union dead was so popular that companies mass-produced the monuments. This monument to the Confederate dead stands in a Springfield, Missouri, cemetery.

Records of the Department of Veterans Affairs

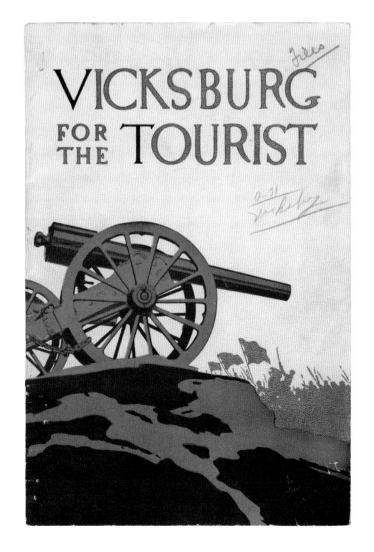

PROMOTING CIVIL WAR SITES

Initially most visitors to Civil War battlefields were veterans. As the Civil War generation passed away, however, railroads began creating promotional materials like this 1929 brochure. It attempted to entice new tourists to ride passenger trains to Civil War battlefields and cemeteries.

National Archives, Records of the National Park Service

"That we here highly resolve that these dead shall not have died in vain"......

POST MAY 28 TH. TO JUNE 15 TH.   WESTINGHOUSE   WAR PRODUCTION CO-ORDINATING COMMITTEE

HELPFUL HERO

In this poster President Lincoln's ghostly image and words from his Gettysburg Address provide the background for a World War II cemetery. World War II posters sometimes featured Civil War heroes like Lincoln and Robert E. Lee to promote patriotic unity and inspire citizens to enlist in the Armed Forces or help out on the home front.

National Archives, Records of the War Production Board

LEE'S APPEAL

This World War II recruiting poster for the United States Navy used Gen. Robert E. Lee's image and memory to inspire men to enlist. It was hoped that Lee's image would have special appeal to people in the South. The poster's words emphasized Lee's—and the enlistees'—loyalty to their home state.

Courtesy of the Virginia Historical Society

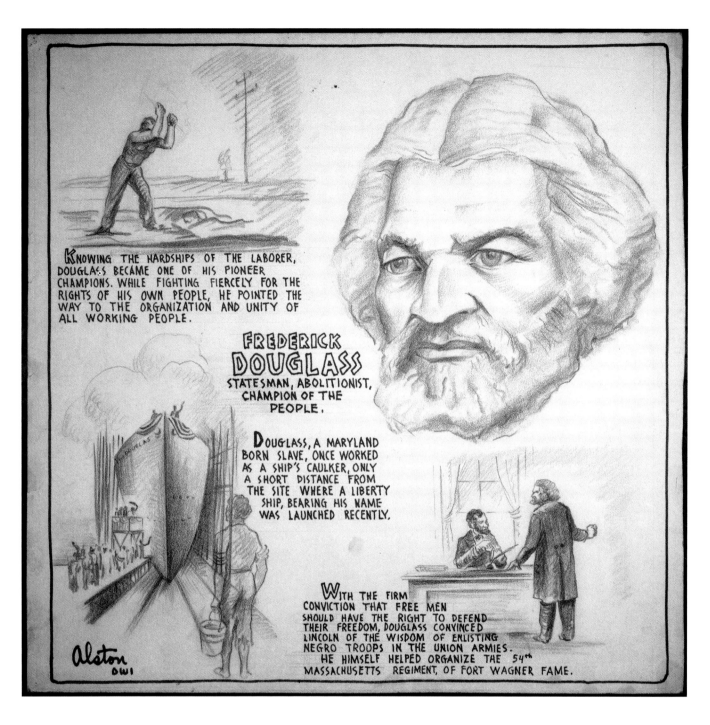

INSPIRATION TO AFRICAN AMERICANS

This World War II-era drawing of the life of Frederick Douglass sought to inspire African Americans to support the war effort. The artist, African American Charles Alston, was employed by the Office of War Information, a Federal agency. Alston created a series of drawings depicting the achievements of black Americans for distribution to African American newspapers.

National Archives, Records of the Office of War Information

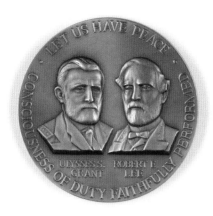 

"LET US HAVE PEACE"

In 1957 Congress created a Civil War Centennial Commission that sponsored and encouraged activities to commemorate the war's 100th anniversary—including battle reenactments, conferences, publications, costume balls, and exhibits. The events emphasized the bravery of soldiers from both sides and national reconciliation after the war. They largely ignored the political and economic causes of the conflict, slavery, African Americans, and postwar violence against blacks.

The Centennial's medal depicted and quoted both Generals Grant and Lee, reflecting the emphasis on reconciliation.

National Archives, Records of the National Park Service

EDUCATION OR ENTERTAINMENT?

On July 21, 1961, more than 50,000 spectators witnessed the centennial reenactment of the Battle of First Manassas (First Bull Run). Some people praised this "living history lesson." Others criticized it as commercialized entertainment that trivialized real battle and its suffering. After the Centennial, the National Park Service banned battle reenactments from Civil War battlefield parks.

National Archives, Records of the National Park Service [79-CWC-5N-1]

PARADES AND PROTESTS

Mississippi's Civil War centennial commission partnered with local organizations to sponsor historical pageants and develop tourist guides to Civil War sites. Ironically, its commemoration—like those in other Southern cities—coincided with African American demands for civil rights. In Jackson, Mississippi, for instance, on the same day a parade commemorated the state's secession, civil rights protestors faced police dogs and tear gas.

National Archives, Records of the National Park Service

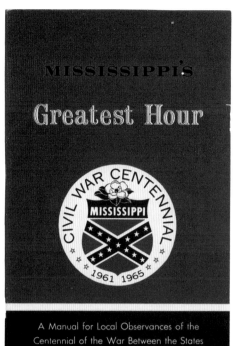

STILL FIGHTING FOR JUSTICE

During the 1963 March on Washington on August 28, 1963, civil rights leaders pose in front of the Lincoln statue at the Lincoln Memorial. Among them is the Reverend Martin Luther King, Jr. (bottom row, second from right).

In his famous "I have a Dream" speech, Reverend King connected the Emancipation Proclamation with the African American civil rights movement, calling it "a joyous daybreak to end the long night of their captivity." Then King added: "But one hundred years later, the Negro still is not free. One hundred years later, the life of the Negro is still sadly crippled by the manacles of segregation and the chains of discrimination."

National Archives, Records of the United States Information Agency [306-SSM-4D-(102)15]

Soldiers' Petition

Because Kentucky did not join the Confederacy, it was not subject to the Reconstruction Acts of 1867 that granted black men the right to vote in former Confederate states. The 170 black Kentuckians who signed this petition were pushing Congress for that right, citing their wartime service to the Union.

Each man noted his regiment and company next to his signature, testifying to the powerful hold the memory of service held among black Civil War veterans. Answering the charge that black men might abandon the Republican Party, the authors again cited their service, arguing "that they were *Soldiers*; they think they fought on the right side; they see no reason to change sides and vote against the *Liberty for which they fought.*"

The petitioners also protested against the rising tide of violence aimed at the recently freed committed by "friends of the 'Lost Cause'"—supporters of the Confederacy. They argued that enfranchisement was the best protection against "the cruel spirit of robbery, arson, and murder in Kentucky." Nevertheless, black men in Kentucky did not receive the right to vote until the 15th Amendment was ratified in 1870.

This petition from 170 black Kentucky men for the right to vote was sent to Congress in July 1867. DETAIL

National Archives, Records of the U.S. House of Representatives

THEY MET AT GETTYSBURG
Darlene McClurkin

A low-budget, black-and-white film provides a rare opportunity to witness the poignant reunion of Union and Confederate soldiers who fought on opposite sides of a bloody national conflict 75 years earlier.

A Confederate and Union veteran shake hands in a frame from the 1938 film *They Met at Gettysburg*.

National Archives, Records of the Office of the Secretary of the Interior

Two Civil War soldiers greet each other and stare back at the movie camera. It is hard to believe that they are not actors in a film dramatization or military reenactment but actual participants of the American Civil War. By the time this footage was shot in July 1938, they were long-lived veterans —two of the 1,845 Civil War soldiers who attended the final reunion of Union and Confederate veterans during the 75th anniversary of the Battle of Gettysburg in Pennsylvania.

The National Archives and Records Administration holds textual, photographic, and audiovisual records of that reunion, including the footage described above. It comes from a film made by the Federal Government entitled *They Met at Gettysburg*. Creating the film was an afterthought, and no funds were budgeted for it. The film is not a complete documentation of the reunion, and it is not equal in caliber to other Government-produced documentary films of the

New Deal era. Nevertheless, it provides evidence of the public's continuing fascination with the Civil War as well as a revealing portrait of the war's participants.

75 Years After the Battle
Fought from July 1 through July 3, 1863, the Battle of Gettysburg was the longest and bloodiest battle of the Civil War and a turning point in the war. The battlefield and nearby national cemetery where President Abraham Lincoln gave his "Gettysburg Address" in 1863 have held special significance for veterans and the general public alike. Veterans have held reunions there since the late 19th century. The first large-scale reunion of both Confederate and Union veterans was organized in 1913 for the 50th anniversary of the battle.

As the 75th anniversary approached in 1938, the United States was in a great economic depression and on the brink

Program from the Blue and Gray Reunion at the 75th anniversary of the Battle of Gettysburg, 1938.

National Archives, Records of the Office of the Quartermaster General

of being swept up in the Second World War. In 1933, the War Department turned over its administration of the Gettysburg National Military Park to the National Park Service (NPS), an agency under the Department of the Interior. Historic sites and battlefield parks such as Gettysburg were becoming popular destinations for a growing number of motorists. NPS officials at the Gettysburg National Military Park (GNMP) made vast improvements to accommodate the anticipated large crowds at the veterans reunion, scheduled for June 29 through July 6, 1938.

Organizing the reunion was a massive undertaking. A Federal commission and a Pennsylvania state commission co-sponsored the reunion, with help from the Grand Army of the Republic (the major organization of Union veterans) and the United Confederate Veterans. The two commissions planned and coordinated every aspect of the event. The U.S. Army, Boy Scouts of America, and Civilian Conservation Corps contributed to the effort as well. Invitations were sent out, not only to the survivors of the Gettysburg battle, but to all Civil War veterans. By 1938, most veterans were well into their 90s and needed attendants, medical care, and other support during the hot summer days of the reunion. Scenes in the Gettysburg film show government and military officials, attendants, and Boy Scouts assisting the aged veterans in various ways.

Memories Captured on Film

Only about 10 minutes long, the film begins with a narration of the events leading to the Battle of Gettysburg and a brief chronology of the battle. The camera pans slowly across the battlefield, then cuts to a montage of battlefield monuments accompanied by martial music. Military troops and the latest armaments appear in review during the reunion's parade. The story of the reunion continues to the tune of "The Battle Hymn of the Republic." The camera pans across the encampment, moving in for close-up shots of veterans sitting together in groups. A wizened veteran in his old army cap captivates a crowd with a story. Unfortunately, we do not hear what he is saying. The camera captures yet another veteran featured in the film, William Henry Jackson, showing a sketch to a reunion official. Jackson became a noted photographer of the American West. He served with Company K of the 12th Vermont Infantry at Gettysburg but saw no battle action. During his military service, he sketched war scenes.

On July 3, President Franklin D. Roosevelt visited the reunion to dedicate the recently completed Eternal Light Peace Memorial. The film shows reunion attendees and throngs of onlookers crowding around a stage to hear the President. Unfortunately, just as the President starts to speak, the film cuts to the end of the speech, as he prepares to leave. The film ends with a ceremonial unveiling of the peace memorial and a brief shot of the fireworks display later that evening.

Most of the reunion footage consists of similar short, choppy scenes filmed in a manner that is more lighthearted and theatrical than what you might expect from a Federal agency.

Veterans reminisce at the 75th-anniversary reunion in a frame from the 1938 film *They Met at Gettysburg*.

National Archives, Records of the Office of the Secretary of the Interior

There is a reason for that: the footage was probably photographed by a newsreel company. In fact, some of the same footage seen in this film appears in a Universal Pictures newsreel story of the same period found among the National Archives' holdings. The U.S. Army Signal Corps agreed to provide photographic coverage of the reunion with still cameras but declined to send motion picture cameramen. As the chairman of the reunion's Federal commission, Secretary of War Harry H. Woodring explained to the Acting Secretary of the Interior that film documentation by the Signal Corps "would be unwarranted and unnecessary" since "[i]t was anticipated that the commercial news reels of the industry would provide a sufficient coverage." Relying on film coverage by commercial newsreel companies, however, might mean settling for an incomplete film record and missing most of the dialogue and background sounds.

Production and Distribution

In the months following the reunion, James R. McConaghie, NPS superintendent at GNMP, received requests from veterans and other groups asking whether films of the reunion were available for loan. As one veteran's son said: "the records of this great reunion should not be buried and forgotten." McConaghie had no budget to produce a film and no film facilities. But he arranged with the Department of the Interior's Division of Motion Pictures to fashion a short educational film about the reunion using footage from the newsreel companies. To supplement this footage, the Motion Pictures staff traveled to Gettysburg and filmed scenic shots of the monuments and surrounding battlefield.

They drafted a script and recorded narration and music. Just before the final editing, a memorandum was sent to NPS Director Arno B. Cammerer announcing that the film "has advanced to the point where we can now exhibit it to you."

NPS records show that there was some demand for the film, but that no funds were available to reproduce and widely distribute it. *They Met at Gettysburg* is not one of the better-known or better-crafted of the Federal documentaries of its era. Yet it informs and expands our understanding of how this war was remembered and commemorated from a distance in time by those who fought in it, and it provides an invaluable opportunity to meet actual participants in the Civil War.

NOTE ON SOURCES

The motion picture film *They Met at Gettysburg* is found in Records of the Office of the Secretary of the Interior, Record Group (RG) 48, National Archives at College Park, Maryland (NACP). Related textual records are found in entry 10, Central Classified File, 1933–49, National Park Service, Gettysburg Military Park, 502–504, Records of the National Park Service, RG 79, NACP.

Other Civil War–related audiovisual records at the National Archives include silent footage of veterans commemorating the 50th anniversary of the Battle of Vicksburg, Mississippi, in 1913 in the Ford Motor Company Collection (Donated Records) and footage of the funeral of a Civil War veteran in Records of the Office of the Chief Signal Officer, RG 111, NACP.

An excellent overview of the reunion is "The Great Reunion: the Seventy-fifth Anniversary of Gettysburg," by National Archives archivist Mitchell Yockelson, *Prologue* 24, no. 2 (Summer 1992): 188–92. Other sources include *Gettysburg: Memory, Market, and an American Shrine* by Jim Weeks (Princeton University Press, 2003); *Race and Reunion* by David W. Blight (Harvard University Press, 2001); and *The American Newsreel, 1911–1967* by Raymond Fielding (University of Oklahoma Press, 1972).

CONTRIBUTORS

SHARON BARRY is an independent exhibit and media writer who has worked on museum exhibits across the nation— including "Discovering the Civil War," "Schoolhouse to White House," and the "Public Vaults" at the National Archives Experience. She was previously the head exhibit writer at the Smithsonian Institution's National Museum of Natural History, where she led a team of writers who wrote text for three major exhibition halls and more than 25 other permanent and temporary exhibits.

BRUCE I. BUSTARD is a senior curator with the National Archives in Washington, DC. He was educated at Hiram College (B.A.) and the University of Iowa (M.A. and Ph.D.). Bruce has been curator of several major National Archives exhibits including "A New Deal for the Arts" and "Picturing the Century: One Hundred Years of Photography from the National Archives." He served as lead researcher for "Discovering the Civil War."

MICHAEL HUSSEY serves on the exhibits and education staffs of the National Archives in Washington, DC. He was educated at Oberlin College (B.A.) and the University of Maryland, College Park (M.A. and Ph.D.). He was a member of the curatorial team for the "Discovering the Civil War" exhibit. He has also served as the curator for the National Archives Rotunda, selecting documents that illuminate U.S. history from the Revolution to the present.

JENNIFER N. JOHNSON is a curator with the National Archives in Washington, DC. She was educated at Texas State University (B.A.) and the University of Maryland (M.A.). Jennifer was the coordinator for the exhibition "Schoolhouse to White House: The Education of the Presidents" and was part of the research team for "Discovering the Civil War."

KENNETH KATO is an archives specialist at the Center for Legislative Archives in Washington, DC. He first came to the Center in 1992, and from 2000 to 2005 worked in the Office of History and Preservation at the U.S. House of Representatives. He earned his Ph.D. in political science at Johns Hopkins University. Kato specializes in congressional development and history.

DARLENE McCLURKIN is an exhibits information specialist with the National Archives in Washington, DC, and has a degree in history from the University of Maryland. She worked in the Motion Picture, Sound Recording, and Video unit at the National Archives for 15 years and has worked with the exhibits staff since 1996. Major National Archives exhibits she has worked on include "American Originals," "The Charters of Freedom," and "The Public Vaults."

WILLIAM J. SANDOVAL is a curator with the National Archives Museum Programs in Washington, DC, and is a 20-year veteran of the U.S. Army. He has degrees in history from The Citadel and Monmouth University, a C.M.S. from Harvard University, and is a graduate of the U.S. Army's Command and General Staff College.

JOEL WALKER serves as the education specialist for the National Archives at Atlanta. He previously worked for the South Carolina Archives and History Center, the Kansas State Historical Society, the National Park Service, and has taught middle school for 10 years. He is the author of *Cottonwood Grove* (2002), a children's book about the Kansas state tree and co-author of *The South Carolina Adventure* (2005), a third-grade social studies textbook.

BUDGE WEIDMAN was the volunteer manager of the all-volunteer Civil War Conservation Corps (CWCC) from its inception in 1994 until her retirement in December 2009. The sole purpose of the CWCC is to preserve Civil War records by microfilming or digitization. The CWCC began by preparing Compiled Military Service Records for microfilming, concentrating on the United States Colored Troops, then prepared the field office records of the Bureau of Refugees, Freedmen, and Abandoned Lands, a five-year effort. The CWCC is currently preparing the Civil War Widows Pension Files for digitization.

TOM WHEELER is managing director at Core Capital Partners in Washington, DC, and past Chairman and President of the Foundation for the National Archives. He has worked at the forefront of telecommunications policy and business development for over three decades, and he led the Obama-Biden Transition for the Federal departments and agencies dealing with science, technology, space, and the arts. He is the author of *Take Command: Leadership Lessons from the Civil War* (2001) and *Mr. Lincoln's T-Mails: The Untold Story of How Abraham Lincoln Used the Telegraph to Win the Civil War* (2006).

INDEX

Page numbers in *italics* refer to illustrations.

INDEX